The Novel in the Victorian Age

A Modern Introduction

Booksellers' men and boys collecting the third number of *Master Humphrey's Clock* from Chapman & Hall's in the Strand. A sketch from Richard Doyle's 'Journal' of 1840; reproduced by courtesy of the Trustees of the British Museum.

The Novel in the Victorian Age

A Modern Introduction

Robin Gilmour

Senior Lecturer in English,
University of Aberdeen

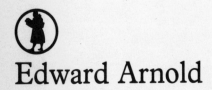

Edward Arnold

13395327
UKM

10-20-86

© Robin Gilmour 1986

First published in Great Britain 1986 by
Edward Arnold (Publishers) Ltd,
41 Bedford Square, London WC1B 3DQ

Edward Arnold (Australia) Pty Ltd,
80 Waverley Road, Caulfield East,
Victoria 3145, Australia

Edward Arnold, 3 East Read Street,
Baltimore, Maryland 21202, USA

British Library Cataloguing in Publication Data

Gilmour, Robin, *1943-*
    The novel in the Victorian age: a modern introduction.
    1. English fiction——19th century——History and criticism
    I. Title
    823′.8′09   PR871

ISBN 0-7131-6487-5
ISBN 0-7131-6468-9 Pbk

Text set in 11/12 pt Compugraphic Plantin
by Colset Private Limited, Singapore
Printed and bound in Great Britain by
Richard Clay (The Chaucer Press) Ltd,
Bungay, Suffolk

Contents

To Liz, with my love

Preface

This book aims to be something more than a study of a few selected Victorian novels, and something less than a comprehensive history or survey of Victorian fiction. As the title suggests, I have attempted to provide an introduction to the work of the major and some minor Victorian novelists that is both critical and contextual; a study which will help the student and general reader find his or her way around a huge field, but which will also suggest some of the ways in which the novelists responded to, and were in turn influenced by, the social and cultural pressures of the age. For this reason the book has been organized mainly in groups of individual authors, focused around themes and issues set out at the start of each chapter. The exception is Dickens, who as the greatest of the Victorian novelists and the one who created the largest and most varied fictional world, has a chapter to himself.

If it is not to degenerate in a welter of names, dates, titles and plot summaries, a study of English fiction from 1837 to 1901 needs to be clear about its boundaries. Since my subject is the novel and the age, I have given less space than I would have wished to the Victorian historical novel, although this decision can perhaps be justified on the grounds that the genre is a relatively discrete one, which has been studied elsewhere (see Select Bibliography for chapter 3); it also reflects my view, argued at some length here, that the true achievements of the historical are to be found in the great mainstream Victorian novels rather than in the historical novel as such – in *Vanity Fair* rather than *The Virginians*, and in *Middlemarch* rather than *Romola*. In the matter of another large subgenre, the novel on religious themes, I have with some regret made a fairly ruthless distinction between those novels which seem to me now of narrowly doctrinal or period interest, and those of more lasting value. At the end of the period, I have interpreted my brief rather strictly to exclude the stories of Kipling and the novels of Conrad (the bulk of whose work falls in the Edwardian period); and in the case of Henry James to confine myself to his novels on English themes, and in that category to those which pre-date his later experimental phase. In this way it is hoped to preserve the shape and coherence of the book, and prevent the kind of diffuse conclusion that tends to result when the policing is lax on that disputed border area between Victorian and Modern.

Finally, this is a study of the English Victorian novel, in its English rather than British context. As a Scot myself I am more than usually aware of the ways in which 'English' tends to appropriate 'British' in cultural (and other) matters, but to have written a history of the British Victorian novel would have made for a much longer and essentially different kind of book. Scottish literature had a profound impact on Victorian fiction through the novels of Sir Walter Scott, but the Scottish novel and the English novel remain in the end different animals, and are best approached – at least initially – in their separate habitats.

Acknowledgments

A book of this kind, ranging widely over a large field, is inevitably the product of many years of reading Victorian novels, and reading, thinking and talking about them. It would be impossible to acknowledge, or even perhaps fully to know, all the intellectual debts one has incurred over these years, but such as I have been aware of in the course of writing this study I have tried to acknowledge, either in the text itself or, more usually, since readability has been a chief consideration, in the footnotes and Select Bibliography. This is also the appropriate place to acknowledge some debts to myself: in chapter 5 I have drawn upon some material from my Introductions to the Penguin English Library editions of *The Warden* and *Barchester Towers*; in chapter 4 from an article on 'Memory in *David Copperfield*', published in *The Dickensian* in 1975; and in chapter 3 from an article on 'Scott and the Victorian Novel', in *Scott and His Influence*, ed. J.H. Alexander and D.S. Hewitt (Aberdeen, Association for Scottish Literary Studies, 1983). I am grateful to the Editors concerned for permission to use this material.

I should like to thank the many friends and colleagues – too many to name individually here – from whose conversations on Victorian and other matters I have profited, and perhaps especially those students, in Aberdeen and Northern Ireland, who chose to take options I have offered in the area covered by this book. Their friendly participation helped me to focus and debate many of the ideas and issues discussed here.

Finally, I should like to thank the staff of the Queen Mother Library in Aberdeen for their friendliness, efficiency and helpfulness.

Note on Texts and References

References in the text are by chapter number, or by book or volume and chapter number, to editions of the novels specified in the *Texts* section which introduces the footnotes to each chapter of this study.

Introduction: The Novel and the Age

The supreme literary achievement of the Victorian age is in its prose fiction. However much we may value the Victorian achievement in poetry, it is in the novels of Dickens and George Eliot, Thackeray and Trollope, Charlotte and Emily Brontë and Hardy, that the creative strengths of the period are most powerfully concentrated. The greatness of these writers is inseparable from the fact that they were working in a great popular form in its heyday. 'We have become a novel-reading people', Trollope wrote in 1870. 'Novels are in the hands of us all; from the Prime Minister down to the last-appointed scullery-maid. We have them in our library, our draw-ing-rooms, our bed-rooms, our kitchens – and in our nurseries.'[1] In retro-spect this seems an enviable situation: produced in huge quantities (it has been estimated that some 40,000 separate titles were published between 1837 and 1901), and consumed with that half-guilty compulsiveness which is surely the frame of mind every novelist would want in his reader, the novel had a directness of relation to the life of Victorian society that poetry on the whole lacked. Trollope observed in his *Autobiography* that people read novels more readily than poetry, 'but they read them, – as men eat pastry after dinner, – not without some inward conviction that the taste is vain if not vicious. I take upon myself to say that it is neither vicious nor vain' (12).

The significance of this popularity was not lost on perceptive contempo-rary observers. The poet Arthur Hugh Clough, for example, taking issue with the austere classicism espoused by his friend Matthew Arnold, asked why it was that people preferred reading *Vanity Fair* or *Bleak House* to reading modern poetry:

Is it. . .that to be widely popular, to gain the ear of multitudes, to shake the hearts of men, poetry should deal more than at present it usually does, with general wants, ordinary feelings, the obvious rather than the rare facts of human nature?. . .The modern novel is preferred to the modern poem, because we do here feel an attempt to include these indispensable latest

---

[1]'On English Prose Fiction as a Rational Amusement', in *Anthony Trollope: Four Lectures*, ed. M.L. Parrish (Constable, 1938), p. 108.

addenda – those phenomena which, if we forget on Sunday, we must remember on Monday – those positive matters of fact, which people, who are not verse-writers, are obliged to have to do with. . .The novelist does try to build us a real house to be lived in; and this common builder, with no notion of the orders, is more to our purpose than the student of ancient art who proposes to lodge us under an Ionic portico.[2]

Poetry is dignified, fiction parvenu and opportunistic, concerned less with the 'orders' than with life. It would be wrong to slight the aesthetic properties of pre-Jamesian fiction, but at the outset it is worth stressing the other side of the coin: the informality and inclusiveness of much Victorian fiction, the easy, unembarrassed way the great novelists brought the crowded stuff of the world into their work, and by interpreting and humanizing it made the novel in fact, what the other literary forms at the time failed to be, the unofficial *magister vitae* of the age.

And yet 'the Victorian novel' is not readily grasped as an entity, however indispensable the phrase may be to literary historians and theorists. It is hard to find a definition that will encompass all the different fictional modes and formal changes occurring between the first numbers of *Pickwick Papers* in 1836 and the publication of *The Wings of the Dove* in 1902, and the difficulty of generalizing about the Victorian novel is similar to the difficulty of generalizing about the period itself. There can be no simple labels for a reign which begins, as one historian has put it, 'with bishops in cauliflower wigs and the great ones of the world driving in coaches with footmen behind, [and] ends with expensive people driving in motor cars and a leader of the House of Commons who rode a bicycle'.[3] The only key to this period of unprecedented change is the fact of change itself, and the Victorians' consciousness of it: they were the first people to prove on their pulses the knowledge that change – social, cultural, intellectual, religious – was not an interruption of an otherwise stable and predictable existence, but the inescapable condition of life in the modern world. Never before, Walter Houghton observes, 'had men thought of their own time as an era of change *from* the past *to* the future'.[4] Several factors combined to thrust this awareness on the first Victorians. There was, as a background to everything else, the unprecedented increase of population. The 1851 census revealed that the population of England and Wales had doubled since the start of the century, from 8.9 to 17.9 million; it was virtually to double again by 1901, to 32.5 million. (In the same period the population of the United Kingdom, which of course included Ireland, rose from 15.9 million in 1801, to 27.4 in 1851 and to 41.5 million

[2]*Victorian Scrutinies: Reviews of Poetry 1830–1870*, ed. Isobel Armstrong (Athlone Press, 1972), pp. 154–6.

[3]G. Kitson Clark, *The Making of Victorian England* (Methuen, 1962), p. 30.

[4]*The Victorian Frame of Mind 1830–1870* (New Haven, Yale, 1957), p. 1.

in 1901).[5] The same census revealed that in 1851 more than half the population of England and Wales was living in an urban environment, and while the definition of 'urban' in this context is a matter for debate, it remains a startling statistic – especially when one considers, as Geoffrey Best points out, that 'no other country in the world approached such a condition until after 1900'.[6] Such rapid urbanization was the result of industrialization, and the spectacular growth of the industrial city, especially in the north of England, was a contemporary wonder and a pressing social problem well before Victoria came to the throne. The first decade of her reign saw the virtual establishment of a national railway network, again a dramatically rapid (and haphazard) development which changed not only the landscape but age-old notions of time and distance.

If the railway engine and the industrial city were the most striking symbols of a new age, witnesses to the awesome power of human technology, then someone born at the start of the century – and Dickens, Thackeray, the Brontës, Trollope, Gaskell and George Eliot were all born in its second decade – would have lived through social, political and religious changes which in retrospect seem scarcely less profound. They would have seen their society make rapid advances in the civilization of everyday life, overhauling the old brutal criminal code with its savage punishment for slight offences, proscribing such cruel practices as the pillory (abolished in 1837) and the baiting of animals, establishing a Metropolitan Police Force in 1829 and extending it to the towns and country in the 1830s.[7] They would have lived in a climate of almost continual debate about parliamentary reform, and through a steady succession of 'blue books', the reports of the various parliamentary commissions appointed to look into almost every area of national life, which laid the groundwork for the great Victorian achievements in reforming legislation. They would have witnessed a series of religious upheavals brought on, initially, by the movement for reform in the relations of Church and State: Catholic Emancipation in the late 1820s, the Oxford Movement in the 1830s, the impact of geology and the 'Higher Criticism' in the 1840s, the public controversy following the publication of Darwin's *Origin of Species* in 1859. Matthew Arnold was not exaggerating when he wrote in 'The Study of Poetry' (1880): 'There is not a creed which is not shaken, not an accredited dogma which is not shown to be questionable, not a received tradition which does not threaten to dissolve.'

Although this consciousness of change runs throughout the period, it was probably most acutely felt during the years which, if we accept the

[5]Figures from Donald Read, *England 1868-1914* (Longman, 1979) pp. 6, 214.
[6]*Mid-Victorian Britain 1851-75* (Weidenfeld & Nicolson, 1971), p. 6.
[7]There is a useful discussion of these reforms in Kitson Clark, *The Making of Victorian England*, pp. 59-62.

tripartite division of the period used by most social historians, we may call the early Victorian era. This phase is bounded by the Reform Bill debates of 1831–2 at one end and by the 1851 Great Exhibition at the other, an event which symbolized the material self-confidence of a people emerging from recent upheavals into the new dawn of Free Trade and industrial supremacy. The first ten years of Victoria's reign, in particular, were a time of acutely felt change and crisis: the years of the coming of the railways, of the rise and decline of Chartism, of the successful activities of the Anti-Corn Law League – a period marked by a great social disaster, the Irish potato famine, and by a great, symbolic legislative decision, the repeal of the corn laws in 1846. The mid-Victorian era can also be seen as a stretch of two decades, from 1851 to the start of the so-called 'Great Depression' in the middle 1870s, a time when the hopes of the Free Traders who had fought for repeal seemed to be realized in a rising prosperity born of Britain's world dominance in commerce and manufacturing industry. In these decades the conflicts of the 1830s and 40s seemed to be settling into a state of balance, and this, to many middle-class observers at any rate, was a sign of the strength and flexibility of Britain's political institutions, and the healthy naturalness of a widely shared moral code based on work, duty, earnestness and the sanctity of the domestic affections. This period of 20 or so years is the high noon of Victorian optimism, and has been called the Age of Equipoise – the title of an influential study by the historian W.L. Burn. The balance starts to go in the later Victorian period, when a number of developments – the challenge to Britain's industrial supremacy and imperial expansion from Germany, political unrest, the fracturing of the mid-Victorian cultural consensus under the impact of new ideas – contribute to a mood of anxiety and slipping confidence. There were important continuities as well, of course, but the sense of a society in transition to less hopeful destinations is marked towards the end of the century.

The development of the novel is not so easily demarcated into early, mid- and late-Victorian phases, because it is dependent on the careers of the major figures and these, inevitably, cut across the historical boundaries. But a tripartite division of the period, flexibly applied, can help us to understand Victorian fiction also, and this is reflected in the shape of the present study. Again, the 1840s are a crucial decade. One has only to think of some of the novels published then – *Vanity Fair, Jane Eyre, Wuthering Heights, Dombey and Son* – to realize what an astonishing period of creative innovation this was. The relations between the novel and society are particularly close and fascinating here: nearly every major novel of the decade can be seen as a response, direct or indirect, to the upheaval of the time. This is true not only of the descriptions of railway construction and travel in *Dombey and Son*, and of novels like *Sybil, Mary Barton* and *Alton Locke* which attempt to explore what Carlyle called the

'Condition-of-England question', but also of the rise of the fictional auto-biography or *bildungsroman* in *Jane Eyre* and *David Copperfield*. The two impulses go together at this time. The search for coherence and stability in the self, for the continuities of personal memory, becomes an urgent task when the individual is confronted with discontinuities in the world out-side. The sense of the present and the sense of the self – the titles of chapters 2 and 3 of this study – need to be seen as complementarities and not opposites, if the character of early Victorian fiction is to be properly understood.

But by the 1850s the mood has changed. Some of the tension, the sense of crisis, has gone. Not from Dickens's fiction, which moves in the 50s and 60s from the buoyancy of *Copperfield* to something like apocalyptic pessi-mism in *Our Mutual Friend*. But in the case of Thackeray, who turns to historical fiction (*Esmond, The Virginians*) and family saga (*The Newcomes*), and in that of Elizabeth Gaskell, who turns to the middle-class experience of social change (*Cranford, North and South*), there is a move-ment towards more relaxed and 'domestic' fictions. By the late 1850s it becomes possible to talk of an 'equipoise' phase in the Victorian novel, extending from the publication of Trollope's *Barchester Towers* in 1857 and George Eliot's *Scenes of Clerical Life* in 1858, to *Middlemarch* in 1871–2. This is the great age of domestic realism, a time of relative stability when novelists could settle to the leisurely depiction of everyday middle-class life; an era of spacious narratives, prolific in sub-plots and running into series, such as Trollope's 'Chronicles of Barsetshire' (1855–67) and Mrs Margaret Oliphant's 'Chronicles of Carlingford' (1863–76). It is a time when an awareness of regional difference, sharpened by recent change and in particular the coming of the railways, inspired the novel of English provincial life, contemporary in Trollope, remembered from childhood and youth in Gaskell's Cranford and Hollingford, George Eliot's St Oggs and Middlemarch. It also sees the rise of another dis-tinctively Victorian genre, the so-called 'sensation novel' associated with Wilkie Collins – the lurid antitype of the domestic novel, dealing melo-dramatically with a hidden world of middle-class nightmare.

The later Victorian period presents a more diffuse picture as novelists like Meredith, James and Hardy grow from Victorian roots into more modern forms of consciousness. Hardy in particular moves within the space of 20 years from the pictureque pastoralism of *Under the Greenwood Tree* (1872), subtitled 'A Rural Painting of the Dutch School', to the tragic rural painting of *Tess of the d'Urbervilles* (1891), where the seduction of a dairymaid can call Providence into question, and the subtitle – 'A Pure Woman' – issues a direct ethical challenge to the Victorian reader. By 1890, too, a perceptible movement inwards has occurred in English fic-tion, away from the crowded canvas of the mid-Victorians towards a more private, psychological kind of novel. If any single work can be said to mark the transition from mid- to late-Victorian, it is *Daniel Deronda* (1876). George Eliot's only novel of near-contemporary life, it makes a break not only with her usual world of memory but also with history and with realism, combining the visionary romance of Deronda's discovery of race and destiny with a pioneering analysis of marital unhappiness and disturbed psychology in the heroine, Gwendolen Harleth. Gwendolen's sisters, in varying degrees spirited, nervous and independent, and trapped in claustrophobic marriages or engagements, are at the heart of the most 'modern' novels of the time: Meredith's Clara Middleton in *The Egoist* and Diana in *Diana of the Crossways*, James's Isabel Archer in *The Portrait of a Lady*, Hardy's Sue Bridehead in *Jude the Obscure*, Laura Fountain in Mrs Humphry Ward's *Helbeck of Bannisdale*, and many others. Nothing, Henry James wrote in 1899, 'is more salient in English life today, to fresh eyes, than the revolution taking place in the position and outlook of women – and taking place much more deeply in the quiet than even the noise on the surface demonstrates'.[8]

The foregoing is a snapshot view of the main lines of development in Victorian fiction. But what of the readers of these novels? Who were they, in what forms did they receive their fiction, and what expectations did they bring to their reading? In the first place, the readership for the novels discussed in this study was predominantly middle-class. Economic factors, and the general level of literacy in England before the 1870 Education Act, ensured that most readers for new fiction would come from the middle classes – a greatly expanded social category in the Victorian age, but still not wide enough to take in many of the poor, for whom other kinds of fiction catered. To Wilkie Collins in 1858 the poor were the 'Unknown Public', a vast potential readership of the future, but at that time reached only by Dickens, and even then less by the monthly instalments of his novels (which at a shilling each were expensive for a working-man) than by his weekly magazines at twopence, and perhaps especially by such admirable ventures as the publication in penny-halfpenny weekly parts of the 'Cheap Edition' of his works.[9] Otherwise most Victorian novelists were conscious of writing for a middle-class and predominantly family audience, increasingly accustomed to the practice of reading aloud in the family circle.

There were three principal outlets available to the aspiring novelist: publication in book form, usually in three volumes, serialization in a magazine or periodical, and serialization in monthly parts. To take serialization first, it was usual throughout the period for magazines like

[8]'The Future of the Novel', in *The House of Fiction*, ed. L. Edel (Hart-Davis, 1957), p. 57.

[9]See R.D. Altick, *The English Common Reader: A Social History of the Mass Reading Public, 1800-1900* (Chicago, University of Chicago Press, 1957), and Louis James, *Fiction for the Working Man* (OUP, 1963; Harmondsworth, Penguin, 1973). Wilkie Collins's article on 'The Unknown Public' appeared in *Household Words* XVIII (1858), pp. 217-24.

Fraser's and *Blackwood's* to carry a certain amount of short fiction and the occasional novel. *Bentley's Miscellany* serialized *Oliver Twist*, and Dickens's *Household Words* carried *Hard Times* and *North and South*. Its successor *All the Year Round*, founded in 1859, contained rather more fiction: *A Tale of Two Cities*, *The Woman in White* and *Great Expectations* were all serialized in its first two years. But the breakthrough in magazine serialization really came with George Smith's decision to set up the *Cornhill Magazine* in 1860 under the editorship of Thackeray. The phenomenal success of this venture in its early years was to spell the end of the other great serial form of the period, the monthly number. This previously 'low' form of popular publication – Deborah Jenkyns in *Cranford*, it may be recalled, considered it ' "vulgar, and below the dignity of literature, to publish in numbers" ' (1) – was revived and greatly expanded by Dickens in *Pickwick Papers*, which established a form which he and Thackeray were to use for many of their novels: that is, 20 monthly instalments published as 19, the last being a double number, each containing 32 pages of text and two or more illustrations, and selling at one shilling. The reader could thus purchase a novel which was significantly longer than the three-decker for two-thirds of the price: 20 shillings against an exorbitant 31/6d. The monthly part helped to create a unique intimacy between the author and his readers, who were used to living with his creations over a long period of time and could influence their development – sometimes dramatically, as Mrs Seymour Hill did when she objected to her incarnation as Miss Mowcher in *David Copperfield* and threatened to sue,[10] or more usually through fluctuating sales, which would lead a novelist to develop a popular character, or initiate a change in direction: Sam Weller in *Pickwick Papers* is an instance of the one, and the American chapters in *Martin Chuzzlewit* of the other, introduced to boost that novel's flagging fortunes. Structurally, the novel in numbers encouraged thematic parallelism as a means of orchestrating a large cast of characters and achieving the necessary effect of the whole moving through the part; and in Dickens's case it probably encouraged his tendency to signal character through a few striking phrases or mannerisms, which make his people immediately memorable and therefore easier to carry across the gap between instalments.

Popular as the monthly number was in the hands of a Dickens, his sales at their best – and they fluctuated greatly[11] – were half that achieved by the early issues of the *Cornhill Magazine*. Carrying two lead serials, Thackeray's *Lovel the Widower* and Trollope's *Framley Parsonage*, plus illustrations, it was selling 100,000 copies at a shilling each. New areas of middle-class readership for quality fiction seemed to have been tapped. The *Bookseller* commented: '*The Cornhill Magazine* has opened our eyes to the great fact of their being a very large, and hitherto overlooked mass of

[10]See J. Butt and K. Tillotson, *Dickens at Work* (Methuen, 1968), pp. 141–2.
[11]See Robert L. Patten, *Charles Dickens and His Publishers* (Oxford, Clarendon, 1978).

readers for literature of high class. Whoever believed that a hundred thousand buyers could be found, month after month, for that serial?'[12] The other big publishing-houses followed the *Cornhill*'s lead, with the result that the magazine soon replaced the monthly part as the chief serial outlet for quality fiction. The standard was high. The *Cornhill* published the last novels of Thackeray, Trollope's *Framley Parsonage* and *The Small House at Allington*, Elizabeth Gaskell's *Wives and Daughters*, some of Henry James's early stories, and two novels by Hardy. Profits were high, too, at least in the early years, and a price in censorship was exacted for this new route to the family reading market. Thackeray was notoriously squeamish about what he would accept, and even Leslie Stephen, when he became editor in 1871, felt compelled by the magazine's reputation to reject *The Return of the Native*, although he had previously published *Far From the Madding Crowd*.

Important as these different forms of serialization are to an understanding of the relationship between the Victorian novelists and their readers, the majority of Victorian novels made their first appearance in three volumes, and were not purchased but borrowed, from the circulating libraries of the time. Chief among these was the Victorian institution known as Mudie's, the lending library started by Edward Mudie from a shop in Bloomsbury in 1842, and which in ten years expanded to dominate the market. A man of evangelical sympathies and keen business sense, Mudie made two decisive innovations in the sleepy world of the lending library as he found it: he cut the annual subscription rate to one guinea per exchangeable volume, or two guineas for four, and he advertised his library as 'Select', thereby announcing the proprietorial control he was prepared to exercise over the books he stocked. The Victorian paterfamilias soon came to know that nothing his wife or daughters borrowed from Mudie's would bring a blush to their cheeks or be considered unseemly on the drawing-room table. Value for money and fitness for family readership, boosted by advertising and efficient distribution throughout the country and overseas, made Mudie's pre-eminent for almost 50 years; and with pre-eminence came the large purchases of new literature (at considerable discount) which gave Mudie his great influence over the fiction market. Other libraries continued to function, but the only serious rival to Mudie's was W.H. Smith, who started their railway bookstalls in 1848 and added lending sections a decade later.

The usual progress for a successful Victorian novel was publication in three volumes, or serialization followed by such publication, adoption by the circulating library – preferably Mudie's – and the consequent large purchase, and then after a year's library circulation, a single-volume reprint, usually at 6/-, followed by a second, cheaper reprint, and possibly

---

[12]Quoted by John Sutherland in *Victorian Novelists and Publishers* (Athlone Press, 1976), p. 43.

a 2/- 'yellowback' for railway bookstalls. The very high price of a guinea-and-a-half for the original inhibited purchase, but of course suited the libraries, which could circulate a single novel to three different subscribers. Success at Mudie's influenced publishers in their decisions on whether to reprint a novel or not, and rejection was usually fatal, except for those who could command a readership through the magazines. Contemporary estimates of the numbers of Mudie's subscribers range from 50,000 at the mid-Victorian peak to half that by 1890, figures that need to be multiplied several times to arrive at the actual readership, when the size of Victorian families and the habit of reading aloud in the family circle are taken into account. The system had obvious disadvantages which critics throughout the period were increasingly to deplore: chiefly, censorship in sexual matters, the straitjacket of the three-decker, and its excessive cost to those who might want to purchase rather than borrow their fiction. There is, however, something to be said on the other side. The circulating library provided a ready and relatively steady market for a large number of novelists, many of them minor writers who would not have survived without the modest returns they could rely on from a Mudie purchase. The censorship exerted on behalf of the young person was no doubt restrictively and, as George Moore was to argue, arbitrarily and hypocritically applied, but the blushing cheek could be forestalled by skilful writing, and the corollary was that Mudie did help to create and sustain a family readership for fiction, which in turn helped to establish the respectability of the novel as a form and its claim to a morally educative role in contemporary society. Even the three-decker form, while it forced the reluctant novelist into prolixity and inhibited the development of shorter fiction, encouraged the spaciousness of narrative description and commentary which gives the great Victorian novels their sweep and moral grandeur.

What expectations did the Victorians have of their fiction? We may be sure that many of them read novels – as most people read novels – for escape and diversion. Charles Darwin was such a reader. He found novels a 'wonderful relief and pleasure' to him in later life, and wrote: 'I like all if moderately good, and if they do not end unhappily – against which a law ought to be passed. A novel, according to my taste, does not come into the first class, unless it contains some person whom one can thoroughly love, and if it be a pretty woman all the better'.[13] This predilection for the happy ending and the loveable character is more deeply rooted in Victorian taste than perhaps we like to think today, and it was potentially in conflict with another assumption of the period, that art should take its material from ordinary life and deal with it in an appropriate manner. The tension between 'idealism' and 'realism', between (to simplify) the happy ending which consoles and the unhappy ending which is true to life, is present in

[13]*Autobiography*, ed. G. de Beer (OUP, 1974), p. 83.

much Victorian fiction and reviewing. The realist impulse led novelists like Thackeray and George Eliot to emphasize the unheroic character of most human behaviour, the determining power of environment, the probability of failure; but it remains just that, an impulse, a tendency, peaking at certain times and in certain classic novels – with *Vanity Fair* (1847–8), *Adam Bede* (1859), *Esther Waters* (1894) – but always existing against the background of other possibilities which the major novelists, for various reasons, were unwilling to relinquish. For convenience, and because the Victorians themselves used the terms, we can class these other possibilities under the heading Romance, and employ Henry James's useful distinction between the 'real' as 'the things we cannot possibly *not* know, sooner or later', and the 'romantic' for 'the things that can reach us only through the beautiful circuit and subterfuge of our thought and desire' (Preface to *The American*). Most of the great Victorian novelists acknowledged the 'real' but were not imprisoned by it; they kept the door open to the transforming energies of romance, with its 'subterfuge' promise that life might be shaped to the heart's desire. So Dickens can say in the Preface to *Bleak House* that he has 'purposely dwelt on the romantic side of familiar things' – an art of the real transfigured by poetry. Romance in its various guises is never very far away, never routed by the periodic onslaughts on its falsifications made by the realist novel. *Vanity Fair* is such a novel, but it was published in the same years as *Jane Eyre* and *Wuthering Heights*, classics of romantic fiction. Trollope aspires to write a fiction 'shorn. . .of all romance',[14] but he does so at a time when gothic romance was all the rage, in the shape of the sensation novel. The 1880s and 90s see a move towards Naturalism, but also a counter-move in the vogue for Meredith and the Stevensonian novel of adventure. Even in ostensibly 'realistic' writers the romantic mode is never banished. Thackeray wrote *The Rose and the Ring* as well as *Vanity Fair*; George Eliot *Silas Marner*, a fable of secular providence, as well as the deterministic *Middlemarch*.

The label 'realistic', then, cannot be applied to the great Victorian novelists without many and continuing qualifications. But there is one sense in which they can be called realists. They may have differed over the modes of their fiction, but they all believed that fiction was an art of the real, that novels could tell the truth about reality, and in doing so exhort, persuade and even change their readers. The modern notion of the novelist as magician or trickster was essentially alien to them. Although Dickens was a brilliant manipulator of his reader, like Nabokov, he could never have written as Nabokov did that 'To call a story a true story is an insult to both art and truth. Every great writer is a great deceiver, but so is that arch-cheat Nature.'[15] All Dickens's statements about his art reveal his

---

[14] *The Letters of Anthony Trollope*, ed. N. John Hall (2 vols., Stanford, Stanford UP 1983) I, p. 238; letter of 18 October 1863.
[15] *Lectures on Literature* (Picador, 1983), p. 5.

passionate sense of responsibility towards his readers and his own gifts, so that he can conclude the writing of *David Copperfield* with the reflection that 'no one can ever believe this Narrative, in the reading, more than I have believed it in the writing' (Preface). The notion of a 'true story' was not to the Victorians the self-evident contradiction it was to Nabokov. 'If I write for you a story,' Trollope said, 'giving you a picture of life as true as I can make it, my story, though a fiction, is not false. It may be as true a book as ever was written.'[16]

And perhaps it was Trollope who came closest to expressing the average Victorian reader's expectations when he defined a novel as 'a picture of common life enlivened by humour and sweetened by pathos' (*Autobiography*, 7). The Victorians wanted the 'real' in the form of ordinary life, but they wanted it heightened, softened and sweetened, made at once more interesting and more consolingly shaped than it is in life itself. They were often contradictory in their demands: reviewers took Dickens to task for his exaggerations of virtue and vice, and Thackeray for his failure to idealize, his cynicism; and when they got the middle range of human experience in Trollope they found it insipid. The novelists responded to these contradictory demands with the mixed form, as it has been called, of their novels. This was a form neither closed and neatly tied, expressing a providential ordering of experience as in comedy, nor open, like the indeterminate and purposely dissatisfying ending of *Vanity Fair*, but combining the features of both: closing intimations of reassurance with the exploration of painful and unreconciled elements in the body of a work. It was a way of holding together a growing sense of life's shapelessness and a longing for shape and order; and as such, James Kincaid argues, it has an analogue in the Victorian state of doubt, with its sense of a God not so much dead as disappeared, gone out of reach.

> He still lingers in memory and perhaps in fact. This tantalizing symbol provided for the Victorians a structure and at least a hint of coherence, but that coherence could not be confidently maintained against the new sense of emptiness and causelessness. So, by extension, a closed form was no longer satisfactory. Still, neither was an open form, for such a form rests on assumptions of incoherence and irrationality which are too certain and too final. The only possible form, then, is one which mirrors that suspended, hesitant state the Victorians talked about as 'doubt'. The form, like the state of mind, refuses to rest in either of the alternate comforts of security or denial.[17]

In this light the mixed form of so many nineteenth-century novels can be seen as an aspect of the Victorian compromise. The central task of Victorian culture was mediatory, seeking always to reconcile and synthesize – reform with tradition, present with past, doubt with duty, romantic

[16] *Anthony Trollope: Four Lectures*, p. 113.
[17] *The Novels of Anthony Trollope* (Oxford, Clarendon, 1977), pp. 21–2.

feeling with domestic stability. The novel shares that impulse, and like the Victorian compromise itself, the mixed form starts to break down as the age advances. The strains are already evident by mid-century, when the unconsoling endings their authors had planned for *Villette* (1853) and *Great Expectations* (1860–61) were altered at the instigations of others, and Thackeray could end *The Newcomes* (1853–5) with a teasing reference to 'happy, harmless Fable-land' where hero and heroine are united to please the sentimental reader. By the 1880s tragedy has broken through in the novels of James and Hardy. The story of the Victorian novel is the story of the novelists' attempts to interpret their changing world, and to hold on to a hopeful vision of the future until the pressure of pessimistic insight at the end of the period could no longer be contained within the reconciling mixed form. That story is the subject of this book.

1

The Novel and Aristocracy: Bulwer-Lytton, Disraeli and Thackeray

There is considerable room for debate about where the Victorian novel as a form may be said to end, but there can be little doubt about where it begins. To contemporary readers and future historians alike, *Pickwick Papers* initiated a new era. Published with symbolic neatness on the point of transition between two reigns, 1836–7, and reviving the monthly part form which was to revolutionize novel publishing, *Pickwick* soon became a legendary book. It was more than just a gloriously funny novel which had immortalized a stagecoaching England that was passing away even as Dickens wrote; with its high spirits and irreverent portrayal of the rituals of English life, and its enormous popularity, it was the portent of a change in the literary climate which Dickens, the young *arriviste* author from the lower middle classes, seemed to typify. Looking back on his career from the 1860s, James Hannay saw in Dickens's popularity a reflection of the tastes of the middle classes enfranchised by the 1832 Reform Act: 'He typifies and represents, in our literary history, the middle class ascendancy prepared for by the Reform Bill; since Sir Walter Scott, with all his fame and his audience, represented mainly the tastes and ideas of the upper class and of the old world'.[1]

Scott and Dickens, old world and new, upper class and middle class: these large antitheses point to the nature of the change that takes place in English fiction in the ten years between Victoria's accession and the publication of *Vanity Fair* in 1847. Scott dominated the world in which the first Victorian novelists started to write; he had done more than any other writer to raise the status of the novel in the early nineteenth century, especially among the new middle classes; and his prestige was further enhanced by

Texts: References to Bulwer-Lytton's novels are to the Knebworth Edition (1873–7). References to Disraeli's *Coningsby* are to the World's Classics edition of the novel. For Thackeray the 1908 *Oxford Thackeray*, edited in 17 volumes by George Saintsbury, has been used, with the exception of *The Book of Snobs*, for which the text taken has been that of John Sutherland's edition (New York, St Martin's Press, 1978). The *Oxford Thackeray* texts of *Barry Lyndon* and *Vanity Fair* have been reissued in the World's Classics series: the latter, comprehensively annotated by Professor Sutherland, is now the best available edition of Thackeray's best known novel. Quotations from Carlyle are taken from his *Collected Works* (Chapman & Hall, 1870).
[1] *Dickens: The Critical Heritage*, ed. Philip Collins (Routledge & Kegan Paul, 1971), pp. 476–7.

the publication of Lockhart's *Life* in 1838. But in creative terms his influence was problematic. Of the two subgenres which grew from the Waverley Novels, the regional novel and the historical romance, the latter soon fell into critical disrepute, despite the popularity of novelists like G.P.R. James (1799–1860) and W.H. Ainsworth (1805–82) at the time. The publisher's foreman who told Trollope that he hoped his new novel was not 'historical' because 'your historical novel is not worth a damn' (*Autobiography*, 6) was expressing a commonly held view, at least by the 1840s. The problem was not simply that in less skilled hands than Scott's the historical romance lost its grasp on history and social change and degenerated into costume drama; it was that the form, even at its best, was not one that the early Victorians could readily use. The historical novel belonged in spirit to an older world: its sympathies were feudal and hierarchical, as Newman recognized when he claimed the Waverley Novels as one of the roots of the Oxford Movement, and it typically dealt in the thrills of the battlefield and the glamour of military heroism even when, as in Scott, its message was a farewell to arms. The leading writers of the new generation, Dickens and Thackeray, were impatient with military heroism, seeing behind it the values of an aristocratic caste for whom physical courage on the battlefield and in defence of personal honour were the supreme qualities. Nothing could be further from the heroic warrior (or even Wordsworth's 'happy warrior') than the plump figure of Mr Pickwick – the type, as G.K. Chesterton said, 'of this true and neglected thing, the romance of the middle classes'.[2] His virtues are private and domestic, and in this he represents what the Victorian critic E.S. Dallas saw as the main direction of modern literature:

> The development of literature in our day. . .has led and is leading to many changes, but to none more important than the withering of the individual as a hero, the elevation and reinforcement of the individual as a private man. This elevation of the private life and the private man to the place of honour in art and literature, over the public life and the historical man that have hitherto held the chief rank in our regards, amounts to a revolution.[3]

By the 1860s, when Dallas was writing, that revolution was complete. Thirty years earlier the picture was rather different. Then the conflict between the hero and the private man, the aristocratic and the bourgeois codes of honour, was much more acute. The 'middle class ascendancy prepared for by the Reform Bill', of which Hannay spoke in connection with Dickens, was in its early stages. The old world of the landowning upper classes was still dominant – in politics, in social life and in literature, for the two dominant subgenres of fiction in the 1830s were the historical romance and the novel of fashionable life, or 'silver-fork' novel,

[2]*Charles Dickens* (Methuen, 1906), p. 77.
[3]*The Gay Science* (2 vols., Chapman & Hall, 1866) II, p. 323.

and both were forms which enshrined the patrician values of pre-industrial England.

One of the ways to understand the conflict of this time is to think in terms of Two Nations – a concept put into currency by the subtitle of Disraeli's novel *Sybil*. Disraeli meant by it the rich and the poor, but in many ways the more important Two Nations of the period are those suggested by the historian Kitson Clark, when he spoke of 'an old nation based upon the old nobility, upon the squires and upon the Established Church, and a new nation based upon commerce and industry, and in religion largely Dissenting'.[4] The conflict between these two nations was sharp, and fought out over the political issue which dominated the 1840s – corn law repeal. The repeal of the corn laws in 1846 was seen at the time as an historic victory for the new nation, which in a way it was. That a predominantly landed and aristocratic House of Commons should have voted to repeal legislation which ensured the protection of home-grown wheat against foreign competition, and therefore in favour of free trade and cheap bread to feed an expanding industrial society, was an event of great symbolic importance. It should have meant the end of aristocratic dominance; in fact, thanks partly to good harvests in the ensuing years, repeal consolidated it, removing the one issue which united the new nation against the old, and demonstrating, through concession to the national interest when it mattered most, the fitness of the landed classes to lead.

The mood of the new nation, if not its particular political grievances, is reflected in the anti-aristocratic thrust of much early Victorian fiction. There is the edgy middle-class defensiveness of *Nicholas Nickleby*, with its villainous baronet, Sir Mulberry Hawk, its posturing dandies and its spoof silver-fork novel, *The Lady Flabella* (28). More ambiguously, since he had a certain attraction to the style of the old nation, there is Thackeray's ten-year campaign against the novels of Sir Edward Bulwer-Lytton, his comic cockney footmen, his anatomy of the disease of snobbery, his delightful parodies, and of course *Vanity Fair*. There is no better introduction to early Victorian fiction than his *Novels by Eminent Hands*, published as 'Punch's Prize Novelists' in 1847, and it is significant that of the seven parodies no less than three are of silver-fork novelists and themes: 'Codlingsby', a hilarious spoof of Disraeli's *Coningsby*, 'Lords and Liveries', a parody of Mrs Catherine Gore (1799–1861), and 'Crinoline', narrated by a footman, James Plush. Another three parodies are of fiction in varying degrees historical: G.P.R. James's historical romances in 'Barbazure', Fenimore Cooper's Leatherstocking (or 'Leatherlegs', as Thackeray has it) tales in 'The Stars and the Stripes', and in 'Phil Fogarty. A Tale of the Fighting Onety-Oneth. By Harry Rollicker', the Irish and military novels of Charles Lever (1806–72). The fun in these parodies –

[4]*An Expanding Society: Britain 1830–1900* (Cambridge, CUP 1967), p. 11.

and they are among the funniest parodies in the language – lies in Thackeray's relish for the falsity, the sheer bare-faced unreality of the originals, and the credulity they suppose in the reader. No blood flows, no orphans are made, in the Napoleonic Wars in 'Phil Fogarty'; no real sense of history informs 'Barbazure', which hops around between the Middle Ages and the seventeenth century with a comical disregard for period consistency but plenty of regard for period upholstery: 'A surcoat of peach-coloured samite and a purfled doublet of vair bespoke him noble, as did his brilliant eye, his exquisitely chiselled nose, and his curling chestnut ringlets'. Thackeray shows how the heroes and heroines of such fiction are upholstery too, impossible paragons of taste, beauty, wit, martial skill and courage. While writing *Novels by Eminent Hands* he was engaged in *Vanity Fair*, the 'Novel Without a Hero' which would digest and reinterpret all the forms he was parodying. It is a novel of the Napoleonic wars in which real blood flows (but offstage) and widows and orphans are made, a historical novel which returns the Victorian reader to the glamorous Regency only to introduce him to characters much like himself, a novel of fashionable life with the dark side of fashion exposed. All these forms feed *Vanity Fair*, but it has most in common with the silver-fork novel, which now needs to be more closely examined.

Bulwer-Lytton, Disraeli and the Silver-Fork Novel

The term 'silver-fork' to describe the novel of fashionable life comes from Hazlitt's 1827 essay on 'The Dandy School', in which he made fun of the novelist Theodore Hook's fascination with the fact that the privileged '*eat their fish with a silver fork*'.[5] The phrase hits off nicely the snobbish preoccupation with the rituals and furnishings of 'exclusive' aristocratic life which these novels catered for. Their popularity reflected a middle-class appetite for information about the way the denizens of May Fair ate, drank, talked, furnished their homes and conducted their lives – as Dickens shows in *Nicholas Nickleby*, where it is the middle-class, social-climbing Mrs Wititterly who swoons over *The Lady Flabella*. The first silver-fork novels appeared in the later 1820s, a product of the continuing fascination with the Regency period and with that quintessential Regency figure, the dandy: the cool, crisply dressed, affectedly unaffected man-about-town, whose supreme exemplar was Beau Brummell. Brummell appears as Trebeck in T.H. Lister's *Granby* (1826) and as Russelton in the novel which virtually invented the genre, *Pelham; or the Adventures of a Gentleman* (1828) by Edward Bulwer-Lytton (1803–73). *Pelham* is the story of a dandy's progress through aristocratic society, and of his development from a posture of foppish gallantry to the seriousness of a prudent

[5]*Complete Works of William Hazlitt*, ed. P.P. Howe (21 vols., Dent, 1934) 20, p. 146.

marriage and a career in politics. Narrated in the first person by Pelham, it combines a delightfully witty display of dandy attitudes and assumptions with an underlying satirical exposure of folly and affectation. It is not a novel to be taken altogether seriously, but taken seriously it was, and by no less a figure than Thomas Carlyle. Bulwer-Lytton had devoted a tongue-in-cheek chapter to the 'science of dress', showing Pelham's fussy preoccupation with such minutiae as his gloves, buttons and the shape of his hat. In *Sartor Resartus* (1834), Carlyle took this chapter and setting the world it described beside the world of a drudging Irish peasant, pointed to the social divisions which the contrast exposed. Bulwer-Lytton stood convicted of frivolity and irresponsibility, fiddling while Rome burnt.

'Close thy *Byron*; open thy *Goethe*' (II, 9) – Carlyle's famous injunction in *Sartor* was taken to heart by Bulwer-Lytton, and in his next silver-fork novel, *Ernest Maltravers* (1837) and its sequel *Alice* (1838), he shows the influence of his reading of Goethe's *Wilhelm Meister*. Like *Sartor*, *Ernest Maltravers* is a partial *bildungsroman* – a term for which there is no satisfactory English equivalent, meaning the 'novel of development', usually the development of an innocent and well-intentioned young man as he progresses through the experience of trial, error and suffering towards a deeper understanding of life and the fullest realization of his potential. Ernest is such a young man. The novel begins with his brief and idyllic love-affair with a virtuous mill-girl, Alice Darvil; they are separated by accident, he travels abroad and experiences many adventures, is betrayed by his best friend, and is left at the end 'a lonely wanderer, disgusted with the world'. *Alice; or the Mysteries* deals with his redemption from this state of disillusionment through the 'mysteries' of Alice's continuing love, which has miraculously endured their 18-year separation:

> Here have I found that which shames and bankrupts the Ideal! Here have I found a virtue that, coming at once from God and Nature, has been wiser than all my false philosophy, and firmer than all my pride!. . .you, alike through the equal trials of poverty and wealth, have been destined to rise above all triumphant, – the example of the sublime moral that teaches us with what mysterious beauty and immortal holiness the Creator has endowed our human nature when hallowed by our human affections! (Chapter the Last)

Maltravers is not named 'Ernest' for nothing: on the threshold of the Victorian age he affirms here many of the characteristic values of the Victorian *bildungsroman* – the superiority of the 'real' to the 'Ideal', the Romantic alliance of 'God and Nature' the sanctity of the affections, the redemptive power of human love. If we do not believe in his affirmations, as we do in those of Jane Eyre or David Copperfield, it is because Maltravers remains a silver-fork hero, well-born, dashing, handsome, witty, described with the habitual hyperbole of the genre, and involved in the usual series of glamorous adventures. Bulwer-Lytton acknowledged his debt to Goethe in his 1840 Preface to *Ernest Maltravers*, where he spoke of his 'more homely plan' where the 'apprenticeship' would be to 'practical life', but this was an ambition that remains largely unrealized in the novel.

Ernest Maltravers is a bridge between the first wave of silver-fork novels in the 1820s and 30s and the second in the 1840s, represented by the 'Young England' trilogy – *Coningsby* (1844), *Sybil* (1845) and *Tancred* (1847) – by Benjamin Disraeli (1804–81) *Sybil*, it is true, is partly concerned with industrial life, and will be considered along with the other 'industrial novels' in the next chapter, but Disraeli was fundamentally a fashionable novelist. He made his name with *Vivian Grey* (1826), described in a publisher's puff at the time as 'a sort of Don Juan in prose, detailing the adventures of an ambitious, dashing and talented young man of high life'.[6] He too was to learn to close his Byron. He published several more romantic and fashionable novels before his election to Parliament in 1837, but when he returned to novel-writing seven years later, in *Coningsby*, it was with a new seriousness of purpose. The high life setting and the political ambition remain, but the aristocracy is seen through a different lens, in terms of its ability to meet the challenge of a new age. Just as *Ernest Maltravers* shows the silver-fork novel becoming a *bildungsroman*, so in *Coningsby* the fashionable-novel-cum-*bildungsroman* turns into the political novel – the first example of that species, indeed, in English fiction. Subtitled 'The New Generation', it is a story of the gilded youth of the old nation coming to terms with the challenge of the new, culminating in a symbolic marriage between Arthur Coningsby, heir of old patrician Toryism, and Edith Millbank, daughter of a millowner.

Disraeli's Young England trilogy is not a trilogy in the usual sense of the word, since it deals with continuing themes and ideas rather than with continuing characters. Disraeli defined his aims in the Preface to the 1870–1 Collected Edition of his novels: 'The derivation and character of political parties; the condition of the people which had been the consequence of them; the duties of the Church as a main remedial agency in our present state; were the three principal topics which I intended to treat, but I found they were too vast for the space I had allotted to myself.' Roughly speaking, *Coningsby* deals with the 'derivation and character of political parties', *Sybil* with 'the condition of the people', and *Tancred* with 'the duties of the Church', in the highly idiosyncratic sense of that institution which Disraeli had. The 'Young England' label refers to the promulgation in *Coningsby* and *Sybil* of the views of a group of young Tory aristocrats who acknowledged Disraeli as their leader, and who believed in the rejuvenation of the Conservative party through an alliance between the 'people' and a regenerated aristocracy. Their members included George

[6]Alison Adburgham, *Silver Fork Society* (Constable, 1983), p. 80.

Smythe, the reputed original of Coningsby, and Lord John Manners, the Lord Henry Sydney of the novel, author of such characteristic expressions of romantic medievalism as *A Plea for National Holy-Days* (1842) and the poem *England's Trust* (1841), which looked back to a time when

> Each knew his place – king, peasant, peer, or priest –
> The greatest owned connexion with the least;
> From rank to rank the generous feeling ran,
> And linked society as man to man.

It was such a spirit of romantic feudalism that Young England sought to recapture for the England of the factory and the 1834 Poor Law. Against what they saw as the utilitarian and secularizing tendency of the age, they affirmed the Crown as a symbol of unity, the Church (then under attack from reformers) as the fountain of faith and imagination, and the 'order' of aristocracy as the natural leaders of the country. It was never an entirely coherent or sensible political programme (although their voting record on factory legislation and other matters affecting the condition of the poor was an honourable one), and it invited the sort of parody Dickens gave it in *The Chimes* (1844):

> O let us love our occupations,
> Bless the squire and his relations,
> Live upon our daily rations,
> And always know our proper stations.

Still, as an imaginative critique of the utilitarian ethos Young Englandism had a certain potency, which linked it to other movements of protest at the time like the Oxford Movement, and politically it had the power to embarrass Peelite Toryism. For the question that Disraeli and his friends asked of the contemporary Conservative party was, as he puts it in *Coningsby*, 'what will you conserve?' (II, 5). And the answer given by Coningsby is – not much: " 'A Crown robbed of its prerogatives; a Church controlled by a commission; and an Aristocracy that does not lead" ' (V, 2). *Coningsby* is an attempt to imagine an aristocracy that might lead, the one enduring monument of a short-lived movement that did not survive its members' divisions over Corn Law repeal in 1846.

The political novel and the *bildungsroman* in *Coningsby* run in parallel. The action covers the period from the 1832 Reform Bill to the Tories' return to power in 1841, and takes Coningsby from a 14-year-old Eton schoolboy to marriage and Parliament at 23. At the heart of the novel is a conflict between two generations of aristocracy and two kinds of Toryism. The older generation is represented by Coningsby's grandfather, a cynical, licentious Tory grandee modelled on the Marquis of Hertford,

Thackeray's Lord Steyne in *Vanity Fair*; and by his factotum Rigby, a brilliantly malicious portrait of John Wilson Croker as a scheming but impotent political hack. Monmouth is in many ways the most remarkable creation in the novel. Whereas Coningsby and his friends are treated with typical silver-fork hyperbole, the old aristocrat is presented with a lively sense of the attractiveness as well as the dissipation and ruthlessness of the old order. His politics are entirely manipulative and self-seeking. At the climax of the novel Coningsby refuses to stand for the family seat because he does not see what 'Conservative principles' Peel stands for. ' "All this is vastly fine," ' Lord Monmouth retorts, ' "but I see no means by which I can attain my object but by supporting Peel. After all, what is the end of all parties and all politics? To gain your object. I want to turn our coronet into a ducal one. . ." ' (VIII, 3). He at least knows what he wants, and Disraeli is at his best in satirizing the party hacks who serve him, like Rigby with his 'slashing' articles, and the party managers Tadpole and Taper.

Beside these keenly etched characters, the Young England figures seem cloudy. Even Coningsby himself only comes to life in relation to Rigby and Lord Monmouth; the account of his Eton schooldays and Cambridge career seem the wish-fulfilling fantasies of Disraeli the outsider, an aspect of the novel mercilessly parodied by Thackeray in 'Codlingsby'. Everything is set at an impossible pitch of beauty and elegance. When Lord Monmouth comes to Montem at Eton, he joins 'an assemblage of the noble, the beautiful, and the celebrated, gathered together in rooms not unworthy of them, as you looked upon their interesting walls, breathing with the portraits of the heroes whom Eton boasts, from Wotton to Wellesley.' There they watch 'Five hundred of the youth of England, sparkling with health, high spirits, and fancy dresses. . . .It was a brilliant spectacle to see them defiling through the playing fields, those bowery meads; the river sparkling in the sun, the castled heights of Windsor, their glorious landscape. . .' (I, 11). It is all too much. One would believe in Coningsby's 'greatness' and 'brilliance' a little more if these were a little less insisted on, and if his behaviour ever escaped into reality from the inertly decorative postures he is seen assuming. 'As he bowed lowly before the Duchess and her daughter, it would have been difficult to image a youth of a mien more prepossessing and a manner more finished' (III, 2). Too much of the novel is in this high-flown vein. The Young England characters do not come to life: they are much less memorable than their houses. Indeed, the contemporary state of the aristocracy is defined more successfully by place than by characterization. There is Beaumanoir, the Palladian castle of Lord Henry Sydney, a symbol of domesticated aristocracy in contrast to Coningsby Castle, Lord Monmouth's house, grand and remote like the old order itself. There is St Geneviève, the Gothic castle of the Catholic Eustace Lyle, which embodies the values of Young England:

the great bell rings for almsgiving (' "I wish the people constantly and visibly to comprehend that Property is their protector and their friend" ', says Eustace Lyle [III, 4]), and the characters celebrate a traditional Christmas there at the end, complete with a Lord of Misrule and a 'Boar's head on a large silver dish' (IX, 1). And there is Millbank's factory, with its churches, schools, institutes, model houses, gardens and 'singing classes' (IV, 3), to show that the feudal spirit of benign paternalism can thrive in the modern world. These different places carry the novel's argument about the condition of England more effectively, in many ways, than the rather formal, set-piece exposition of political principles by the narrator and Coningsby.

If Coningsby represents one aspect of Disraelian wish-fulfilment, then the mysterious figure of his mentor Sidonia represents the other. Dark, cosmopolitan, fabulously wealthy and privy to every secret of all the councils of Europe, Sidonia is an idealized projection of Disraeli the Jewish outsider and political manipulator. He too is described in hyperbolic terms – 'Sidonia had exhausted all the sources of human knowledge; was master of the learning of every nation, of all tongues dead or living, of every literature, Western and Oriental. He had pursued the speculations of science to their last term, and had himself illustrated them by observation and experiment. . . .' (IV, 10). He utters some of the novel's more ridiculous sayings, such as that ' "the Jews. . .are essentially Tories" ' (IV, 15) and ' "The tendency of advanced civilization is in truth to pure Monarchy" ' (V, 8), and as he flits in and out of Coningsby's life he encourages him to aspire to greatness and live according to ' "the heroic principle" ' (V, 2). Sidonia cries out for the parody he received in 'Codlingsby', as Rafael Mendoza of Holywell Street:

> They passed under an awning of old clothes, tawdry fripperies, greasy spangles, and battered masks, into a shop as black and hideous as the entrance was foul. '*This* your home, Rafael?' said Lord Codlingsby.
> 'Why not?' Rafael answered. 'I am tired of Schloss Schinkenstein; the Rhine bores me after a while. It is too hot for Florence; besides they have not completed the picture-gallery, and my place smells of putty. You wouldn't have a man, *mon cher*, bury himself in his chateau in Normandy, out of the hunting season? The Rugantino Palace stupefies me. Those Titians are so gloomy. . .'

Thackeray is Disraeli's most astute critic. In 'Codlingsby', in his two reviews of *Coningsby*, and implicitly in *Vanity Fair*, he raised the same question about Disraeli's novel that Lord John Manners came to ask about Disraeli's political commitment – was it real? He concluded that for all its charm and intelligence, *Coningsby* was still essentially a silver-fork novel, a 'glorification of dandyism':

> It is the fashionable novel, pushed, we do really believe, to its extremest verge, beyond which all is naught. It is a glorification of dandyism, far beyond all

other glories which dandyism has attained. Dandies are here made to regener-
ate the world – to heal the wounds of the wretched body politic – to infuse
new blood into torpid old institutions – to reconcile the ancient world to the
modern – to solve the doubts and perplexities which at present confound
us – and to introduce the supreme truth to the people, as theatre managers do
the sovereign to the play, smiling, and in silk stockings, and with a pair of wax
candles.[7]

Professing to affirm the seriousness of a 'new generation', Disraeli had
really affirmed the old exclusive spirit of aristocracy, Thackeray thought,
had given his dandies new clothes in which to play the old roles. *Vanity
Fair* grew out of his discontent with novels like *Coningsby*. There
Thackeray would give a fresh, middle-class slant to the notion of a 'new
generation'; by setting his novel in the time of the Regency he would
portray in Amelia and Dobbin a more serious generation growing to
maturity in the aftermath of Waterloo, and through their experience he
would question 'the heroic principle' as a guide either to conduct or to
novel-writing. He would also borrow Lord Monmouth for his 'Wicked
Nobleman', Lord Steyne, both characters being based on the notorious
Lord Hertford. Above all, he would question the assumption of aristocratic distinction and leadership which underlay the whole silver-fork
genre, and put in its place his own notion of the gentleman, redefined, as
Gordon Ray has said, 'to fit a middle-class rather than an aristocratic
context'.[8]

Thackeray

William Makepeace Thackeray (1811–63) is best-known today as the
author of *Vanity Fair* and *The History of Henry Esmond*, which also
happen to be the only two of his novels to have remained regularly in print
in recent years. The student who wants to read more is usually advised to
try *Pendennis* and *The Newcomes*, thus completing the quartet of his agreed
major novels, and yet he or she might be better advised, and Thackeray's
reputation better served, by a recommendation to move backwards from
Vanity Fair instead, at least initially – to *Barry Lyndon* rather than
Esmond, and to *The Book of Snobs* rather than *Pendennis* or *The Newcomes*.
It is not that these earlier works are better than the later, mature novels, as
John Carey has argued in a recent study,[9] but they are shorter and sharper,
and being the work of a younger, more iconoclastic Thackeray, they help
us to see his satirical vision, and thus his relation to the age, more clearly.
There is an important truth in Geoffrey Tillotson's remark that Thackeray
'had nothing fresh to say, except perhaps certain things in *Esmond* and

[7] *Thackeray's Contributions to the 'Morning Chronicle'*, ed. G.N. Ray (Urbana, University of Illinois
Press, 1955), p. 39.
[8] *Thackeray: The Uses of Adversity* (OUP, 1955), p. 13.
[9] *Thackeray: Prodigal Genius* (Faber, 1977).

Dennis Duval, after *Vanity Fair*, even after *The Book of Snobs*'.[10] The later novels are triumphs of manner, they represent the stylish elaboration of an achieved vision; the earlier works are less mellow, but in many ways satirically sharper.

The title-page of the first monthly part of *Vanity Fair* is a reminder of this early Thackeray. It shows a clown with donkey's ears standing on a tub preaching to a congregation of clowns, and carries the subtitle 'Pen and Pencil Sketches of English Society', and the address of the *Punch* office. These are pointers to the Thackeray the reader of 1847 would have been familiar with – a writer of sketches, reviews, parodies, burlesques, often illustrated by himself (as was *Vanity Fair*), published in the satirical magazines – the *Private Eyes* in effect – of the time, *Fraser's* and *Punch*. Although *Vanity Fair* was published by Bradbury and Evans, the publishers of Dickens and *Punch*, the use of the *Punch* office as the address was clearly an attempt to capitalize on the topical success of *The Book of Snobs*, then being serialized as *The Snobs of England* in the magazine. And the self-mocking image of the narrator as clown, addressing his 'brother wearers of motley' (19), is much closer to the author of the Snob Papers, who subtitled them 'By One of Themselves', than to the world-weary, detached moralist of the novel's preface, 'Before the Curtain', which was written after *Vanity Fair* was completed, when Thackeray had discovered his mature authorial tone.

From the start of his career in 1837 Thackeray showed himself obsessed with two subjects, which he returned to again and again in the ensuing decade: the falsity of contemporary fiction, and the English preoccupation with rank, or as we would put it today, social class. *Catherine* (1839–40), is an attack on the then fashionable 'Newgate Novel' of criminal life. *Barry Lyndon* (1844) is a spoof memoir mocking sentimental visions of the eighteenth century and the novel of military adventure, specifically Charles Lever's 'Harry Lorrequer' novels of high-spirited Irish adventurers; Thackeray's Irish hero is a self-condemned upstart, braggart, gambler and fortune-hunter, and his account of battle shows even his revulsion from its random brutality. 'A Shabby Genteel Story' (1840) explores the borderline of gentility with humour and compassion, and in his first success, the *Yellowplush Papers* (1837–8), high life is seen irreverently through the memoirs of a footman. These early works were all published in *Fraser's* and, *Catherine* apart, are well worth recovering today, but Thackeray's career as a significant contemporary satirist really dates from his writing for *Punch*. He joined the magazine in 1844, shortly before the mania for speculation in railway shares reached its height. It was a time when huge fortunes were being made overnight, and the mushrooming of new wealth threatened to turn the social system topsy-turvy. *Punch*

---

[10]*Thackeray the Novelist* (Cambridge, CUP, 1954), p. 18.

captured the mood with its famous cartoon, 'King Hudson's Levee', which showed George Hudson, the railway entrepreneur, receiving homage from a kneeling deputation of peers, bishops, judges, army officers and society ladies – the old nation on its knees before the new. Thackeray provided his own comic version of Hudson's rise in 'The Diary of C. Jeames de la Pluche, Esq.' (1845–6), the story of a cockney footman who makes a fortune in railway shares and finds himself courted by the 'haristocracy'. Snobbish and anti-snobbish at the same time – since it mocked the gentry for cultivating Jeames for his money, and Jeames for his aspiring footman's English – 'The Diary' was a move into territory that came to be distinctively Thackeray's own, and its topical success prepared the way for the most important of his *Punch* offerings, *The Book of Snobs*, which ran weekly from February 1846 to February 1847. Thackeray did not invent the word 'snob', which was Cambridge undergraduate slang for a townsman, but he gave it a decisive push towards its modern meaning of one who has a false respect for rank and social position.

The Book of Snobs may not be a classic of Victorian fiction, but it is a classic piece of Victoriana, and deserves to be better known by students of the period. Quite as much as *Sybil* or *Mary Barton* it is a despatch from the front, from the social battlefield of the 1840s. The very weaknesses of the book, its repetitiveness and failure to define or develop adequately the theme of snobbery, are evidence of its urgent topicality; they show how eagerly Thackeray had seized on the social fluidity of the time, brought about by the beanstalk growth of new money and the restless pursuit of old status by groups newly enfranchised politically and economically. Take, for example, Lady De Mogyns (née Flack), married to Sir Alured Mogyns Smith De Mogyns (né Alfred Smith Muggins), their title created by the editor of *Fluke's Peerage*; she begs and bribes her way in to Lady Clapperclaw's ball, then cuts her:

> In the race of fashion the resolute and active DE MOGYNS has passed the poor old CLAPPERCLAW. Her progress in gentility may be traced by the sets of friends whom she has courted, and made, and cut, and left behind her. She has struggled so gallantly for polite reputation that she has won it; pitilessly kicking down the ladder as she advanced, degree by degree. (VII).

Fittingly, the son of this ruthless social climber is a Young Englander. 'He is the only man in the country who believes in the DE MOGYNSES, and sighs for the days when a DE MOGYNS led the van of battle. He has written a little volume of spoony puny poems. He wears a lock of the hair of LAUD, the Confessor and Martyr, and fainted when he kissed the POPE's toe at Rome.' Then there are those who have been ruined by their exposure to rank, like Tom Sniffle, a useful country curate until invited to dine with Lord Brandyball, as a result of which he falls in love with Lady Fanny Toffy, acquires expensive clothes and habits, changes his name to T. D'Arcy

Sniffle, and is eventually ruined.

As these and other names (Snobky, Crawley, Lady Susan Scraper) suggest, Thackeray was working with a broad brush. The mood varies from slapstick farce to solemn moral exhortation, and the famous definition of a snob as '*He who meanly admires mean things*' (II) does little to bring the aim of the collection into focus. But the unevenness does not greatly matter when one considers that it is probably the price Thackeray had to pay for writing at this speed and with such inventiveness: he had found a subject, and a stance before that subject, which released his satirical imagination. Later novels would flesh out the insight, here gleefully announced, of the processes by which wealth and rank adapted to each other in English society:

> It used to be the custom of some very old-fashioned clubs in the City, when a gentleman asked for change for a guinea, always to bring it to him in *washed silver*: that which had passed immediately out of the hands of the vulgar being considered 'as too coarse to soil a gentleman's fingers.' So, when the City Snob's money has been washed during a generation or so; has been washed into estates, and woods, and castles and town-mansions; it is allowed to pass current as real aristocratic coin. Old PUMP sweeps a shop, runs of messages, becomes a confidential clerk and partner. PUMP THE SECOND becomes chief of the house, spins more and more money, marries his son to an Earl's daughter. PUMP TERTIUS goes on with the bank; but his chief business in life is to become the father of PUMP QUARTUS, who comes out a full-blown aristocrat, and takes his seat as BARON PUMPINGTON, and his race rules hereditarily over this nation of snobs. (VIII)

Thackeray's strength as a satirist is his continual awareness of the part which money plays in this process, and the 'washing' metaphor catches it brilliantly. He never forgot the truth of the old saying that 'gentility is but ancient riches'. His weakness, some would say, is that he could not sufficiently separate himself from the system he attacked. Not for Thackeray the moral detachment of a Dickens or a Carlyle. His stance as 'Snobographer' is that of someone who shares the disease he dissects. Consequently he was driven to find a point of vantage within the system from which he could denounce and mock all that he distrusted – snobs, silver-fork novels, Young England, heroes and heroism – and he found this in the concept of the gentleman, redefined and moralized.

The Snob Papers, the *Punch* parodies of contemporary fiction, the reviews and parody of *Coningsby*: these anticipate the themes of *Vanity Fair* (1847–8), but they do not account for the greatly increased power of that novel over anything Thackeray had hitherto written. If there can be a single reason for this transformation, it lies in the satirical purchase on his society Thackeray achieved by sinking the action in time to the period of the Regency and its aftermath. The world of *Barry Lyndon* was too remote for effective contemporary satire, but by opening *Vanity Fair* when 'the present century was in its teens' (1) he was recreating a period still in living memory. This historical dimension served Thackeray's aims in a number of ways. First, it restored his fashionable novel to the period from which all subsequent fashionable novels had taken their bearings: the 'teens' of the Regency, when Beau Brummell ruled the clubs and the future George IV ruled, or misruled, at Carlton House. The irony is that we meet neither of these glamorous figures, but instead a stockbroker's family in Russell Square, the Sedleys, and the dandy son of a City merchant, George Osborne – characters, in other words, very like Thackeray's own middle-class readers. The Regency is evoked, only to be divested of its glamour. Second, it enabled him to evoke the Battle of Waterloo, and to divest that event of its glamour also, by the simple – but brilliant – stroke of refusing to treat it directly. Thackeray's answer to the military novel was to let the fighting happen offstage, and concentrate instead on the comedy and tragedy of those left behind: the comedy of fat Jos Sedley leaving Brussels in a panic because he thinks the French have won, the suffering of his sister Amelia who loses her husband in the battle. Third, the historical setting helped Thackeray achieve, securely and for the first time, the 'long retrospective vision' which Percy Lubbock recognized as the distinctive mark of his genius: 'as surely as Dickens tended towards the theatre, with its clear-cut isolation of events and episodes. . .so Thackeray preferred the manner of musing expatiation, where scene melts into scene, impressions are foreshortened by distance, and the backward-ranging thought can linger and brood as it will'.[11] And last, the setting was not *too* historical. The teens and twenties were close enough in memory for Victorian readers to see a continuity with their own society, and therefore the contemporary applicability of Thackeray's satire. Like so many Victorian novels, *Vanity Fair* is a novel of both past and present.

Lubbock's distinction between the panoramic method of Thackeray and the dramatic method of Dickens is a valuable one. Thackeray could manage the striking dramatic scene, such as Rawdon Crawley's confrontation with Becky and Lord Steyne in chapter 53, but he was more at home with the longer perspective of memory, holding his characters at a distance and surrounding their action with the flow of narrative commentary. The narrator is an important part of our experience of a Thackeray novel, and is not to be identified necessarily with Thackeray himself. In *Vanity Fair* he is a shifting presence, at first a fellow-wearer of motley, latterly the melancholy 'Manager of the Performance' with his box of puppets. He comes forward as a man contemporary with the characters (and thus some 15 or 20 years older than Thackeray himself when he wrote the novel), and he is a master of narrative distance, achieving some of his finest effects, paradoxically, by his refusals – backing off from the famous battle, for example, or declining the privileges of omniscience to remind us of the limits of worldly moralizing:

[11] *The Craft of Fiction* (Cape, 1921), p. 96.

There was only Amelia to stand by and support with her gentle arms the tottering, heart-broken, old man. We are not going to write the history; it would be too dreary and stupid. I can see Vanity Fair yawning over it *d'avance*. (56)

The effect generally is one of a temporal density richer than in any previous English fiction. The action is steeped in time and history, giving a special authority to Thackeray's portrayal of changing manners. In one way the 'message' of *Vanity Fair* is not very different from that of the now-forgotten silver-fork novels: their theme too is the vanity of human wishes, the disillusionment that lies in wait for the seeker after pleasure and fashion. But what is a cliché in *Ernest Maltravers* or Mrs Gore's *Cecil* becomes a felt experience for the reader of *Vanity Fair*, as life's evanescence is brought home by Thackeray's command of the long perspective of time.

Subtly interwoven with the individual lives of the characters are the impersonal forces of history. Although Waterloo itself is refused, the return of Napoleon which led to it is kept continually before the reader in the first half of *Vanity Fair*. There is a running parallel between Becky and Napoleon: both are French (she claims her mother is a Montmorency), both upstarts and adventurers, both engaged in skilful campaigns against the old order (see, for example, the titles of chapters 2 and 3). Napoleon's return to France brings ruin to Amelia's father:

So imprisoned and tortured was this gentle little heart, when in the month of March, Anno Domini 1815, Napoleon landed at Cannes, and Louis XVIII fled, and all Europe was in alarm, and the funds fell, and old John Sedley was ruined. (18).

The sentence enacts the impact it records, stepping down from the grandeur of 'Anno Domini 1815' to the ruin of 'old John Sedley'. And history in *Vanity Fair* takes even Napoleon and Waterloo in its stride, for its central subject is the experience of a generation which grew up with the century itself, and lived to see Waterloo as the receding landmark of a different society. The marriage of Dobbin and Amelia exemplifies Dallas's 'elevation of the private life and the private man. . .over the public life and the historical man'. As Gordon Ray says, *Vanity Fair* is 'the capital illustration in literature of the revolution in manners that occurred between the reigns of George IV and Victoria'.[12]

Waterloo divides the novel. It marks not only a turning-point in the lives of the characters (on one side youth and expectation, on the other parenthood, ageing, disillusionment) but a noticeable change in the novel's mood and pace. The tone of the early chapters, as Becky moves briskly up the social ladder, is irreverent and self-mocking in the manner of *The Book*

[12]*Thackeray: The Uses of Adversity*, p. 418.

of Snobs. Insignificant details are emphasized (a green silk purse, a bowl of punch), the larger ambitions of the fashionable or military novel mocked. The mystique of aristocracy is debunked when Becky meets Sir Pitt Crawley and discovers that the uncouth old baronet is ' "not what we silly girls, when we used to read *Cecilia* at Chiswick, imagined a baronet must have been. Anything, indeed, less like Lord Orville cannot be imagined. Fancy an old, stumpy, short, vulgar, and very dirty man, in old clothes and shabby old gaiters, who smokes a horrid pipe, and cooks his own horrid supper in a saucepan. He speaks with a country accent, and swore a great deal at the old charwoman. . ." ' (8). As the novel gets under way, however, Thackeray starts to try out a wider range of tones. Different moods are brought into conjunction, and the melancholy of Vanity Fair is registered beside its greed and selfishness. So the frenzy and 'baffled desire' of Sir Pitt when he discovers that Becky has married Rawdon strike a more sombre note:

> One day after he went to Queen's Crawley, he burst like a madman into the room she had used when there – dashed open her boxes with his foot, and flung about her papers, clothes and other relics. Miss Horrocks, the butler's daughter, took some of them. The children dressed themselves and acted plays in the others. It was but a few days after the poor mother had gone to her lonely burying-place; and was laid, unwept and disregarded, in a vault full of strangers. (16)

These are the mixed effects of the mature Thackeray, bringing into a single paragraph the old man's lust and anger, the servant's acquisitiveness, the indifference of the children, and the pathos of the dead and ignored wife, lying in 'a vault full of strangers'. It is a fitting prelude to the Sedley auction in the following chapter, an event 'which Satire and Sentiment can visit arm-in-arm together; where you can light on the strangest contrasts laughable and tearful: where you may be gentle and pathetic, or savage and cynical with perfect propriety. . .' (17). And just as the auction itself is the perfect emblem of the instability of life in Vanity Fair, so the contrasting attitudes of Satire and Sentiment which it stimulates form the unsettling crosscurrents of Thackeray's narration.

After Waterloo, as Thackeray settles to a longer perspective and a looser chronology, the balance of Satire and Sentiment changes. Becky continues her upward rise, moving at last into the aristocratic set of Lord Steyne and his cronies; but her struggle 'to Live Well on Nothing a Year' (the title of chapter 36), besides being doomed, takes place against the background of the sad and lonely lives of the other characters. Rawdon changes from a young buck into an old buffer, Dobbin pines for Amelia in India, Amelia struggles on in a house soured by the poverty of her elderly parents. The account of her sufferings and eventual capitulation (chapters 38, 46, 50) is one of the finest things in the novel. Thackeray did not sentimentalize poverty, as Dickens was inclined to do; he knew how it can change people for the worse, and he had a feeling heart for the obscure and unglamorous domestic servitude of the Amelias of Victorian England. 'How many thousands of people are there, women for the most part, who are doomed to endure this long slavery? – who are hospital nurses without wages, – sisters of Charity. . .without the romance and the sentiment of sacrifice, – who strive, fast, watch, and suffer, unpitied; and fade away ignobly and unknown' (57). Time erodes in the second half of *Vanity Fair*, but it also winnows; the long perspectives rob fashion of its glitter and the characters of their illusions, but reinforce the qualities embodied in Dobbin. When the narrator comes to affirm Dobbin's true gentlemanliness at the end, the affirmation carries with it the authority of his long service to Amelia, his true chivalry:

> And it must be remembered, that this poor lady had never met a gentleman in her life until this present moment. Perhaps these are rarer personages than some of us think for. Which of us can point out many such in his circle – men whose aims are generous, whose truth is constant, and not only constant in its kind, but elevated in its degree; whose want of meanness makes them simple: who can look the world honestly in the face with an equal manly sympathy for the great and the small? We all know a hundred whose coats are very well made, and a score who have excellent manners, and one or two happy beings who are what they call, in the inner circles, and have shot into the very centre and bull's-eye of the fashion; but of gentlemen how many? Let us take a little scrap of paper and each make out his list.
>
> My friend the major I write, without any doubt, in mine. (62)

Dobbin is Thackeray's answer to Coningsby and Ernest Maltravers – a rather ambiguous answer, it might seem, since he then goes on to point out the major's lisp and yellow complexion and remind us of his clumsy hands and feet. Yet even these reminders of Dobbin's lack of style can be seen to serve Thackeray's anti-fashionable point. It is important we should register Dobbin's ungainliness at this moment because it is related to qualities which have no place in the silver-fork novel: indifference to appearance, the absence of false pride and affectation, clear-sightedness, constancy, real chivalry to the weak as opposed to the bogus chivalry of Young England. And Dobbin is the son of a grocer: there is nothing aristocratic about him.

The ironies remain to the end of this most pervasively ironic of novels. Dobbin may be a true gentleman, but it is hinted that the 'prize' of Amelia may not after all have been worth the long waiting, and that he too is a victim of time. The ending is no more consoling to the reader's romantic expectations than the rest of the novel has been, and the last words are of the vanity of human wishes:

> Ah! *Vanitas Vanitatum*! Which of us is happy in this world? Which of us has his desire? or, having it, is satisfied? – Come, children, let us shut up the box and the puppets, for our play is played out.

Vanity Fair is the most important novel of its decade, perhaps the most important English novel since *Persuasion* (1817). Thackeray's contemporaries saw almost at once that it had raised Victorian fiction to a new level of intellectual seriousness and satirical power, and had set new standards of realism. Charlotte Brontë's embarrassingly effusive Preface to *Jane Eyre*, which she dedicated to Thackeray, expresses the general excitement at the arrival of a major talent ('an intellect profounder and more unique than his contemporaries have yet recognized. . .the first social regenerator of the day. . .He resembles Fielding as an eagle does a vulture. . .'). What of the novel's 'realism'? *Vanity Fair* is not a realistic novel in the sense that *Adam Bede* is; that is to say, it does not aim at a sustained representation of middling human nature in a closely observed, ordinary environment which is seen largely to condition the possibilities and the actualities of character and conduct. The elements of such a novel are certainly present in *Vanity Fair* – the account of Amelia's widowhood in her parent's home is one example – but Thackeray's method is much more playful and unstable than George Eliot's. His characteristic procedure is to undermine fictional stereotyping by pointing always to a real world beyond the fictional, which is the ultimate standard and judge of the truthfulness of novels. His narrator is in touch with that real world, mediating between it and the fiction he might be writing, and the fiction he is writing. Parody and puppeteering go together. Thackeray feels his way into *Vanity Fair* by inverting the familiar Romance antithesis (his 'fair' heroine is the villainess, his 'dark' heroine the domestic angel), by teasing the reader with the ways he might have treated his humble subject-matter if he had been Bulwer-Lytton, or Scott, and he fades out by reminding the reader that the puppets must go back in the box and the play is over. All this was very disconcerting to the Victorians, who looked for an uninterrupted illusion in fiction, but it makes Thackeray, paradoxically, a much more modern writer in this respect than George Eliot. At a time when the fictionality of fiction is all the rage, it is strange that Thackeray is not more widely ready today, although there is one contemporary novelist who seems to have profited from his example. John Fowles's handling of the omniscient point of view in *The French Lieutenant's Woman* is playful and teasing in the Thackeray manner, and it is interesting to find him in the notes on the novel praising *Lovel the Widower* as 'a brilliant technical exercise in the use of "voice".' 'I cannot believe that it is a dead technique', Fowles goes on. 'Nothing can get us off the charge of omniscience. . .'[13]

Thackeray's next novel, *The History of Pendennis* (1848–50), continues his critique of aristocracy and the silver-fork novel with the story of a young man's initiation into experience and the world. Arthur Pendennis, one of the 'gentlemen of our age. . .no better nor worse than most

[13]'Notes on an Unfinished Novel', in *The Novel Today*, ed. M. Bradbury (Fontana/Collins, 1977), p. 143.

educated men' (Preface), is the son of an apothecary and petty squire, who grows up in the period of Thackeray's own youth and early manhood to experience some of his generation's characteristic social and emotional uncertainties. The transitional character of the 1830s is embodied in the two parent-figures who dominate Pen's life. His mother, Helen, is the pure-minded guardian of the values of hearth and home, both loving and possessive; his uncle, Major Pendennis, is an ageing Regency dandy, concerned that Pen should learn the ways of the world and advance in society. One looks forward to the Victorian angel in the house, the other back to the worldly sophistication of the Regency, and Pen is caught between them. (The cover of the original monthly parts is again revealing: it shows a young man divided between domesticity, represented by a dark-haired woman and two children, and the world and the flesh, represented by a blond mermaid and two infant devils, one brandishing a coach and a coronet.) The central subject is announced and developed in the novel's masterly opening sequence, where Major Pendennis is summoned from his London club to sort out Pen's youthful infatuation for an Irish actress. Thackeray chooses to set his account of Pen's background and upbringing within the frame of the indiscretion it has led to: we are shown how a fatherless only boy, reared as a little prince by an over-protective mother, will naturally seek his heart's desire impulsively, how there is generosity and decency mixed up with his folly, and how the Major's worldly experience is necessary to save him from worse folly. Neither the unworldly nor the worldly perspctive is fully endorsed, and Pen swings between the two. He reacts against his youthful impetuousness by cultivating a nonchalant dandyism at 'Oxbridge', and this hardens to cynicism in his lackadaisical pursuit of Blanche Amory, the heiress his uncle wants him to marry. From being the saviour of Pen, 'his selfish old mentor' (17) threatens to become his Mephistopheles. But Pen cannot be a wholehearted dandy and man of the world either; there is a feeling heart beneath his cynical exterior, and in London he encounters a second mentor, the bluff Warrington, who offers an alternative style of plain 'manliness' which the novel advances as superior to dandyism and an index of true, innate gentlemanliness: 'The young man was perfectly easy and unembarrassed', we are told when the Major meets Warrington for the first time, 'He was dressed in a ragged old shooting-jacket, and had a bristly blue beard. He was drinking beer like a coal-heaver, and yet you couldn't but perceive that he was a gentleman' (28).

Pendennis should have been Thackeray's masterpiece, the great intellectual *bildungsroman* of a period rich in the fiction of childhood but not so strong in the handling of early adult sexuality and self-doubt. That the novel is not quite what it might have been can be attributed partly to the near fatal illness which interrupted its writing, and partly to Thackeray's inability, through reluctance or censorship or a mixture of both, to deal adequately with Pen's sexual experience. 'Since the author of Tom Jones was buried, no writer of fiction among us has been permitted to depict to his utmost power a MAN', he protested in the Preface. 'We must drape him, and give him a certain conventional simper.' The drape falls most damagingly over Pen's affair with the porter's daughter Fanny Bolton. In life, and in the contemporary French novel, Pen would have seduced Fanny, but he is saved by the bell of a providential illness. The sexual dimension of a worldly education is hinted at in Blanche Amory, and through such conventional filters as the French prints on Harry Foker's walls and the actresses he entertains at Richmond:

> 'Twopence-halfpenny for your thoughts, Fokey!' cried out Miss Rougemont, taking her cigar from her truly vermilion lips, as she beheld the young fellow lost in thought, seated at the head of his table, amidst melting ices, and cut pineapples, and bottles full and empty, and cigar-ashes scattered on fruit, and the ruins of a dessert which had no pleasure for him. (40).

The spoiled feast is a characteristic Thackerayan touch, intimating the waste and self-disgust of life in Vanity Fair, but it is a minor character who experiences these feelings. Pen is not allowed his Miss Rougemont. Another reason for the novel's relative failure may lie in its lack of psychological inwardness. Thackeray's conception of his art as 'a sort of confidential talk between writer and reader' (Preface) worked against the vivid notation of individual consciousness one gets in Charlotte Brontë or George Eliot. The narrator's presence is less marked than in *Vanity Fair*, but it still surrounds and interprets Pen's consciousness, voicing his conflicts within a Seven-Ages-of-Man vision of human life rather than in particular psychological terms. 'We alter very little', this voice declares (59). Pen does not change, or grapple with his own nature, or achieve any spiritual insight which alters the direction of his life; he merely grows into a sceptical but kind-hearted worldliness, which we are then asked to excuse because, after all, he is just like the rest of us – 'knowing how mean the best of us is, let us give a hand of charity to Arthur Pendennis, with all his faults and shortcomings, who does not claim to be a hero, but only a man and a brother' (75).

The 'man and brother' tone with which *Pendennis* ends was to become the preferred tone of Thackeray's subsequent novels. Pen's development stops at the point where the 'wisdom' of his compassionate worldliness merges with that of the narrator, and the two voices flow together in *The Newcomes* (1853–5) and *Philip* (1861–2), where Pen is the friend and confidant of the central characters and the editor of their stories. This device creates a rich texture of reminiscence: characters from earlier novels are recalled parenthetically, or reappear in person, as Major Pendennis does in *The Newcomes*, and the impression grows of a densely peopled world with the narrator at the centre of a web of gossip and recollection.

Increasingly the weight of dramatic interest in Thackeray's work shifts from action to narration, and within the narration towards the recollection and resurrection of the fictional world he has created in previous novels. As one contemporary reviewer noted, *Philip* 'gains its most distinguishing peculiarity from the habit which the author has of reflecting on his own compositions'.[14] Thackeray, who began his career by parodying the fiction of others, comes perilously close to ending it by parodying himself.

'Thackeray is the novelist of memory', Chesterton said, ' – of our memories as well as his own'.[15] Memory is the hidden subject of *The History of Henry Esmond* (1852), his elegant pastiche memoir by 'A Colonel in the Service of Her Majesty Q. Anne', telling of his involvement in the Marlborough Wars, his disillusionment with Jacobite politics, and his emigration to the New World. *Esmond* is the most successful Victorian solution to the problem of historical fiction because the movement it charts is essentially a progress out of history as the Victorians understood it from their reading of Scott, a heroic world of battles and duels and romantic heroines, into the private life of the domestic affections which Rachel Esmond symbolizes. By making 'History familiar rather than heroic' (I, Preface), Thackeray was doing for the eighteenth century what he had done for the Regency in *Vanity Fair*. Esmond is a Victorian in Augustan dress. In his 'secret mind' (II, 5) this exile from the eighteenth century makes the modern recognition that the essence of personality is to be found, not in loyalty to class or country or political cause, but in the continuity of the inner life, in memory:

> Who, in the course of his life, hath not been so bewitched, and worshipped some idol or another? Years after this passion hath been dead and buried, along with a thousand other worldly cares and ambitions, he who felt it can recall it out of its grave, and admire, almost as fondly as he did in his youth, that lovely queenly creature. . .such a past is always present to a man; such a passion once felt forms a part of his whole being, and cannot be separated from it. . .just as the wound I had at Blenheim, and of which I wear the scar, hath become part of my frame and influenced my whole body, nay spirit, subsequently, though 'twas got and healed forty years ago. Parting and forgetting! What faithful heart can do these? Our great thoughts, our great affections, the Truths of our life, never leave us. Surely, they cannot separate from our consciousness; shall follow it whithersoever that shall go; and are of their nature divine and immortal. (III, 6).

In such passages one recognizes in Thackeray the Victorian Proust.

Henry Esmond deserves its classic status, but in the final analysis it risks less, and achieves less, than the one later novel which, if any, can challenge *Vanity Fair* for the title of Thackeray's masterpiece. *The Newcomes* is

---

[14] *Thackeray: The Critical Heritage*, ed. G. Tillotson and D. Hawes (Routledge & Kegan Paul, 1968), p. 310; from an unsigned review in the *Saturday Review*, 23 August 1862.
[15] *The Victorian Age in Literature* (Williams & Norgate, 1913), p. 126.

today probably the least read and most underrated of major Victorian novels, and yet it is in many ways Thackeray's most ambitious social fable. Subtitled 'The Memoirs of a Most Respectable Family', the novel tells the story of a family who have risen from weaver origins in the eighteenth century, via a prudent marriage into Clapham Sect Evangelicalism to banking prosperity and aristocratic connections in the early Victorian period. It is a sombre gloss on the 'City Snobs' chapter in *The Book of Snobs*, where old Pump's money is 'washed' through the generations into 'real aristocratic coin' (VIII). Upper-class society is portrayed as a ruthless marriage-market; rank is bartered for wealth and in the process lives are destroyed and the natural human affections betrayed. There are two branches of the family, Sir Brian and his brother Hobson Newcome, prosperous, self-seeking bankers, and Colonel Thomas Newcome, a Don Quixote figure of antique simplicity and courtesy, who returns from service in India to find he has no place in this society, and ends as a pensioner in Grey Friars School (Charterhouse). Foolish though he is in his pursuit of wealth for his son Clive, there is an archetypal grandeur about the Colonel that remains untouched by his ruin and makes his life and death – a famous monument of Victorian pathos – a complexly moving judgement on Thackeray's society.

Although *The Newcomes* is a magnificent summation of his characteristic interests, it also makes us aware of the historical boundaries of Thackeray's world. The movement from Major Dobbin to Colonel Newcome is a step back into the eighteenth century and into archetype; in making it, he seems to acknowledge that true gentlemanliness can have no place in his society, and – ironically, in view of the anti-heroic bias of *Vanity Fair* – resurrects the image of the noble warrior to reproach an unheroic, materialistic age. *The Newcomes* confirms the impression that Thackeray was essentially a novelist of the first phase of Victorian society, and that by 1855 his important work had been done. He portrayed the struggle between the old nation and the new where it was keenest, on what one contemporary called 'the debateable land between the aristocracy and the middle classes';[16] he pondered the past that fed the Victorian present, and brought it to bear on the interpretation of the present. But the anatomy of the present, in all those modern manifestations that lay outwith the domain of Vanity Fair, was a task for other novelists.

[16]W.C. Roscoe, 'W.M. Thackeray, Artist and Moralist', *National Review*, 1856; *Critical Heritage*, p. 272.

2

The Sense of the Present: Disraeli, Charles Kingsley and Elizabeth Gaskell

In his apocalyptic *Latter-Day Pamphlet* on 'The Present Time' (1850), Thomas Carlyle expressed his sense of the uniqueness of the changes through which his countrymen were passing – 'in the days that are now passing-over us, even fools are arrested to ask the meaning of them; few of the generations of men have seen more impressive days. . . .It is a Time to make the dullest man consider; and ask himself, Whence *he* came? Whither he is bound?' These questions are asked at all times of rapid social transformation, but never with such urgency as by the early Victorians. Carried forward into the future at breakneck speed on the Great Victorian Express, they looked back wistfully and anxiously at the familiar landmarks they were leaving behind, and in their writings sought to develop a continuity between past and present, to uncover what Tennyson in another context called 'A link among the days, to knit/The generations each with each' (*In Memoriam,* lyric 40). It is no accident that the 1840s should see the simultaneous rise of the social-problem or 'Condition-of-England' novel (*Mary Barton, Alton Locke*) and the fictional autobiography or *bildungsroman* (*Jane Eyre, David Copperfield*). Different as the two forms are, they can and should be seen as linked responses to the dislocations of a time of profound change; the same pressures which drove one novelist outward to map the landscape of a changing society drove another – or in Dickens's case the same novelist – to explore the continuities and discontinuities in the history of the self. The impulse to engage with society and the impulse to retreat from it, to find a refuge in the memory of a more stable past or, in the case of Charlotte Brontë's heroines, in a home of the heart beyond change, reflect the contemporary sense of crisis and upheaval. This predicament accounts for a feature of early Victorian fiction which is still too little understood, although it has a significant bearing on any consideration of these novels as historical documents: the novelists' tendency to set the action of their novels back in time. All the novelists of

Texts: Quotations from *Sybil* and *Coningsby* have been taken from the World's Classics editions, those from Elizabeth Gaskell's novels from the Penguin English Library editions. The Dickens editions used in this study are specified in the textual note to chapter 4. For *Alton Locke*, the World's Classics edition has been used, and for *Yeast*, the Eversley Edition (Macmillan, 1881). All quotations from Carlyle are taken from his *Collected Works* (Chapman & Hall, 1870).

this generation are in varying degrees subject to what Kathleen Tillotson has called 'the drag of the past and the pull of the present'.[1] I shall have more to say about the 'drag of the past' in the next chapter; here I want to consider the 'pull of the present' and the challenge it presented to the novelist.

Industrialism and the Novel

The most vivid symbol of changing times was the coming of the railways in the 1830s and 1840s. Between 1830, when the duke of Wellington opened the Liverpool and Manchester line, and 1850, some 6,000 miles of railway were opened, over 3,600 in the five years from 1846 to the end of 1850.[2] No alert contemporary could avoid being struck by this dramatic development, whether in the form of the changing landscape, the railway mania in the City, the increased speed of communications (for the new electric telegraph went hand in hand with the railway), or the shrinking distance between different parts of the kingdom, in particular between the provinces and London. 'Railways are shifting all Towns of Britain into new places', Carlyle observed in 'Hudson's Statue' (1850), 'railways have set all the Towns of Britain a-dancing. Reading is coming up to London, Basingstoke is going down to Gosport or Southampton, Dumfries to Liverpool and Glasgow. . .' Time itself was altered by the coming of the railways which, by establishing Greenwich time as 'railway time' through the train timetable, standardized regional differences and imposed a new and urgent sense of the present.

The early Victorians were fascinated and bewildered by the railway. This juggernaut of progress typified all the forces which were transforming their society faster than anyone could assimilate; it marked, as Thackeray recognized in his essay 'De Juventute', a profound dividing-line in their history and experience; yet it was also a dramatic witness to the energy and resourcefulness of their generation. Something of the taut ambivalence in the contemporary response is caught in the classic fictional account of a railway journey, Mr Dombey's trip from Euston to Birmingham in chapter 20 of *Dombey and Son* (1846–8). Dickens describes the train as a 'monster', and to Dombey's grief-stricken eye it is 'a type of the triumphant monster, Death', yet the excited rhythm of the prose testifies to a transforming energy at odds with Dombey's sullen introspection, 'tingeing the scene of transition before him with the morbid colours of his own mind, and making it a ruin and a picture of decay, instead of hopeful change, and promise of better things. . .'. Dickens was prepared to give the railway the benefit of the doubt, and he saw, in

[1]*Novels of the Eighteen-Forties* (Oxford, Clarendon, 1954), p. 111.
[2]Figures from Michael Robbins, *The Railway Age* (Harmondsworth, Penguin, 1965), p. 31.

addition, that the directness of the railway line had opened up a new perspective on the city, cutting a cross-section through the slums which the middle-class traveller had hitherto been able to avoid. The railway which brought the towns of Britain closer together also let the light of day in on the realities of urban squalor partly created by industrialization, making the Victorian traveller sharply aware of the contrasts and divisions within his society. It made what Carlyle called the 'Condition-of-England question' hard to avoid or evade.

This question was posed in an acute form by the industrial cities that had sprung up in the first half of the nineteenth century. Of these Manchester, the 'shock city' of the 1840s as Asa Briggs has called it, was the type and symbol. Already famous as a cotton town at the end of the eighteenth century, it achieved notoriety through the incredible rapidity of its growth in the early decades of the nineteenth: by 1831 its population had increased 'nearly six times in sixty years, and by nearly 45 per cent in the previous decade'.[3] In the 1830s and 1840s Manchester became the most visited and written about provincial city in Britain. Here the miracles, and the cost, of Britain's industrial revolution could be seen in their most dramatic shape – the almost fabulous power of the new machinery, the energy and independence of a new urban aristocracy of employers, but also the breakdown of traditional patterns of social relationship, the segregation of the different classes into increasingly self-enclosed districts, the squalor in which many of the poor lived, and the suffering and destitution which were the inevitable consequences, it seemed, of violent trade fluctuations. ' "The Age of Ruins is past" ', Sidonia declares in an often-quoted passage in *Coningsby*. ' "Have you seen Manchester?" ' (III, 1). To see Manchester, as de Tocqueville found in 1835, was to be overwhelmed by the sense of contrast:

> Look up and all around this place you will see the huge palaces of industry. You will hear the noise of furnaces, the whistle of steam. These vast structures keep air and light out of the human habitations which they dominate; they envelop them in perpetual fog; here is the slave, there the master; there the wealth of some, here the poverty of most; there the organized effort of thousands produce, to the profit of one man, what society has not yet learnt to give. Here the weakness of the individual seems more feeble and helpless even than in the middle of a wilderness. . . .From this foul drain the greatest stream of human industry flows out to fertilize the whole world. From this filthy sewer pure gold flows. Here humanity attains its most complete development and its most brutish; here civilization works its miracles, and civilized man is turned back almost into a savage.[4]

In the almost violent paradox of the last three sentences, de Tocqueville

[3]Asa Briggs, *Victorian Cities* (Harmondsworth, Penguin, 1968), p. 89.
[4]Alexis de Tocqueville, *Journeys to England and Ireland*, ed. J.P. Mayer (Faber, 1958), pp. 107–8.

can be seen struggling to reconcile the opposed attributes of the new industrial society. The civilization/savage antithesis was used by several contemporary observers. In *Hard Times* (1854) Dickens describes Coketown as 'a town of unnatural red and black like the painted face of a savage' (I, 5). One of the Sub-Commissioners on the Children's Employment Commission wrote in 1842 of a 17-year-old Halifax pit-girl: 'This girl is an ignorant, filthy, ragged, and deplorable-looking object, and such an one as the uncivilized natives of the prairies would be shocked to look upon.'[5] The paradox is seized by Dickens in *Bleak House* (1852-3) and turned against a society which applauds missionary work among the 'savages' of Africa, but ignores Jo the crossing-sweeper on its doorstep, who 'is not softened by distance and unfamiliarity. . .is not a genuine foreign-grown savage' but 'the ordinary home-made article' (47), one of the many examples in the novel of 'how civilization and barbarism walked this boastful island together' (11) in 1852.

But if the huge mills in the industrial north were satanic, they were also titanic, and the element of wonder and romance is never far from the contemporary response. De Tocqueville called the Manchester factories 'huge palaces of industry', and this phrase becomes almost a cliché of the period. In *The Age and its Architects* (1850) E.P. Hood wrote that 'the factories illuminated seem in the distance like the fairly temples of labour and industry' (p. 29). Distance lent enchantment, of course, but the ambiguity is distinctively Victorian. Even Dickens in *Hard Times* refers to the Coketown factories as looking 'when they were illuminated, like Fairy palaces', although he qualifies it with ' – or the travellers by express-train said so' (I, 10). References to the *Arabian Nights* abound, as when in *North and South* (1855) Mr Thornton explains to Mr Hale 'the magnificent power, yet delicate adjustment of the might of the steam-hammer, which was recalling to Mr Hale some of the wonderful stories of subservient genii in the Arabian Nights. . .' (10)

In considering the contemporary response, fictional and otherwise, to the experience of industrialization and urbanization, it is important to bear in mind the unprecedented nature of the upheaval through which the first generation of Victorians lived, the sheer rapidity with which they moved into uncharted territory. Their reaction to what must have seemed chaotic and haphazard change was not stony-hearted indifference, justified by *laissez-faire* ideology (as a certain tradition of social-cum-cultural history would have us believe); on the contrary, there was a sustained attempt at the political level to chart the uncharted territory and legislate accordingly. Inevitably, some of the legislation designed to adapt the traditional social framework to modern needs, such as the infamous 1834 Poor Law Act, increased the suffering it was designed to alleviate, but it is still too easy for

[5]Quoted in Sheila Smith, *The Other Nation: The Poor in English Novels of the 1840s and 1850s* (Oxford, Clarendon, 1980), p. 140.

the student of literature to read, say, *Oliver Twist* (1838) as an attack on society for maltreating and neglecting orphan children, which it is, and forget that the first of several Factory Acts had been passed in 1833, controlling the exploitation of children in the cotton mills. As George Watson has said, 'it is supremely ironical that the first age in our history successfully to limit by legislation the abuse of child labour should today be widely regarded as especially guilty of the exploitation of children.'[6] Similarly, while Mr Gradgrind's naive faith in blue books and statistics is a justifiable target for Dickens's satire on aggressive factualism in *Hard Times*, one should remember also that those same blue books – the various reports of the Children's Employment Commission and the Sanitary Boards, for example, or Edwin Chadwick's great *Report on the Sanitary Condition of the Labouring Population of Great Britain* (1842) – laid the foundation of information upon which the substantial Victorian achievement in reforming legislation, especially in the field of Public Health, was laid. To point this out is not to minimize the extent of human suffering involved in the process of industrialization, merely to state the obvious but often neglected truth that the publicity the Victorians gave to their problems, as a prelude to reform, is a witness to the awakened social conscience of the age, not to its unique callousness or inhumanity.

The novelists played an important part in publicizing the Condition-of-England question. The rise of the social-problem novel in the 1830s is closely related to contemporary interest in such matters as the New Poor Law of 1834 and factory legislation, as the full titles of works like *Oliver Twist; or the Parish Boy's Progress* and Mrs Trollope's *The Life and Adventures of Michael Armstrong, the Factory Boy* (1840) indicate. Frances Trollope deserves credit for having introduced the factory system and its evils to English fiction, although her book's restriction to the issue of child-labour and avoidance of adult efforts at 'combination' set it rather apart from the so-called 'industrial novels' of the later 1840s and 1850s, novels responding to the challenge of Chartism, such as *Sybil*, *Alton Locke* and *Mary Barton*, or to the topical concern with trade unions and industrial strikes, like *Hard Times* and *North and South*. The term 'industrial novel' is not entirely satisfactory, since *Alton Locke* is not concerned with *industrial* labour as such, but is better than Cazamian's 'social novel' (are not most novels 'social'?) or 'Condition-of-England novel', a much wider category. It denotes a group of novels which, with the partial exception of Elizabeth Gaskell's, are frankly opportunistic in exploiting the findings of contemporary observers and in following, after a certain inevitable time-lag, the contours of contemporary concern and debate. The documentary element is often close to the surface and only partly digested. It is known that Disraeli drew extensively on Parliamentary reports when writing

[6]*Politics and Literature in Modern Britain* (Macmillan, 1977), p. 139.

Sybil, that Kingsley was stimulated to write *Alton Locke* as a result of reading an article by Henry Mayhew in the *Morning Chronicle*, that Dickens's visit to Preston in January 1854 to witness the strike there inspired the industrial scenes in *Hard Times*, begun at the same time.[7] The price of topicality in some of these novels is a shallow-rooted and external vision of the industrial scene, and a correspondingly exaggerated rhetoric of moral indignation.

Yet industrial life was a genuinely new subject for the novel, and its incorporation within the conventions of early Victorian fiction posed inevitable problems of form and treatment, to say nothing of the ideological problems inherent in the subject itself. Work, and especially the routine work of factory or mill, is something that novelists have always had difficulty in making interesting, and the same is true of social problems when these are not dramatic or romantic in nature. In the industrial novel the documentary impulse towards the patient observation of the everyday is always potentially at odds with the inherent tendency of the form towards exciting plots and romantic entanglements. 'It is admitted that a novel can hardly be made interesting or successful without love', Trollope observed half-regretfully in his *Autobiography* (12), and all these novels fall back on love as a means of sustaining interest, spinning the plot, or generally sugaring the pill. In a letter to the editor of the magazine serializing *Yeast*, Kingsley wrote that misunderstanding of his message was not a cause for worry: 'There is love and murder enough to satisfy "sweet-toothed" readers.'[8] The trouble with the resort to 'love and murder', though, is that these tend to run away with a novel, distorting the social theme in the process. Elizabeth Gaskell's original title for the novel that became *Mary Barton* was *John Barton*, and it was to have been a study of the struggles and sufferings of a typical working-man. *Mary Barton* is partly that, of course, but the plot of which Mary is the centre, with its melodramatic elements of rival lovers, murder, trial, and last-minute rescue, transforms it into a different, more conventional kind of book than *John Barton* might have been. The formal problem of marrying a new kind of interest and subject-matter to the available conventions is satisfactorily resolved in only one of these novels, *North and South*, and significantly this is achieved by making the central consciousness a middle-class character not very different in background and outlook from Elizabeth Gaskell herself.

For the industrial novel, in the last analysis, is a middle-class enterprise. It reveals the fears and fantasies, as well as the generous sympathies, of

[7]The term 'industrial novel' to describe this group of novels is used by Raymond Williams in *Culture and Society 1780-1950* (Harmondsworth, Penguin, 1961). The novelists' use of documentary material is fully discussed in Sheila Smith, *The Other Nation*. For Dickens's visit to Preston and his response to the strike there see K.J. Fielding, 'The Battle for Preston', *Dickensian* 54 (1954), pp. 159–62, also the article by G. Carnall mentioned in Select Bibliography.

[8]Quoted Smith, *The Other Nation*, p. 232.

writers confronted by what were then strange new areas of experience. Its essential context was the fear of Chartism, the predominantly working-class movement for political reform which flourished and declined in the first ten years of Victoria's reign. Chartism was born of disappointment with the 1832 Reform Bill and took its name from the 'People's Charter' proclaimed in 1838, with its famous 'six points' designed to secure working-class representation in Parliament. There were mass meetings and demonstrations of Chartists throughout this period, and much talk of the need for force if Parliament refused to grant their demands, but their aims were primarily constitutional, as is shown by the fact that they brought their petition three times to the House of Commons: in July 1839, in May 1842, this time with three million signatures, and in April 1848. On each occasion it was rejected. In 1848 the fears of the authorities were aroused by revolutions on the continent and rioting at home; London was packed with soldiers and special constables under the command of the duke of Wellington, but the Chartist demonstration went off quietly, dampened by the rain.

If the fear of Chartism was the inspiration for most of the industrial novels, then it is hardly an exaggeration to say that Carlyle's pamphlet, *Chartism* (1839), was the light by which the novelists learned to read the new phenomenon. Published in the same year as the first Chartist petition to Parliament, it offered a potent (and characteristic) blend of topical analysis and social prophecy. Carlyle began by castigating Parliament for busying itself with trivial issues like the 'Queen's Bedchamber question' while the most important question close to home remained undiscussed: 'Surely Honourable Members ought to speak of the Condition-of-England question too' (1). In raising this question Carlyle showed himself deeply sympathetic to the sufferings of the working classes but condescending to their political aims: he saw the Chartist meetings and demonstrations not as a demand for political reform, which they were, but as the sign of a deep-rooted sickness which political democracy was powerless to cure. Carlyle was both more sympathetic than other observers, and more apocalyptic.

> What are all popular commotions and maddest bellowings, from Peterloo to the Place-de-Grève itself? Bellowings, *in*articulate cries as of a dumb creature in rage and pain; to the ear of wisdom they are inarticulate prayers: 'Guide me, govern me! I am mad and miserable, and cannot guide myself!' Surely of all 'rights of man' this right of the ignorant man to be guided by the wiser, to be, gently and forcibly, held in the true course by him, is the indisputablest. Nature herself ordains it from the first. . . .Not towards the impossibility, 'self-government' of a multitude by a multitude; but towards some possibility, government by the wisest, does bewildered Europe struggle. (6)

Carlyle's rhetoric answered to the contemporary sense of crisis, and the appeal of his analysis at the time lay in the fact that while his language was apocalyptic, his message was highly conservative: the poor need to be led, by those in authority freshly enlightened as to their true condition. A revolution was needed, but in the hearts and minds of the ruling classes rather than in the structure of society. It was a call for responsible leadership. The analysis looks forward to Carlyle's later writings on the nature of true leadership in *Heroes and Hero-Worship* (1840) and *Past and Present* (1843), and back to his earlier, Romantic antithesis in 'Signs of the Times' (1829) between an external faith in *'mere political arrangements'* and the internal workings of conscience and imagination. In this respect *Chartism* is a pivotal work in Carlyle's career, and with *Past and Present* was to have a great influence on the industrial novel, despite the fact that it has remarkably little to offer in the way of specific suggestions. *Hard Times* is dedicated to Carlyle, *Alton Locke* shows his influence on almost every page, *Sybil* reads at times like a fictionalized *Past and Present*, and even *Mary Barton* ends, like *Alton Locke*, with Carlyle's favourite panacea of emigration.

Disraeli and Kingsley

Carlyle went on to develop his ideas about the nature of the leadership necessary for the new industrial society in *Past and Present*. Building on an ironic contrast between the modern workhouse and the medieval monastery – the past and present of the title – he argued that the existing aristocracy had to reassume leadership by casting off their idleness and throwing themselves into the work of reform, beginning with the corn laws; and, rather more originally, he suggested that they should be assisted in this task by a new aristocracy drawn from the ranks of capital, 'Captains of Industry' (Carlyle's influence owed much to his genius for the catchphrase) espousing a new 'Chivalry of Labour', who would bring to the leadership of society a working knowledge of industrialism. These ideas, and many more from the rich stockpot of nineteenth-century medievalism, are to be found in Disraeli's *Coningsby* and *Sybil*, which for all their faults have a lively and intelligent topicality. *Coningsby* was considered in the previous chapter in relation to the fashionable novel, and *Sybil* partly belongs there too. It is more usefully seen, however, as a Condition-of-England novel, and has even some claim to be considered the first in that now richly populated field. Previous novels had dealt with particular issues, like the employment of children in factories, and Coningsby had come north to meet a Carlylean Captain of Industry in Oswald Millbank, but *Sybil*, published in 1845, is the first novel to make Chartism and the industrial city (Disraeli's 'Mowbray' is Manchester) central to a vision of the nation as a whole.

Sybil, or The Two Nations, to give the book its full title, spans the acute phase of Chartist agitation. It opens in 1837, with the death of William IV and the accession of the young Victoria, takes in the first Chartist petition of 1839, and ends with the plug riots that followed rejection of the second petition in 1842. Around these topical events is woven the improbable and tedious plot of the love affair between the young aristocrat Charles Egremont and sybil Gerard, daughter of the Chartist Walter Gerard, who turns out to be the true heir to Mowbray Castle and an aristocrat of more ancient lineage than any of the noblemen in the book. This romantic-fashionable nonsense should not be allowed to obscure, however, the deeper and more interesting logic of *Sybil*, which is one of contrast. As Egremont shuttles between his mother's political salon in London, his brother's estate at Marney Abbey, where agricultural distress is acute, Mowbray Castle and Mowbray town, and the home of Sybil, a diagram of the Condition of England emerges. Using the technique of contrast he had learned from *Past and Present*, and possibly from *Oliver Twist*, Disraeli presents a series of ironic parallels between the Two Nations of the subtitle. We see the society hostesses in London discussing trivial issues like the Jamaica bill and the Bedchamber plot, and then Widow Carey and the working girls flirting and debating politics in a Mowbray pub. In one chapter the young swells of Mowbray, Dandy Mick and Devilsdust, toast 'Confusion to Capital', in the next we are at Mowbray Castle and Lord de Mowbray is holding forth against 'the levelling spirit of the age' (II, 10, 11). The deficiencies of aristocracy are mocked in the pagan industrial town of Wodgate, a place with 'no churches, chapels, town-hall, institute, theatre', without law or police or sanitation – and thus an image of the England Carlyle's 'Do-Nothing Aristocracy' will eventually create – and yet run by the master workmen, and so, Disraeli says with bitter irony, by

> a real aristocracy; it is privileged, but it does something for its privileges. It is distinguished from the main body not merely by name. It is the most knowing class at Wodgate; it possesses indeed in its way complete knowledge; and it imparts in its manner a certain quantity of it to those whom it guides. Thus it is an aristocracy that leads, and therefore a fact. (III, 4)

There is in passages like these a bold imaginative grasp of a total situation which is the real strength of *Sybil*; it goes with Disraeli's talent for the eye-catching slogan (like 'the Two Nations') and the power of vigorous caricature evident in such often-quoted scenes as the description of the tommy-shop in Book III, chapter 3. In detail, he is always vulnerable. His landscapes drip with stage paint, his humbler characters talk either in stilted heroics or in a literary cockney quite out of keeping with the regional setting, much of his social realism gives the impression of being, as one contemporary reviewer put it, 'not drawn from life, but concocted from second-hand sources, and out of materials which the painter was incompetent to appreciate or mould'.[9] These weaknesses matter in any

9[W.R. Greg], *Westminster Review* 44 (1845), p. 143.

final assessment of Disraeli as a novelist, but they should not be allowed to detract from his achievement here in bringing the Condition-of-England question to a vivid fictional focus.

Sybil is less obviously an expression of the ideas of the Young England movement than *Coningsby*. Young Englandism appears in the high-church vicar, Aubrey St Lys, and in Sybil's Roman Catholicism and convent breeding, and in the ruined Marney Abbey with its 'Portal of the Poor', a symbol – like Carlyle's monastery of St Edmundsbury – of the medieval Church which once cared for the people. It lies behind the novel's most operatic moment, when among the ruins of the Abbey, flushed with the setting sun and ringing with 'the evening hymn to the Virgin', Sybil pronounces on the divided nation England has become:

> 'Two nations; between whom there is no intercourse and no sympathy; who are as ignorant of each other's habits, thoughts, and feelings, as if they were dwellers in different zones, or inhabitants of different planets. . .'
> 'You speak of—' said Egremont, hesitatingly.
> 'THE RICH AND THE POOR.'
> At this moment a sudden flush of rosy light, suffusing the grey ruins, indicated that the sun had just fallen; and, through a vacant arch that overlooked them, alone in the resplendent sky, glittered the twilight star. (II, 5)

The atmosphere of this scene is very much of its period, combining the values of Young England and the Anglo-Catholic Oxford Movement (it is worth recalling that Newman went over to Rome in the year *Sybil* was published) with an idealized, medievalized vision of maidenhood that looks forward to Pre-Raphaelitism at the end of the decade. It is an ambience subjected to critical scrutiny in a first novel serialized in *Fraser's Magazine* in 1848, Kingsley's *Yeast: A Problem* (1851).

Charles Kingsley (1819–75) is remembered today as a novelist for one classic historical-novel-cum-adventure-story, *Westward Ho!* (1855), one dubiously classic work of Victorian fantasy, *The Water Babies* (1863), and one greatly interesting, although not quite great social-problem novel, *Alton Locke, Tailor and Poet* (1850). Until recently *Westward Ho!* was usually read in childhood, and it is in childhood that some of Kingsley's narrative gifts are perhaps best appreciated – his feeling for nature, especially for the Devon countryside in which this tale of Elizabethan exploration and conquest begins, and the relish in his descriptions of physical activities like sailing and fighting. The adult reader soon becomes aware of the pugnacious Protestant nationalism that underlies the simple adventure story, making the war between England and Spain a struggle between Protestantism and Catholicism, the virgin queen and the Virgin Mary. This side of *Westward Ho!* has origins both psychological and topical, in Kingsley's passionate identification with the Allied cause in the Crimean War and with the inflamed Protestantism that followed the restoration of the Catholic hierarchy to England in 1850, and the label of 'muscular Christianity' has stuck to him ever since. But there is more to Kingsley than this. He deserves to be remembered also as a leading member of the Christian Socialist movement in Victorian England and contributor to its two short-lived but influential journals, *Politics for the People* (1848) and *Christian Socialist* (1850–51), a movement for social reform born out of the collapse of Chartism and seeking to Christianize its ideals (but not its political aims) and to campaign for sanitary reform and working-men's associations. 'Socialism,' the first issue of *Christian Socialist* declared, 'the latest born of the forces now at work in modern society, and Christianity, the eldest born of those forces, are in their natures not hostile, but akin to each other, or rather. . .the one is but the development, the outgrowth, the manifestation of the other.'[10] If there is some intellectual simplification in this declaration, there is also something attractive in the energy with which Kingsley threw himself into the task of writing his 'Parson Lot' tracts and articles and spreading the message in his sermons and speeches. Few Anglican clergymen of the day can have been prepared, as he was, to stand up in a meeting of working-men when the Church was under attack and declare 'with the stammer which always came at first when he was much moved, but which fixed every one's attention at once – "I am a Church of England parson" – a long pause – "and a Chartist" '.[11] Kingsley's sympathy with the political aims of Chartism was in fact limited, but no novel of the period goes further than *Alton Locke* in trying to understand the grievances which inspired Chartism and to recreate them in their context.

Yeast was described by Kingsley as an attempt 'to show what some at least of the young in these days are really thinking and feeling' (Preface, 1851) – a novel about young England to counter Young England. The central character is one Lancelot Smith, the name combining ancient chivalry and modern middle-class reality, and in so far as this hotch-potch of a novel can be said to have a controlling theme it is that suggested by the hero's name: the conflict of past and present, the struggle of a romantic chivalrous youth, the son of a merchant but aroused by romantic literature and the medieval revival, to confront the problematic present, 'to be emancipated. . .from selfish dreams; to learn to work trustfully in the living Present, not to gloat sentimentally over the unreturning Past' (3). The theme is not worked out very successfully, but there is at least a sporadic attempt to project Lancelot's inner debate onto society at large and sound out the contemporary adequacy of the high-church, paternalist, medievalizing nostrums of Young England.

Much more successful is *Alton Locke*, a novel saved from the shapelessness of *Yeast* by the intensity of Kingsley's involvement with his

[10]Quoted Louis Cazamian, *The Social Novel in England 1830–1850*, trans. Martin Fido (Routledge & Kegan Paul, 1973), p. 251.

[11]Thomas Hughes, 'Prefatory Memoir', *Alton Locke* (Macmillan, 1884), p. xix.

Chartist hero and the element of cultural typicality in the story he unfolds. Writing on board an emigrant ship taking him to the United States, Alton recalls his impoverished childhood in London, his ambitions to become a poet, and the experiences of exploitation and urban destitution which turn him into a Chartist and lead to his imprisonment for inciting a riot of farm-labourers. The first part of the novel traces his development from disillusionment with his mother's Calvinism, through his discovery of a father-figure in the old Scots bookseller and 'moral force' radical who adopts him, to involvement with 'physical force' Chartism; the second takes him through disillusionment with the Chartist demonstration of 1848 to physical recuperation and Christian conversion at the hands of an aristocratic lady. Kingsley's choice of a first-person narrative for his tailor-poet's story enabled him to incorporate in a bold and original way the knowledge of working-class life he had obtained from his acquaintance with self-educated artisans like Thomas Cooper and the Chartist poet Gerald Massey. He may fail to capture their tone – the polemical urge to rebuke the 'scented Belgravian' (8), the fashionable reader, works against verisimilitude – but the story Alton tells has a convincing and, in the early chapters at least, moving representativeness. The Dissenting household in which he is brought up by his widowed mother, with its stern distrust of the imagination; the awakening of the boy's imagination through reading the Bible and *Pilgrim's Progress*, and the parallel discovery of the beauty of the natural world; the hunger for books leading to the discovery of Milton and Byron, and then the nights spent in illicit, eyesight-ruining reading in the garret-bedroom – all these aspects of Alton's early life can be paralleled many times in the history of working-class self-education in the nineteenth century.[12] Kingsley is particularly good at conveying the way the hungry imagination of the poor boy struggles out of its physical and spiritual prison, feeding itself on such scraps of colour as the description of the Pacific islands in the missionary tracts:

> And one day, I recollect it well, in the little dingy, foul, reeking, twelve-foot-square back-yard, where huge smoky party-walls shut out every breath of air and almost all the light of heaven, I had climbed up between the water-butt and the angle of the wall for the purpose of fishing out of the dirty fluid which lay there, crusted with soot and alive with insects, to be renewed only three times in the seven days, some of the great larvae and kicking monsters which made up a large item in my list of wonders: all of a sudden the horror of the place came over me; those grim prison-walls above, with their canopy of lurid smoke; the dreary, sloppy, broken pavement; the horrible stench of the stagnant cesspools; the utter want of form, colour, life in the whole place, crushed me down, without my being able to analyse my feelings as I can now; and then came over me that dream of Pacific Islands, and the free, open sea; and I slid

---

[12]See Richard Altick, *The English Common Reader* (Chicago, University of Chicago Press, 1957), and David Vincent, *Bread, Knowledge and Freedom* (Europa, 1981).

down from my perch, and bursting into tears threw myself upon my knees in the court, and prayed aloud to God to let me be a missionary. (1)

In this moment of negative epiphany Kingsley transcends his usual rhetoric of sympathy and indignation to give us a piercing sense of Alton's predicament that is at once individual and general. We see the how and why of the poetry he will later write, its 'spiritual wedding' of 'Childe Harold and the old missionary records' (8), and the sheer crushing power of urban ugliness. In such an environment, we are made to feel, poetry and religion can only be means of escape.

It is in moments of sympathetic insight like these, as well as in the more famous and familiar accounts of the sweatshops and the slums, that *Alton Locke* succeeds. The novel's other considerable success is Sandy Mackaye, the largely self-taught Carlylean sage who is the principal agent of Alton's liberation and education after he rejects his mother's narrow religion and leaves home. Mackaye is Kingsley's tribute to all that Carlyle had done for him as a spiritual teacher and social prophet, and he tends to overshadow the other characters in this most Carlylean of novels. This is in some respects unfortunate for the book's political theme, since Kingsley had started by balancing Mackaye's moral persuasiveness with the political idealism of John Crossthwaite, a sympathetically conceived Chartist activist whom Alton meets in the tailors' workroom. In chapter 10, 'How Folks Turn Chartists' (the pedagogic intent is typical of the industrial novel), Crossthwaite is seen attempting to organize a protest strike against the employers' decision to close the workshop and return to piece-work, and justifying the aims of the Charter in terms of the middle-class political reform that had preceded and inspired it:

'Why, didn't they tell us, before the Reform Bill, that extension of the suffrage was to cure everything? And how can you have too much of a good thing? We've only taken them at their word, we Chartists.'

It is an unanswerable point, which the novel proceeds to deflect. Alton becomes a Chartist, but his later, narrating voice instructs us in the folly of this faith in 'outer' system: 'It was within, rather than without, that I needed reform' (10). Mackaye embodies this Carlylean message. Just as Carlyle's rhetoric had responded to the contemporary sense of crisis while disdaining '*mere political arrangements*', so Sandy Mackaye combines a lifetime's service in the cause of the 'people' with indifference to the political manifestation of that cause in Chartism. His speech in refusing to sign the petition is a magnificent piece of rhetoric –

'tell 'em that ane o' fourscore years and mair – ane that has grawn grey in the people's cause – that sat at the feet o' Cartwright, an' knelt by the death-bed o' Rabbie Burns – ane that cheerit Burdett as he went to the Touer, an' spent his wee earnings for Hunt an' Cobbett. . .sends them the last message that e'er he'll send on airth; tell 'em that they're the slaves o' warse than priests and kings – the slaves o' their ain lusts and passions – ' (33)

– but like his symbolic death on the morning the petition is presented to Parliament on 10 April 1848, it serves to disinherit Chartism from the tradition of democratic radicalism to which it belongs and which Mackaye here invokes. Still, our final image of 'the old warrior dead upon his shield' (34) crowns an impressive creation. The loneliness and integrity of the self-made man is well caught, and the intermingling of political and religious yearnings in his personality rings true to the period. Mackaye may at times seem more of an aristocrat than a democrat, but that too is in keeping with the type he belongs to.

In common with other novels on this subject, *Alton Locke* portrays the failure of working-class movements as both inevitable and brought about by violence and false leadership. Alton's attempts to prove his loyalty to 'The Cause' by preaching Chartism to farm labourers ends in rioting and his own imprisonment; the failure of the 1848 Chartist petition is laid at the door of Irish rogues and hotheads. In the end Kingsley follows Carlyle and Disraeli in locating true leadership in a regenerated aristocracy. It is through Alton's chance encounter with the middle-class clerical family, the Winnstays, that he meets their relation Eleanor Staunton, who as the widowed Lady Ellerton leads him to Christian redemption at the end of the novel. Here *Alton Locke* enters the area where class-consciousness and sexuality struggle in the soul of the poor boy striving to improve himself, almost a new area for fiction and one to be explored further in novels like *Great Expectations, The Princess Casamassima* and *Born in Exile*. For much of the action Alton is hopelessly in love with a 'lady', the worldly Lillian Winnstay, and her eventual marriage to his cousin George, a cynical and sceptical clergyman, typifies all that Kingsley saw as corrupt and irresponsible in the contemporary Church of England. His loss of Lillian coincides melodramatically with the collapse of the Charter, and in his ensuing illness he is nursed back to health and a new Christian vision by Eleanor. After the remarkable 'Dream Land' chapter (36), a visionary account of Alton's rebirth in terms of current evolutionary theory, the ending of the novel becomes a virtual sermon, with Eleanor Christianizing the Carlylean analysis that has underlain the book:

> 'Yes,' she continued, 'Freedom, Equality, and Brotherhood are here. Realize them in thine own self, and so alone thou helpest to make them realities for all. Not from without, from Charters and Republics, but from within, from the Spirit working in each; not by wrath and haste, but by patience made perfect through suffering, canst thou proclaim their good news to the growing masses, and deliver them, as thy Master did before thee, by the cross, and not the sword. Divine paradox!' (41)

The social grievances at the root of Chartism, so sympathetically explored and denounced in the early chapters, are here baptized by an aristocratic lady: we are back momentarily in the world of *Sybil* and that strange, very Victorian blend of rank, religiosity and paternalism. And it is as a novel of its period that *Alton Locke* is perhaps best approached today. It is not a timeless classic but very much a work of the mid-century, brightly lit and brimming with significance like a Pre-Raphaelite painting, rather hysterical in places, but full of the enthusiastic sympathies and aversions of a warm-blooded, impulsive man who responded with commendable intensity to the human suffering of the time.

Elizabeth Gaskell

It is a fair criticism of Disraeli and Kingsley in their social-problem novels, and even of Dickens in *Hard Times*, to say that they were too aware of their characters as aspects of a 'problem' to let them breathe freely, but the same could hardly be said with justice of Elizabeth Gaskell (1810–65). The great strength of her work is a quality of patience in the handling of character, born of confidence in her own knowledge; an ability to see her characters not only in relation to the problems of Chartism or industrial strife, but in relation to themselves and each other, as individuals living together a life which inevitably contains much that has no bearing on social problems as such. This gives her two industrial novels – *Ruth* is a rather different case – a solidity and authenticity which no others of the genre possess.

Elizabeth Gaskell is the health visitor among the Victorian novelists. Her characteristic procedure is to take the reader into the homes of her characters, observing the smallest details of household decoration and routine and the texture of daily life, and only then to move outward into the contended area of 'social problems'. In the early chapters of *Mary Barton* (1848) this approach of patient observation yields a uniquely full and sympathetic account of working-class life in Manchester. The Bartons are introduced in the setting of their home and its furnishings; their holiday meal in chapter 2 is carefully itemized and priced, its little luxuries (the ham and rum Mary is sent out to buy) explained in terms of the traditions of working-class hospitality. The hard-won decency of Alice Wilson's life in her cellar-room comes across in details like the description of 'her unlackered, ancient, third-hand tea-tray arranged with a black tea-pot, two cups with a red and white pattern, and one with the old friendly willow pattern, and saucers, not to match. . .' (4). It is the respect for her characters implied by such observation that is at the root of her success in communicating the totality of their lives; not just their sufferings (though these are never far away) but also the social rituals, and the friendships and affections and memories and interests that sustain them and make them individual – old Alice with her memories of her childhood home in the country, which she longs to revisit and never does, or the weaver-entomologist Job Legh, whose walls are hung with 'rude wooden frames of impaled insects' (5). The fact that these characters are shown to be capable of leading dignified and independent lives, given half a chance, makes more terrible the sufferings of those who cannot cope, like the dying Davenport in his cellar, where 'three or four little children [were] rolling on the damp, nay wet, brick floor, through which the stagnant, filthy moisture of the street oozed up; the fire-place was empty and black; the wife sat on her husband's chair, and cried in the dank loneliness' (6).

Gaskell's method of undogmatic observation leads her to imagine contrasts and juxtapositions which are sometimes more disturbing in their social implications than her reconciling authorial commentary can quite encompass. In chapter 6 we are taken from the cellar in which Davenport is dying to the millowner's house where, though trade is bad and workers are laid off, the Carson family can still idle over their substantial cooked breakfast. The contrast may be a little crude, but it makes John Barton's retort to the conventional wisdom about the 'sufferings' of the masters a devastating one: ' "Han they ever seen a child o' their'n die for want o' food?" ' (6). In a way these contrasts are the more powerful because of Gaskell's attempts to soften the impression of a cruel injustice which they leave behind. The authorial voice seeks to explain and reconcile, but the observing eye records the ineluctable fact that when times are bad it is the workman and his children who starve.

> Carriages still roll along the streets, concerts are still crowded by subscribers, the shops for expensive luxuries still find daily customers, while the workman loiters away his unemployed time in watching these things, and thinking of the pale, uncomplaining wife at home, and the wailing children asking in vain for enough of food, of the sinking health, of the dying life of those near and dear to him. The contrast is too great. Why should he alone suffer from bad times?
>
> I know that this is not really the case; and I know what is the truth in such matters: but what I wish to impress is what the workman feels and thinks. (3)

But Gaskell does not say what is 'really' the case here; the authorial commentary backs away from acknowledging the full implications of the contrast which her observing eye has perceived, which in turn might have led her to a more sympathetic view of John Barton's political activites, his trades unionism and involvement with Chartism.

The first ten chapters give a tantalizing glimpse of what the originally conceived *John Barton* might have been, a novel rooted in a sense of individual lives but recognizing that their sufferings required cure at a more general level, through social and political reform. The truth, however, is that politics chills Gaskell's imagination, and Barton's inevitable involvement with politics, born as she shows it out of concern for others as well as himself, leads to a simplification of his character, as he takes to opium and then murders Harry Carson. The violence of that act is an expression of the violence she senses in the 'awful power' of working-class 'combination' (15), since Barton is forced to act against his nature by the binding power of a secret oath. It is characteristic that her largely sympathetic account of the strike in chapter 15 should end with the statement: 'So much for generalities. Let us now return to individuals.' This resort to individuals is a source of both strength and weakness in *Mary Barton*. It enabled Gaskell to particularise the Condition-of-England problem with a precision and sympathy that no other novelist of the period can match, and it gives real force to her plea for mutual forbearance and understanding between masters and men. But it also led her at the end to offer the deathbed reconciliation between Mr Carson and his son's murderer as a symbolic reconciliation of master and man, and that is a drastic simplification of the social vision unfolded in the early chapters. The John Barton we first meet is a man feeling his way through personal loss to political action and some general understanding of the suffering around him; the man who dies in Carson's arms is a guilty sinner reaching for forgiveness. Whether the deathbed moves us or not, its assertion of social reconciliation – 'Rich and poor, masters and men, were then brothers in the deep suffering of the heart' (35) – is hollow, because Barton has ceased to represent his class in any recognizable way. This is not to slight Gaskell's message of reconciliation as such, merely to recognize that it fails to meet the problem of rich and poor glimpsed in the early chapters – a problem structural and impersonal, inherent in the violent trade fluctuations of early industrial capitalism.

Her next industrial novel, *North and South* (1855), is more satisfying as a whole, though perhaps less moving in its parts, than *Mary Barton*. It followed *Hard Times* (1854) in Dickens's periodical *Household Words* and the two novels make an instructive comparison. *Hard Times* has the vigorous simplicity of a brilliant cartoon, impatiently piercing through surface appearance to moral judgement. *North and South* is more patient with surface, recognizing the profound effect which changes in environment have on individuals (it is one of the novel's major themes), and much more tentative in coming to conclusions. Dickens sees the north like a sharp-eyed Londoner on a flying visit, which of course he was on his trip to Preston, and cannot conceal how alien and incomprehensible it all is to him:

> It contained several large streets all very like one another, and many small streets still more like one another, inhabited by people equally like one another, who all went in and out at the same hours, with the same sound upon the same pavements, to do the same work, and to whom every day was the same as yesterday and to-morrow, and every year the counterpart of the last and the next. (I, 5)

He would never have described the inhabitants of Clapham as he describes Coketown here. Gaskell not only knew the north much better, she was concerned in a way Dickens was not to balance the claims of north and south at this moment in history and evaluate their contribution to national life. The sense of the present is rarely keener in Victorian fiction than it is in this novel, where different ways of life, old habits and new possibilities, contend in the heart and mind of the heroine, Margaret Hale.

Gaskell's original title was *Margaret Hale*, and the concentration on the experience of a central protagonist is mostly a gain. Something of *Mary Barton*'s sense of a whole community is missing, and with it the sharpness of conflict in the earlier novel; but the shrinking of the industrial theme to representative individuals – Thornton the prickly self-made mill-owner, Higgins the articulate striking workman – is not only more congenial to Gaskell's eye-level approach to social problems, it also allows a much more extensive debate about the issues than before. The strike may end in predictable violence, the reconciliation between master and man at the end may seem wishful rather than earned, but the chapter ('What is a Strike?') in which Higgins explains his motives for striking goes further than any previous novel in allowing the case for such action to be put:

> 'And so you plan dying, in order to be revenged upon them!'
> 'No,' said he, 'I dunnot. I just look forward to the chance of dying at my post sooner than yield. That's what folk call fine and honourable in a soldier, and why not in a poor weaver-chap?'
> 'But,' said Margaret, 'a soldier dies in the cause of the Nation – in the cause of others.'
> He laughed grimly. 'My lass,' said he, 'yo're but a young wench, but don't yo' think I can keep three people. . .on sixteen shilling a week? Dun yo' think it's for mysel' I'm striking work at this time? It's just as much in the cause of others as yon soldier – only, m'appen, the cause he dies for it's just that of somebody he never clapt eyes on, nor heerd on all his born days, while I take up John Boucher's cause, as lives next door but one, wi' a sickly wife, and eight childer. . .' (17)

This was a daring exchange to put in a novel written at the time of the Crimean War, and published in the same year as such bellicose offerings as *Maud* and *Westward Ho!*

The industrial matter is set in a larger framework of personal and social change. *North and South* is a partial *bildungsroman* dealing with the early adulthood of a woman caught between two worlds, south and north, past and future, bewildered (as she reflects at the end) by 'being whirled on through all these phases of my life, in which nothing abides by me, no creature, no place. . .' (46). The novel opens with Margaret leaving her cousin's leisured London home to return to her vicarage home in a Hampshire village, Helstone, where she finds the relations of childhood reversed: her parents now depend on her, and in place of the anticipated renewal of early certainties she comes face to face with her father's religious 'doubts', which necessitate removal to Milton-Northern

(Manchester). There is a whole chapter of Victorian middle-class history in the ensuing account of how the family respond to the upheaval: the departure from the idyllic Hampshire vicarage, with its echoes of Tennyson's *In Memoriam* (6), the struggle to adjust to life in the industrial north where feudal deference no longer holds, the illness and death of parents (the peevish mother, the willing but weak father) who fail to adapt, the conflict in Margaret herself between the pull of nostalgia and the urge to new life and fresh relationships. The central section of the novel is deeply of its time in this struggle to accommodate change, and the Tennysonian echoes are more than merely decorative. Walt Whitman's comment on Tennyson as the poet of his age defines Margaret's predica-ment as well: 'We are like the voyagers of a ship, casting off for new seas, distant shores. We would still dwell in the old suffocating and dead haunts, remembering and magnifying their pleasant experiences only, and more than once impell'd to jump ashore before it is too late, and stay where our fathers stay'd, and live as they lived.'[13] North and south are real locations but also places of the mind, symbols of a larger cultural upheaval which Gaskell underlines with analogies drawn from the English Civil War. Mrs Hale comes from the Royalist Beresford family, Mr Hale dies in Oxford, associated in this novel with feudalism and traditional culture, and set against the puritan and practical Milton-Northern, where Mr Thornton speaks in admiration of Cromwell (15). And this conflict of values is focused and developed in the turbulent relationship of Margaret and John Thornton, an affair of sharp oppositions managed by Gaskell with a fine sense of the sexual piquancy that lies in the mutual attraction of two proud and powerful natures.

The climax of the novel is not the sudden coming together of the two lovers in the last chapter but Margaret's return to Helstone after the death of her parents, when she can check the idealized memory which has sustained her in Milton-Northern with the reality of change in the village. Familiar landmarks have gone, households have changed, the old vicarage is being modernized; back at the inn Margaret looks across at the light shining in her old bedroom and realizes that there is no home to return to. Her initial sense of perplexity and loss gives way, next morning, to an acceptance of the inevitability of change: ' "If the world stood still, it would retrograde and become corrupt. . . .Looking out of myself, and my own painful sense of change, the progress of all around me is right and necessary" ' (46). The recognition is painful yet needs to be made if she is to take hold of the present in this changing society, which she does by accepting Thornton at the end. Their union is less a reconciliation of north and south than a meeting of kindred spirits, alike in their energy and independence, and in their orientation towards a future in which the best

[13]'A Word about Tennyson' (1887), in *Tennyson: The Critical Heritage*, ed. J.D. Jump (Routledge & Kegan Paul, 1967), p. 350.

part of the feudal past, the sense of social interdependence, will survive in Thornton's determination to cultivate 'some intercourse with the hands beyond the mere "cash nexus"' (51) in the new business which Margaret's money makes possible.

The critical esteem currently enjoyed by *Mary Barton* and *North and South* reflects our new-found appreciation of Elizabeth Gaskell as a novelist of social change, and it has involved a corresponding decline in the prestige of *Cranford* (1851–3), for long her most popular work. *Cranford*, and sometimes *Wives and Daughters*, are now taken to represent the vein of period charm in Gaskell which her more ambitious works are seen to transcend.[14] And yet, as Peter Keating demonstrates in his fine introduction to the Penguin edition, *Cranford* is far from innocent of the concerns which animate her other novels at this time. It too is informed by a sense of the present, even though it opens in the 1830s and deals with the lives of spinster ladies and widows in a county town seemingly remote from the great social changes of the age. The story of Miss Matty's thwarted life at the hands of her dominating elder sister Deborah and the Cranford 'strict code of gentility' certainly has a period charm, but it is set subtly in a larger context of historical change which reveals this as a dying way of life and introduces the characteristic Gaskell preoccupation with the survival of the past in the present. The mediating consciousness here is that of the narrator Mary Smith, more an observer than a character in the novel, and being young at the time, and a native of the nearby manufacturing town of Drumble, able to record the contortions of genteel poverty with an amused modern eye, while learning at the end that the bustling modern world will be a poorer place without the compensating Cranford virtues of kindness and neighbourliness.

Cranford began as a sketch for *Household Words* and then grew into something more as Gaskell realized the potential that lay in the subject of provincial life in the recent past. It is not a timeless idyll: running through it are the forces of the future which will leave Cranford stranded in the past, deftly indicated by such markers of change as the new railways, *Pickwick Papers*, the poems of Tennyson, the bank failure that ruins Miss Matty, the industrial rumble from nearby Drumble. These are set against a deepening awareness as we read of the power of the past in the characters' lives. The narrative reaches back from the opening debate between Miss Deborah and Captain Brown on the relative merits of Dr Johnson and Dickens to the story of Miss Matty's thwarted youthful love for Mr Holbrook, now an elderly, dying bachelor, and then in chapter 5, where Mary and Miss Matty read through the family letters after Deborah's death, to the eighteenth century:

---

[14]As they are by John Lucas, for example, one of Gaskell's best modern critics, who describes them as 'beautiful idylls' in *The Literature of Change* (Hassocks, Harvester, 1977), p. 2.

The letters were as happy as letters could be – at least those early letters were. There was in them a vivid and intense sense of the present time, which seemed so strong and full, as if it could never pass away, and as if the warm, living hearts that so expressed themselves could never die, and be as nothing to the sunny earth. I should have felt less melancholy, I believe, if the letters had been more so.

These long perspectives confer sympathy and understanding. The glimpse of Miss Matty's childhood, and her parents' devotion (they hope that ' "little Matty might not be vain, even if she were a bewty" '), make us feel the pathos of what might have been, of hopes never realized, and the ironic contrast between what Miss Matty was then and what she is now. We see too that while her parents lived in the age and wrote in the idiom of Dr Johnson, Miss Matty and her sister have not been able to grow into their own time and their own idiom. The perpetuation of old gentility far beyond its day has disinherited Miss Matty from the fulfilment her parents had known. Hence the many references in the novel to her love of children and babies, the thwarting of that impulse being beautifully caught in the characteristic little detail of the sisters' attitude to eating oranges:

> Miss Jenkyns did not like to cut the fruit; for, as she observed, the juice all ran out nobody knew where; sucking (only I think she used some more recondite word) was in fact the only way of enjoying oranges; but then there was the unpleasant association with a ceremony frequently gone through by little babies; and so, after dessert, in orange season, Miss Jenkyns and Miss Matty used to rise up, possess themselves each of an orange in silence, and withdraw to the privacy of their own rooms, to indulge in sucking oranges. (3)

There is comedy, pathos, acute observation of manners here: that is the distinctive *Cranford* note. But we should remember also, while admiring Gaskell's gentle exposure of a dying way of life, that Cranford has something to teach the modern world. Financial ruin comes to Miss Matty from the failure of the Drumble bank, but the qualities that enable her to meet ruin with dignity are generated within the old world, in the scrupulous honesty of Miss Matty herself and the rallying-round of her friends. The final impression left by the novel is not one of loss, but of kindness and community.

The close interplay of past and present which marks *North and South* and *Cranford* is not so keenly felt in Gaskell's later novels, where the time-gap widens into something more purely historical or picturesque. *Sylvia's Lovers* (1863) is a full-dress historical novel, set in Yorkshire in the 1790s against the background of the French Wars, and *Wives and Daughters* (1864–5) deals with English provincial life in the 1820s, a 40-year gap more typical of Thackeray and George Eliot (whose provincial novels may have been an influence). *Wives and Daughters* belongs to a later, more relaxed phase of Gaskell's art, and to a slightly later phase of Victorian society; and I shall return to it in discussing mid-Victorian domestic realism, of which it is a notable monument, in chapter 5.

There remains the superb novella *Cousin Phillis* (1863–4), a well-nigh perfect distillation of Gaskell's art and themes. Set in the 1840s, it tells of the love a farmer's daughter, Phillis Holman, comes to have for a railway engineer brought to the farm by her naive young cousin, who is also the narrator. In this modern version of pastoral the farmer, Ebenezer Holman, is no simple rustic but a classical scholar and Independent minister (a 'whole man' as his name suggests), and the engineer, Holdsworth, no conventional seducer but a lively practical man whose love for Phillis if fleeting and undeclared. All is beautifully understated, yet running through the story and its rich pastoral symbolism are the forces of change which bring Holdsworth to the farm and take him away again, to railway-building and marriage in Canada. It is a tale of loss, but done with such poise and delicacy that elegiac seems the wrong word to describe its effect. Brief as it is, *Cousin Phillis* is close to the heart of the Elizabeth Gaskell modern criticism has been most excited to rediscover – a novelist of change, in whose finest work the social and the personal are subtly interrelated.

3

The Sense of the Self: Autobiography, the Brontës and the Romantic Inheritance

The Sense of the Past and the Autobiographical Impulse

One cannot read very far in the early Victorian novelists without encountering Kathleen Tillotson's 'drag of the past' as well as 'the pull of the present'. We have seen how Thackeray's imagination tended to stray back to the Regency, and beyond, into the eighteenth century, and how Elizabeth Gaskell's subtle sense of social change comes from an awareness of the past surviving in the present (*North and South*) and the present growing in the past (*Cranford, Cousin Phillis*). A retrospective tendency can be found in many of the classic Victorian novels. The first word of *Wuthering Heights* (1847) is a date, 1801, and the novel is carefully and elaborately plotted back to its start in the 1770s. *Shirley* (1849) takes place in the Yorkshire of 1811–12. *Adam Bede* (1859) is set back 60 years to the last year of the eighteenth century, *Middlemarch* (1871–2) 40 years to 1831–2. Sometimes past and present mingle, as in *Vanity Fair* or *Jane Eyre*, set without great precision or consistency in the first quarter of the nineteenth century but dealing with the then (1847) topical issue of the governess; sometimes they are kept distinct, as in *Shirley, Wuthering Heights*, and all George Eliot's novels except for *Daniel Deronda*. When all allowances have been made for the natural tendency of novelists to set their fictions back in time, this impulse is too widespread and too thorough to be explained away happily in terms of the breathing-space necessary for plots to unfold and characters to grow or age. Without being quite historical novels, all these works in their very different ways invoke, and recreate, an historical perspective, either by returning to a formative past (*Vanity Fair*), or to a historical turning-point (*Adam Bede, Middlemarch*), or to the remembered world of childhood (*The Mill on the Floss, Wives and Daughters*).

What we are faced with in this phenomenon is not the objectivity of the

Texts: References to *Jane Eyre* and *Villette* are to the editions in the Penguin English Library, to *Agnes Grey* and *The Professor* to the texts in the Haworth Edition (1899–1903), and to the new World's Classics edition for *Wuthering Heights*. The latter is based on the first edition of the novel, which was published in 2 volumes: in most modern reprints the chapters in volume II are numbered from 15 to 34.

historical novelist sitting in comfortable detachment from a past which is well and truly gone and has to be resurrected from sources, but something altogether more personal and subjective, in which memory and nostalgia play their part, as well as the desire of the individual in an age of rapid change to orientate himself or herself in relation to past and present by discovering, or more precisely uncovering, a sense of personal and social continuity and stability. These novelists are concerned with the recent past of their society as an aspect of their concern with the personal past – the past of childhood memory and (what is often a powerful ingredient in the memory of our childhood) the memory of parents' memories. George Eliot observed in her essay 'Looking Backward' that the age of Pitt 'never seemed prosaic' to her because it was 'the time of my father's youth' and 'came to my imagination first through his memories, which made a wondrous perspective to my little daily world of discovery'.[1] And it is that double reach of individual memory which frames the historical limits of the retrospective Victorian novels, in George Eliot's case extending from the time of her father's youth in *Adam Bede* and *Silas Marner* to the time of her own childhood and youth in *The Mill on the Floss*. Elizabeth Gaskell has a similar command of her own and others' memories, acknowledging in 'The Last Generation in England' (1849) her desire 'to put upon record some of the details of country town life, either observed by myself, or handed down to me by older relations. . .'.[2] George Eliot took the germ idea for *Adam Bede* from a story told her by her Methodist aunt in 1839, when she was 20, and the Brontës found material for their fiction in the recollections of past Yorkshire life handed down to them by the family housekeeper, Tabby Ackroyd.

The important point is that history and autobiography, the social and the personal, are not really separable here. The concern for changing ways is bound up with the experience of having lived through these changes, or of knowing others who have, and with a sense of the unprecedented nature of the changes themselves. Thackeray's *Roundabout Paper*, 'De Juventute', is a classic expression of this feeling. 'We who have lived before railways were made, belong to another world', he wrote:

> *Then* was the old world. Stage-coaches, more or less swift, riding-horses, packhorses, highwaymen, knights in armour, Norman invaders, Roman legends, Druids, Ancient Britons painted blue, and so forth – all these belong to the old period. . . .But your railroad starts the new era, and we of a certain age belong to the new time and the old one. . . .There it lies on the other side of yonder embankments. You young folks have never seen it; and Waterloo is to you no more than Agincourt, and George IV than Sardanapalus. We elderly

---

[1] *The Impressions of Theophrastus Such* (1879), variously reprinted.
[2] Reprinted as an appendix to E.P. Watson's edition of *Cranford* (Oxford, OUP, 1977), p. 161–68; p. 161. The essay is also reprinted in the Penguin English Library edition of *Cranford and Cousin Phillis*.

people have lived in that prae-railroad world, which has passed into limbo and vanished from under us. I tell you it was firm under our feet once, and not long ago. They have raised those railroad embankments up, and shut off the old world that was behind them.

Those iron lines, that embankment, underscore a change more profound, as Kathleen Tillotson observes, than any subsequent generation has known. 'The sense of division, of belonging to two ages. . .can never have been so strong as for those authors who grew up into the railway age. Cut off abruptly from the stagecoach world in their youth, they prolonged and idealized it in memory. By constantly recreating it, they made good their age's seeming betrayal'.[3]

The novelists were encouraged in their task of imaginative recreation by the example of Scott and by the Romantic poets, especially Wordsworth. Scott's was an ambiguous inheritance, as we saw in chapter 1. He was the founding-father of the historical romance, which in the hands of imitators like W.H. Ainsworth and G.P.R. James very quickly fell into critical disrepute. In 1832, the year of Scott's death, a writer in *The Athenaeum* was already referring to Scott's imitators as 'The Wardrobe School of Novelists', and by the time of George Henry Lewes's attack on 'Historical Romance' in the *Westminster Review* in 1846, and Thackeray's *Punch* parody 'Barbazure' (1847), this aspect of the Scott inheritance was widely seen to be bankrupt.[4] When novelists began to take history seriously again, as Thackeray did in his 'Novel Without a Hero', they wrote in conscious reaction against historical romance and so, to some extent, in reaction against Scott also. But Scott was also a novelist of regional life, and much could be learnt from his example in the recording of changing customs and manners. If many Victorian novels are 'novels of the recent past', in Kathleen Tillotson's phrase, then a precedent for this kind of semi-historical fiction existed in Scott's own novels of the recent past, like *Guy Mannering* (1815) and *The Antiquary* (1816) – novels of regional life and change, set comfortably within living memory, and evincing that domestication of the historical sense which is Scott's chief legacy to Victorian fiction. The novel of remoter historical events was a formal challenge to be attempted once or twice in their careers, but the deeper creative influence is to be seen in the use to which the Victorian novelists put Scott's example in recording the impact of change upon the provincial communities they lived in or remembered – Cranford, Middlemarch, Casterbridge. I shall return to this aspect of the Scott inheritance when considering *Wuthering Heights*.

The importance of Wordsworth is obvious. The prominence he gave to

[3]*Novels of the Eighteen-Forties*, pp. 106–7. Thackeray's essay was published in the *Cornhill Magazine* in 1860, and reprinted in his *Roundabout Papers* (1863), variously reprinted.
[4]See James C. Simmons, *The Novelist as Historian: Essays on the Victorian Historical Novel* (The Hague, Mouton, 1973).

childhood, his sense of a 'natural piety' linking the different stages of human growth, and his stress on the redemptive power of memory, were all deeply congenial to the first generation of Victorian novelists. It was they rather than the Victorian poets who took over the mission Wordsworth envisaged for the poet in his Preface to the *Lyrical Ballads*, of being 'an upholder and preserver, carrying everywhere with him relationship and love'.[5] A partial exception should be made for Tennyson: he too was important in contributing a note of elegy to the Victorian imagination of change, and his poems, especially the 1842 volumes and *In Memoriam*, passed very quickly into the literary bloodstream. Tennyson's 'passion of the past', which acknowledges a picturesqueness in the receding view just because it is receding, may seem more purely nostalgic, and therefore less valuable, than Wordsworth's more intellectually rigorous concept of memory, but by mid-century the two influences were mingling. For the student of Victorian Romanticism there is something richly suggestive in the publication, in 1850, of *The Prelude, In Memoriam* and *David Copperfield*; and David DeLaura is surely right to see the autobiographical impulse as not merely symptomatic of the time but central to its creative enterprise:

> This presentation of one's own past, as part of a search for new meanings in a deteriorating cultural situation, is perhaps the most central binding activity of serious nineteenth-century literature. It is the great 'task', a kind of implicitly shared program for the century. This everywhere evident autobiographical pressure of the period, deriving most obviously from the example of Wordsworth, reaches a kind of climax around mid-century – most obviously, in such works as *In Memoriam*, the poetry of Arnold and Clough, the fiction of Charlotte Brontë, Thackeray's *Pendennis*, Dickens' *David Copperfield* and *Great Expectations*, and George Eliot's *Mill on the Floss*.[6]

Of the novels mentioned here, those of Charlotte Brontë (1816–55) are the most original, the most radically innovative in the imagination and presentation of the self. By invoking the larger context of cultural crisis and discontinuity which made the act of autobiography compulsive, DeLaura valuably reminds us that *Jane Eyre* and *Villette* do not exist in isolation from the social pressures of the time. Deeply private as these novels are, their concern with selfhood and fulfilment is urgent in a way that more ruminative fictions of the self, *David Copperfield* or *Mill on the Floss*, are not; their cry of need is a contemporary one. Lady Eastlake's remark, that *Jane Eyre* was the product of 'the tone of the mind and thought which has overthrown authority and violated every code human and divine abroad, and fostered Chartism and rebellion at home', is not so fatuous as it sounds

---

[5]Wordsworth and Coleridge, *Lyrical Ballads*, ed. R.L. Brett and A.R. Jones (Methuen, 1965), p. 259.
[6]'The Allegory of Life: The Autobiographical Impulse in Victorian Prose', in G.P. Landow (ed.), *Approaches to Victorian Autobiography* (Athens, Ohio, Ohio UP, 1979), p. 338.

in the light of subsequent knowledge of Charlotte Brontë's life and opinions: there is radicalism of feeling in that novel, despite its author's Tory, Anglican allegiances. We will not find Chartism in *Villette*, but we will find something like its domestic correlative, the 'hunger, rebellion and rage' that so shocked Matthew Arnold when he read the book.[7]

'You will see that "Villette" touches on no matter of public interest', Charlotte Brontë wrote to her publisher. 'I cannot write books handling the topics of the day; it is of no use trying'.[8] Her novels are not topical in the sense that *Mary Barton* or *Hard Times* were topical, but they are not as free from topicality as this disclaimer would suggest. *Jane Eyre* (1847) was published at a time when the situation of the governess was in the public eye, with the activities of the Governesses' Benevolent Institution founded in 1843, and the founding of Queen's College in 1848 to provide education for ladies in general and lady-governesses in particular. *Villette* (1853) has autobiographical roots in Charlotte's two visits to Brussels, but its anti-Catholicism is partly shaped by her awareness of the current scare over 'Papal Aggression' following the restoration of the Roman Catholic hierarchy to England in 1850. *Shirley* (1849) is partly a response to Chartism, distanced and transposed to the Yorkshire Luddite riots of 1811–12. More generally, the Brontë novels are 'social' in the sense that they were consciously writing regional novels, among the first of the kind in the Victorian period, and were pioneers in initiating a shift of scene away from the London axis of Dickens, Thackeray and the fashionable novelists. This was sufficiently unusual for one French reviewer of *Jane Eyre* to call it 'quite simply a novel of country life. This book contains not a hint of a description of a London season, a stay at a watering-place, or a point-to-point race; no social lions appear, nor even the briefest sketch of the Beau Brummell or the Count d'Orsay of the day'.[9] An awareness of ways of life very different from the metropolitan norm, and of the need to introduce the southern reader to what may be strange or unfamiliar, is built into the title of Anne Brontë's *Tenant of Wildfell Hall* (1848), and into the very structure of *Wuthering Heights* (1847); and is seen besides in the Brontës' care, following Scott, over dialect, topography, local custom and folklore, period detail. *Shirley* is an indifferent Condition-of-England novel but a superb Condition-of-Yorkshire novel, capturing as few other novels of the period do the romance and conflict of the first phase of the Industrial Revolution in its impact on rural Britain. And just as in that novel Caroline Helstone's emotional hunger is seen in the context of the physical hunger of the Luddites, so Charlotte Brontë's fictions of the self draw their

[7]These contemporary comments can be found in Miriam Allott (ed.), *The Brontës: The Critical Heritage* (Routledge & Kegan Paul, 1974), pp. 109–10, 201.

[8]Elizabeth Gaskell, *Life of Charlotte Brontë* (1857), ed. Alan Shelston (Harmondsworth, Penguin, 1975) II, 11, p. 483.

[9]Eugène Forçade, *Revue des Deux Mondes*, 31 October 1848; *Critical Heritage*, p. 102.

power from an implicit awareness of the wider context which made the exploration of the self, and the search for continuity and relationship, urgent tasks.

Fictions of the Self: *Agnes Grey, Jane Eyre, Villette*

The plight of the governess was topical in the 1840s, but it was not an entirely new subject for fiction. Lady Blessington in *The Governess* (1839), Harriet Martineau in *Deerbrook* (1839), Elizabeth Sewell in *Amy Herbert* (1844) had treated the figure of the governess sympathetically, if mostly peripherally, as had Dickens in Ruth Pinch of *Martin Chuzzlewit* (1843–4). Becky Sharp is a governess, although not for long, and not in ways likely to increase subscriptions to the Governesses' Benevolent Institution. The fullest and most sympathetic fictional treatment, fuller in this respect than *Jane Eyre*, is in Anne Brontë's *Agnes Grey* (1847), where many typical features of the governess's lot are handled with a quiet realism that illuminates Charlotte's novel by contrast. As the daughter of an impoverished clergyman, forced to work to supplement the family income, Agnes is in the classic situation of the Victorian governess: educated in taste and feeling to be the equal (at least) of her employers, but condemned to an indeterminate status – too well-bred for the servants' hall, too poor and dependent to be always welcome in the drawing-room. Elizabeth Sewell wrote in 1865 that 'the real discomfort of a governess's position arises from the fact that it is undefined. She is not a relation, not a guest, not a mistress, not a servant – but something made up of all. No one knows exactly how to treat her'.[10] Such indeterminacy of status was a literary opportunity, and one reason for the increased visibility of the governess in the fiction of the 1840s may be the heightened awareness of class differences at the time, and the fact that many more middle-class families were able to lay claim to the social prestige of employing a governess. Agnes Grey's situation is in this respect the opposite of Becky's: the ambiguities which give Becky her chance to rise in society are a constant source of humiliation for Agnes, interpreted by her employers and her charges in ways that trample on her dignity as a human being. Whereas Becky aspires upwards, Agnes yearns backwards, to 'the village spire, and the old grey parsonage beyond it' which she leaves at the start of the novel and which remains her standard of delicacy and right conduct throughout her subsequent exposure to boorish employers and undisciplined children. *Agnes Grey* is sometimes described as a mild novel, but its vision of the governess's lot is one of casual, arbitrary cruelty – children who torture animals, parents who alternate long neglect with sudden, humiliating reproach, grown charges who

---

[10]Quoted by M. Jeanne Peterson, 'The Victorian Governess: Status Incongruence in Family and Society', in Martha Vicinus (ed.), *Suffer and Be Still: Women in the Victorian Age* (Bloomington, Indiana UP, 1972), pp. 3–19; pp. 9–10.

ignore the governess in company and pester her with impossible demands in private. The scene where Agnes stones the nestlings to death rather than see them tortured by Tom Bloomfield is a powerful emblem of her situation (5); it was apropos of this scene that Charlotte told Elizabeth Gaskell

> that none but those who had been in the position of a governess could ever realize the dark side of 'respectable' human nature; under no great temptation to crime, but daily giving way to selfishness and ill-temper, till its conduct towards those dependent on it sometimes amounts to a tyranny of which one would rather be the victim than the inflicter.

– following it with the story of the little boy who declared at table that he loved her, only to be rebuked by his mother: ' "Love the *governess*, my dear!" '.[11]

Agnes Grey is a more thorough exploration of the humiliations of governess life than *Jane Eyre*, of that 'estrangement from one's real character' that Charlotte saw as the chief evil of the job.[12] 'Already I seemed to feel my intellect deteriorating, my heart petrifying, my soul contracting; and I trembled lest my very moral perceptions should become deadened. . . beneath the baneful influence of such a mode of life' (11). But it is also a more conventional book. Agnes suffers in silence and is rewarded with marriage to the curate; Jane may suffer less, indeed hardly at all, as a governess, but her challenge to the social barriers that would keep her apart from Rochester is radical, and no one who has read the novel can fail to be stirred by her cry:

> 'Do you think I can stay to become nothing to you? Do you think I am an automaton? – a machine without feelings? and bear to have my morsel of bread snatched from my lips, and my drop of living water dashed from my cup? Do you think, because I am poor, obscure, plain, and little, I am soulless and heartless? You think wrong! – I have as much soul as you – and full as much heart! And if God had gifted me with some beauty and much wealth, I should have made it as hard for you to leave me, as it is now for me to leave you. I am not talking to you now through the medium of custom, conventionalities, nor even of mortal flesh: it is my spirit that addresses your spirit; just as if both had passed through the grave, and we stood at God's feet, equal – as we are!' (23)

The originality of *Jane Eyre* lies not only in the thrilling intensity of such moments of rebellious feeling, but in the way they express conflicts within the character of Jane herself – conflicts of duty and desire, assertion and restraint – which vitalize the narrative at every point, and are grounded in the formative experiences of childhood.

Like *Vanity Fair*, but more starkly, *Jane Eyre* opens with a famous act of defiance. Becky throws the copy of Dr Johnson's *Dictionary* back into Miss

[11]Gaskell, *Life*, I, 8, pp. 186–7.
[12]Gaskell, *Life*, I, 10, p. 217.

Pinkerton's garden, Jane retaliates when her cousin John Reed throws a book at her. There is no comic-nostalgic evocation of childhood days here: we are thrust straight into the heart of a child's conflict, and into a setting which is instinct with poetic symbolism – the frost outside, the 'death-white realms' of the illustrations in Bewick's *Birds*, then the flame of rebellion, imprisonment in the red-room, and fear of the oppressor turning into fear of the self, as Jane glimpses her image in the looking-glass: 'the strange little figure there gazing at me with a white face and arms specking the gloom, and glittering eyes of fear moving where all else was still, had the effect of a real spirit: I thought it like one of the tiny phantoms, half fairy, half imp, Bessie's evening stories represented as coming out of lone, ferny dells in moors, and appearing before the eyes of belated travellers' (2). There is a range and intensity of feeling in these opening chapters, a sense of the self being shaped by conflicting forces within and without, which is new in the English novel.

The form of *Jane Eyre* follows a psychological rather than a merely chronological progress: it is dictated by, and in its turn amplifies and develops, the rhythm of need and rebellion established in the opening chapters. Jane's is a story of pilgrimage, invoking at several points the symbolic journey of Christian but altering its destination, from a Celestial City beyond the world to a spiritual and emotional goal within it, a home of the heart.[13] There are five stages, each with its symbolic house: childhood at Gateshead, school at Lowood, early womanhood and romantic love at Thornfield Hall, sisterhood and independence at Moor House, marriage at Ferndean. Each stage builds upon the last, as Jane struggles to reconcile her sense of the possibilities of life with the limiting and sometimes humiliating conditions in which she is required to live hers. Only those experiences relevant to the story of her growth are given extended treatment in the narrative. Thus the Lowood chapters (5–9) centre largely on her friendship with Helen Burns, for the untidy, otherworldly Helen, first encountered reading *Rasselas*, offers an example of Christian stoicism in face of injustice from which Jane can learn. And she does learn: when she tells the story of her 'sad childhood' to Miss Temple the bitterness has gone, and she convinces her teacher of the truth of her version. But we are also shown why Helen's way can never be hers, because Jane is too hungry for life: 'Helen had calmed me; but in the tranquillity she imparted there was an alloy of inexpressible sadness' (8). The Lowood chapters further the design of the book: through a sisterly love she has never known before Jane grows in self-respect and self-mastery, but with the death of Helen, cradling Jane in her arms, this phase of Jane's growth has been sufficiently intimated, and the action moves swiftly forward to Jane at 18.

The phases of the novel build upon one another, and also interrelate and

[13]The significance of the Bunyan analogy is discussed by Michael Wheeler in his chapter on the novel in *The Art of Allusion in Victorian Fiction* (Macmillan, 1979).

echo in ways that are both structural and essentially poetic. Jane's Cinderella situation at Gateshead, for example, with her cousins Eliza and Georgiana Reed as the ugly sisters, is repeated and reversed at Moor House, where she discovers true intellectual equality and kinship in her cousins Mary and Diana Rivers. John Reed the physical bully at Gateshead, becomes St John Rivers the spiritual bully at Moor House. Our sense of the continuity of Jane's being is reinforced by numerous echoes and parallels of a less obvious kind. Her first meeting with Rochester on the country lane, when he thinks she has bewitched his horse, recalls the reflection of herself in chapter 2 as 'a real spirit' a fairy 'appearing before the eyes of belated travellers', and an unobtrusive link is made between the bullied child and the about-to-be-beloved woman. One thinks, also, of Jane spending the night before her wedding with Adèle in her arms, 'the emblem of my past life' (25), as Helen Burns had cradled her, or at the end bringing the blind Rochester a glass of water, a metaphor become narrative event, recalling her earlier cry to him: ' "Do you think I. . .can bear to have my morsel of bread snatched from my lips, and my drop of living water dashed from my cup?" ' (23). Such purposeful echoes as these, to say nothing of the binding power of natural imagery and colour symbolism, make it hard to see how this could ever have been considered a formless novel.

The depth and intensity of feeling in *Jane Eyre* exposes the inadequacy of the term *bildungsroman* to describe the creative innovation this novel represents. Jane's pilgrimage is an altogether more urgent affair than the leisurely sentimental education of Ernest Maltravers or Pendennis, or even David Copperfield. It is at once more private and more radically 'social', because the questions Jane asks pierce below the obvious public issues to the conditions of fulfilment her society offers to the plain, poor, single gentlewoman, and the adequacy of its religious professions and religious consolations. ' "You ask rather too many questions" ', Helen tells Jane (5). Jane questions Helen's resignation as she had earlier questioned her aunt's injustice, and her questioning continues even at Helen's deathbed where, movingly, it is the younger child who clings to life and will not settle for the conventional reassurances:

> 'But where are you going to, Helen? Can you see? Do you know?'
> 'I believe; I have faith: I am going to God.'
> 'Where is God? What is God?'. . . .
> 'You are sure, then, Helen, that there is such a place as heaven; and that our souls can get to it when we die?'. . . .
> 'And shall I see you again, Helen, when I die?'. . . .
> Again I questioned; but this time only in thought. 'Where is that region? Does it exist?' And I clasped my arms closer round Helen; she seemed dearer to me than ever; I felt as if I could not let her go; I lay with my face hidden on her neck. (9)

Passages like these, which so keenly reinforce our sense of Jane's individuality, remind us that *Jane Eyre*, with its pilgrim heroine who feels 'as a wanderer on the face of the earth' (21), is also a religious novel. Its interrogation of contemporary Christianity is part of a larger spiritual enquiry which daringly seeks to combine the Romantic quest for emotional fulfilment with the Christian search for salvation and true being. In that quintessentially Victorian enterprise of reinterpreting the Romantic and Christian inheritances, *Jane Eyre* is a key document.

At this point, something more specific needs to be said about Charlotte Brontë's relation to the Romantic movement. She and her sisters were deeply read in Romantic poetry and in the novels of Scott: 'For fiction, read Scott alone;' she wrote to Ellen Nussey in 1834, 'all novels after his are worthless'.[14] The influence of Scott and Wordsworth was almost wholly positive, but Byron's influence was both more deeply formative and more disturbing. She and her brother Branwell created in their family stories a fantasy-world, Angria, which has deeply Byronic in character, a world of dominant, aristocratic males and submissive females, engaged in the restless pursuit of passion and military conquest. She was involved in elaborating this fantasy for ten years, from the age of about 13 to 23, and she came to see that it was an imaginative drug from which she had to break free if she was to grow as a human being and as an artist. At the end of that period she wrote: 'I long to quit for a while that burning clime where we have sojourned too long – its skies aflame – the glow of sunset is always upon it – the mind would cease from excitement and turn now to a cooler region where the dawn breaks grey and sober, and the coming day for a time at least is subdued by clouds.'[15] She broke from Angria, but that opposition between the 'burning clime' and the 'cooler region' was to remain with her as the poles of her imagination. All her life she oscillated between them: at the generic level between the glow of Romance and the cool solidity of Realism, at the moral level between those personified abstractions – Duty and Desire, Conscience and Passion, Reason and Imagination – whose hands are so often at each other's throats in the novels. What is sometimes called, rather misleadingly, the 'domestication of Romanticism' in her work is really her refusal to surrender either the transforming energies of romance or the saving stabilities of the real, her struggle to incorporate the one in the other. Her 'faculty of discerning the wonderful in and through the commonplace', as one contemporary reviewer put it,[16] is the hallmark of her genius; it is evident in all her novels, but only perhaps in *Jane Eyre* is the fusion of the two realms, the mundane and the visionary, completely successful.

The Romantic elements in *Jane Eyre* are of several kinds. There is, first,

[14]Gaskell, *Life*, I, 7, p. 152.
[15]Quoted Tillotson, *Novels of the Eighteen-Forties*, p. 273.
[16]*Critical Heritage*, p. 91; from a review of *Jane Eyre* in *The Christian Remembrancer*, April 1848.

the vestigial Romance structure of the book, with its devices of contrast and parallelism (Jane's two lovers, the dark Rochester, the blond Rivers; her two sets of cousins), its quest plot and fairy-tale coincidences. Then there is the centrality of Nature, the use of landscape and weather to symbolize psychological states and provide narrative rhythm (so that, for example, we move with Jane from the frost of Lowood and its pinched régime to the midsummer fullness of the orchard where Rochester proposes in chapter 23). Equally important is a less figurative emphasis on nature in and for itself, as 'rocks and stones and trees', a delighted evocation of landscape and seasonal change as a Wordsworthian resource of health and vitality. Third, there is the much-discussed 'Gothic' element provided by Thornfield Hall, its dark Byronic owner and the mad wife in the attic, and the use made in the novel of dreams, omens and supernatural solicitings. Charlotte Brontë's resort to Gothic effects can be compared to the essentially psychological treatment of the supernatural by Wordsworth and Coleridge in *Lyrical Ballads*, and as with Gothic, so with the other Romantic elements in *Jane Eyre*: they serve to release her 'real talent', as Robert Heilman put it, 'the talent for finding and giving dramatic form to impulses and feelings which, because of their depth or mysteriousness or intensity or ambiguity, or of their ignoring or transcending everyday norms of propriety or reason, increase wonderfully the sense of reality in the novel'.[17]

For most readers, though, the central Romantic feature of *Jane Eyre* is the love affair between Jane and Rochester. Here Romance (in the pejorative modern sense) and Romanticism are perilously close, yet a myriad derivatives have done nothing to dim its emotional and spiritual intensity. Rochester is Byronic, of course; with his dark features and darker past, he brings a larger, cosmopolitan world into Jane's provincial seclusion at Thornfield. 'A rill from the outer world was flowing through it. It had a master; for my part, I liked it better' (13). His patrician status is important: Jane can accept him as her 'master' because he is generously above the Gateshead/Lowood equation of money and respectability under which she has suffered hitherto. The dignity and independence she finds in her new rôle is well caught in their dialogue, where Rochester reveals himself to be as inveterate a questioner as Jane herself. The lively play of challenge and response between them bespeaks quickness of sympathy and a healthy polarity. Rochester is earthy, and his name suggests Restoration sensuality and worldliness; Jane is spirit, as her name implies with its suggestions of 'Ariel' and 'eyrie'. He is pulled to earth by his passions, a Vulcan to Rivers's Apollo (37); she is drawn to high places and the distant view, like the roof at Thornfield where she can look out on a world ordered by the height of her vision (11), or the 'breezy mountain nook in the

---

[17]'Charlotte Brontë's "New" Gothic', in *From Jane Austen to Joseph Conrad*, ed. R.C. Rathburn and M. Steinmann (Minneapolis, University of Minnesota Press, 1958), pp. 131–2.

healthy heart of England' (31) where she has her school. If Rochester is Byronic to Jane, there is something of the spiritual elusiveness of Wordsworth's Lucy in his sense of her: he calls her a spirit, a fairy elf, a sprite. Their union is as elemental as these complementary attributes suggest, and as profoundly constitutive of each other's being. Rochester is the 'master' in whom Jane finds the 'new servitude' (10) she seeks on leaving Lowood, she is the 'prop and guide' (37) on whom he leans at the end of the novel.

Although *Jane Eyre* deals with the heroine's growth to independence and maturity, there is a sense in which she learns nothing more about Rochester, nothing essential about her feelings for him, after she leaves Thornfield than she knew before. The discovery of the mad wife prevents their marriage, but it does not alter her intuitive conviction of the rightness, even the inescapability, of their love. There is no growing beyond him, only a growing back to him, and this is what makes their parting so painful. The full resources of Charlotte Brontë's poetic-dramatic prose are brought to bear on the description of Jane's discovery and loss, the violent wrenching of her being from its true centre; and the Psalms are invoked to convey the depth at which the self is being shaken:

> Self-abandoned, relaxed, and effortless, I seemed to have laid me down in the dried-up bed of a great river; I heard a flood loosened in remote mountains, and I felt the torrent come. . . . it came: in full heavy swing the torrent poured over me. The whole consciousness of my life lorn, my love lost, my hope quenched, my faith death-struck, swayed full and mighty above me in one sullen mass. That bitter hour cannot be described: in truth, 'the waters came into my soul; I sank in deep mire: I felt no standing; I came into deep waters; the floods overflowed me.' (26)

No novelist, not even D.H. Lawrence with whom she is sometimes compared, excels Charlotte Brontë in portraying the life-and-death struggles of the psyche.

Charlotte Brontë's second great novel of the self, *Villette* (1853), is in several respects a reworking, from a more austere and self-conscious perspective, of themes and situations from her previous novels. Like her first novel, *The Professor* (1857, unpublished in her lifetime), it derives from her experience of M. Heger's school in Brussels, the most important episode in Charlotte's emotional life, and deals centrally with a master–pupil love-affair. But whereas *The Professor* was avowedly 'plain and homely' (Preface), with a male autobiographer who marries his English–Swiss pupil and establishes himself successfully in life, *Villette* is a tale of loss and largely unrequited need, told by the female pupil in a prose that is dramatic and poetic, employing the 'vivid contrasts of light and shade' eschewed by the narrator of *The Professor* in his pursuit of an unadorned tale of 'real life' (19). Like *Jane Eyre*, *Villette* portrays an emotional and spiritual quest, but it lacks the romantic optimism and vigorous forward movement of Jane's pilgrimage; it is a novel of silent suffering, bravely confronting the morbidity in the heroine's situation. Written at a time of great unhappiness in Charlotte's life, it develops the 'old maid' theme of *Shirley*, transporting a heroine as emotionally starved as Caroline Helstone from Yorkshire to Belgium, and exposing her loneliness and need to the rigours of a foreign culture and an alien religion. 'You say that she may be thought morbid and weak,' Charlotte wrote of Lucy Snowe to her publisher, 'unless the history of her life be more fully given. I consider that she *is* both morbid and weak at times; her character sets up no pretensions to unmixed strength, and anybody living her life would necessarily become morbid.'[18]

Considered as autobiographical narrative, *Villette* is less fluid than *Jane Eyre* and more oblique in its presentation of the central character. Lucy Snowe is not so warm-blooded as Jane, and less easy for the romantic reader to identify with: 'A *cold* name she must have', Charlotte wrote to her publisher.[19] When Jane looks in the mirror she sees a 'spirit' with 'glittering eyes', Lucy sees 'a faded, hollow-eyed vision. Yet I thought little of the wan spectacle. The blight, I believed, was chiefly external: I still felt life at life's sources' (4). The contrast between external and internal is much more extreme in *Villette*, snow on the surface – and Lucy narrates as an old woman with white hair 'under a white cap, like snow beneath snow' (5) – hunger below. We are told nothing of Lucy's childhood or family, beyond the fact that she is an orphan and alone, and she seems much more of a spectator than an actor in her own destiny. The opening chapters lead us to expect that little Polly Home is to be the central protagonist, and it is only on a second reading that we take in the full irony of Lucy's protested detachment from the storms of emotional need that buffet Polly. 'She seemed growing old and unearthly. I, Lucy Snowe, plead guiltless of that curse, an overheated and discursive imagination. . .' (2). Later, it is Lucy who will feel 'unearthly' in the loneliness of Brussels, and confess to the solace she finds in the imagination (21).

What may at first seem a rather clumsy opening to *Villette* reveals on further acquaintance a powerful concentration of symbolic and thematic effects. Little Polly, in her passionate attachment first to her father and then to Graham Bretton, is an externalization of Lucy's sensibility, as Q.D. Leavis pointed out, 'suffering for its delicacy and proud refinement as ordinary souls do not'.[20] Similarly Miss Marchmont, the invalid to whom she becomes a companion in chapter 4, prefigures Lucy's subsequent destiny of unmarried widowhood. The effect is to highlight the central preoccupation of the novel – a woman's loneliness and need – and

[18]Gaskell, *Life*, II, 11, p. 485.
[19]Gaskell, *Life*, II, 11, p. 485.
[20]'*Villette*', in *Collected Essay*, ed. G. Singh, I (Cambridge, UP, 1983), pp. 212–13.

to dramatize three different responses to it, all of which have been or will be Lucy's: the vulnerability of the child, the self-repression of the young adult, the stoicism of an older woman looking back sadly but without bitterness to the aborted happiness of her youth.

In taking Lucy to schoolteaching in Brussels, Charlotte Brontë was not simply drawing on the most painful area of her own past, she was also subjecting her heroine to extremes of emotional and spiritual isolation no previous character in her novels had had to endure. Caroline Helstone can fall back on friendship, good works and the consolations of the English landscape. Lucy has none of these. She responds to the challenge of teaching in a foreign country, but the long vacation tests her English, Protestant spirit to breaking-point and, alone in the deserted school with only a servant and the 'crétin' for company, she falls ill and in her desperate loneliness goes (as Charlotte herself had done) to confess to a Catholic priest. This climactic scene, which ends volume I of the first edition, is one of the most striking passages in Victorian fiction, and illustrates the ambivalence with which Roman Catholicism is handled in the novel: resisted at the level of doctrine, and blamed for encouraging hypocrisy in its adherents, it also offers the promise of authority and psychological release for which the lonely Protestant heroine yearns. Elizabeth Gaskell noted a similar ambivalence in the response of Charlotte and Emily to Brussels: 'The great solemn Cathedral of St Gudule, the religious paintings, the striking forms and ceremonies of the Romish Church – all made a deep impression on the girls, fresh from the bare walls and simple worship of Haworth Church. And then they were indignant with themselves for having been susceptible of this impression, and their stout Protestant hearts arrayed themselves against the false Duessa that had thus imposed upon them.'[21]

Lucy's breakdown is followed by rescue at the hands of her Bretton godmother and her son, now installed in Brussels (a fairy-tale coincidence that recalls Jane's discovery of her Rivers cousins after her wanderings on the moor). The second movement of the novel shows Lucy restored to the family relationship of the opening, but with the roles reversed: it is she, not Polly, who now loves desperately, and Polly returns, now a woman and confident in her powers, to claim Graham Bretton. The second volume, like the first, moves towards crisis, as Lucy's life opens out into the wider life of Villette with the companionship of Graham Bretton and then shrinks back on the reappearance of Polly as the Countess de Bassompierre. It is at this point that the mysterious nun is introduced, who interrupts Lucy reading Graham's letter in the attic and again when she attempts to bury his letters in the garden. The device has been criticised as a dash of Gothic spice, which it partly is, but the nun works on symbolic and

[21]Gaskell, *Life*, I, 11, p. 226.

pyschological levels as well. Madame Beck's house had once been a convent, and its ghostly legend tells of a nun who had been 'buried alive, for some sin against her vow' (12). This is Lucy's fate too. In the chapter titled 'A Burial', when she inters the letters in the roots of an old tree in the garden and with them her hopes, the nun surfaces as a symbol of her loneliness and self-repression, and the silence to which she is condemned by her own nature and by circumstances:

> 'Who are you? and why do you come to me?'
> She stood mute. She had no face – no features: all below her brow was masked with a white cloth; but she had eyes, and they viewed me. (26)

Lucy is similarly 'mute', and hides behind the masking civilities of ordinary social intercourse. It takes the abrupt, unpredictable interrogations of M. Paul Emmanuel to unwind the cloth around her mouth, and challenge her into speech and relationship. He makes possible her hard-won movement to health, and control of the spectres of the imagination, at the end of the novel, although she is not given the happy-ever-after destiny of Jane Eyre. There is a haunting nun in the third volume, but this is no longer the sinister *alter ego* of the *pensionnat* garden but Paul Emmanuel's dead fiancée, Justine Marie, whose memory is manipulated by her unscrupulous relatives to prevent him marrying Lucy. The obstacles to fulfilment are now objective rather than subjective – the family opposition and religious differences which threaten to separate the lovers, the physical shipwreck which finally does.

And shipwreck, rather than pilgrimage, seems the controlling metaphor of *Villette*. Although there are several references to *Pilgrim's Progress* and to life as a pilgrimage (a particularly striking one at the start of chapter 38), and although Lucy's beloved is given the name of a Christian saint, Paul, and Emmanuel, the Hebrew word for Messiah, 'God with us',[22] *Jane Eyre*'s optimistic fusion of the Romantic and religious traditions is lacking. Paul Emmanuel is indeed Lucy's saviour, he leaves her at the end in freedom, independence and health, and yet the controlling deity of *Villette* is the 'King of Terrors' (37), who will not chime events with the heart's desire and of whom Lucy says: 'His will be done, as done it surely will be, whether we humble ourselves to resignation or not' (38). The sense of fate in the novel is close to that of Arnold's lines, published in the year Charlotte Brontë wrote *Villette*:

> Who ordered, that their longing's fire
> Should be, as soon as kindled, cooled?
> Who renders vain their deep desire?
> A God, a God their severance ruled;

---

[22]As Barry Qualls points out in *The Secular Pilgrims of Victorian Fiction* (Cambridge, CUP, 1982), p. 80.

> And bade betwixt their shores to be
> The unplumbed, salt, estranging sea.
>
> ('To Marguerite, Continued')

And her sense of the emotional shipwreck which threatens to overwhelm Lucy for most of the novel recalls another poem, which Charlotte Brontë certainly read, Cowper's 'The Castaway':

> No voice divine the storm allayed,
>   No light propitious shone,
> When, snatched from all effectual aid,
>   We perished, each alone;
> But I beneath a rougher sea,
> And whelmed in deeper gulfs than he.

To invoke these comparisons is to recognize that *Villette* is not just one of the great Victorian novels, but one of the great religious novels of the period.

Wuthering Heights

'When Charlotte wrote she said with eloquence and splendour and passion "I love", "I hate", "I suffer". Her experience, though more intense, is on a level with our own. But there is no "I" in *Wuthering Heights*.' Virginia Woolf's comment points to an obvious but fundamental distinction between Charlotte and Emily. *Jane Eyre* and *Villette* are intensely 'I' novels, and belong recognizably to the tradition of the *bildungsroman* in nineteenth-century fiction. But Emily, Virginia Woolf said, 'was inspired by some more general conception. The impulse which urged her to create was not her own suffering or her own injuries. She looked out upon a world cleft into gigantic disorder and felt within her the power to unite it in a book.'[23] The claim of *Wuthering Heights* (1847) to be considered the greatest of the Brontë novels lies in its combination of the characteristic Brontëan intensity of feeling and spiritual aspiration with something more, a formal control serving a more than individualistic reading of experience. One feels that remarkable qualities of intelligence went into its conception and composition. The unusual 'head for logic' which M. Heger observed in Emily, when a pupil of his, is evident in the extreme care with which she planned a timetable for the action of her novel, so that nearly every significant event has a date which can be deduced from

---

[23] '*Jane Eyre* and *Wuthering Heights*', in *The Common Reader* I, ed. Andrew McNeillie (Hogarth Press, 1984), p. 159.

internal evidence.[24] And intelligence of a more profound kind can be seen in the imagination and exploration of the opposition between Heights and Grange on which the novel is built. Whether we talk about this opposition generically, in terms of the polarities of Romance, or metaphysically, in terms of Lord David Cecil's distinction between 'the principle of storm' and 'the principle of calm', or sociologically, in terms of the contrasted relationship between two ways of life, it is clear that it is fundamental to the book's conception, and that the narrative method (the use of several, variously reliable narrators, the skilful shifts in point of view) serves to keep the reader from settling too quickly for one side or the other. The conflict between Heights and Grange, Earnshaws and Lintons, is a true 'contrary', of the kind defined in Blake's *Marriage of Heaven and Hell*: opposite or discordant qualities which do not cancel each other out, but exist in a state of creative tension:

> Without Contraries is no progression. Attraction and Repulsion, Reason and Energy, Love and Hate, are necessary to Human Existence.

So the 'contraries' of Heights and Grange may be said to be 'necessary' to the universe of *Wuthering Heights* in the sense that the Grange characters are continually drawn to the Heights, to complete themselves by opposites; and 'necessary' in the reader's mind also, since no fully responsive reading of the novel can side entirely with Heights against Grange, or vice versa.

These 'contraries' can be defined in various ways, but Dorothy Van Ghent came close to the heart of the matter when she spoke of 'a tension between two kinds of reality: the raw, inhuman reality of anonymous natural energies, and the restrictive reality of civilized habits, manners, and codes'.[25] It is a tension between a way of life, located at the Heights and embodied at its extreme in Heathcliff, which is powerfully physical and instinctive, has essential affinities with the amoral energies of nature, and is in important ways uncivilized; and the way of life represented by Thrushcross Grange and embodied in Edgar Linton, which is civilized, restrained, temperate and (we may feel) lacking in natural vitality. The Heights is a small community bound together by the disciplines of manual labour, but where people are harsh and aggressive in their relations one with another; a place which sets no value on culture – Catherine as a child throws 'The Helmet of Salvation' into the dog-kennel, ' "vowing I hated a good book" ' (I, 3) – and which, apart from Joseph's cruel and comic Calvinism, has little use for religion. It is an austere way of life, yet not one in which the bodily needs of food and warmth are neglected: there is the

---

[24]M. Heger's praise of Emily's intellectual powers can be found in the Gaskell *Life*, I, 11, p. 230. For the meticulous planning of the novel's time-scheme, see C.P. Sanger, 'The Structure of *Wuthering Heights*', *Hogarth Essays*, 19 (Hogarth Press, 1926); reprinted in the *Casebook* and *Twentieth-Century Views* volumes mentioned in the Bibliography.

[25]*The English Novel: Form and Function* (New York, Harper & Row, 1961), p. 157.

great fire burning in the house-place, and continuing to burn there despite the gradual dilapidation of domestic life at the Heights through the course of the novel. Thrushcross Grange, on the other hand, is situated in the valley and surrounded by a protective park: the life lived there is recognizably genteel and middle-class – Edgar Linton does not work for his living, and the servants are kept out of sight, not sharing meals with their employers as the Heights servants do. Though isolated to some extent, the Lintons obviously enjoy the status of local gentry: Edgar is a magistrate and sets an example of pious Anglicanism. Unlike the Heights, the civilizing arts have a place in the Grange; there is a library there and Edgar Linton is habitually seen in it. His bookishness is despised by his wife Catherine, yet it is an inheritance he passes on to his daughter. When Lockwood comes down after his night of terror in the Heights he sees young Cathy 'kneeling on the hearth, reading a book by the aid of the blaze' (I, 3), and her posture is symbolic of the restoration of balance in the second generation which she helps to bring about: the fire of the Heights, the civilizing influence of the Grange, the restored hearth.

There is nothing abstract about the way these places are imagined. Heights and Grange exist in a particular locality at a particular time, Yorkshire in the last quarter of the eighteenth century. The characters are subject to the disciplines of work, the influence of social class (which is after all the trigger of the plot, drawing Catherine to the Grange and away from Heathcliff), the laws of property and entail. At the realistic level, *Wuthering Heights* is a great regional-historical novel, and although to put it that way is to ignore much of central importance in everyone's experience of reading the novel, it does have the merit of emphasizing two aspects which are often neglected: that, as with Charlotte's novels, the 'social' dimension is much more prominent than traditional romantic readings allow, and that while it may seem eccentric in relation to a 'great tradition' drawn from Jane Austen, *Wuthering Heights* is not at all eccentric in relation to a different tradition stemming from the Waverley Novels.

The Brontës, as we know, were steeped in the Waverley Novels. Emily lacked Scott's interest in the larger patterns of history, but there can be little doubt that she meant us to see the world of the Heights historically, as a primitive way of life which is in many ways less civilized than the more recognizably 'modern' Grange. The influence of Scott can be seen in the careful backdating of the action (around the 'Sixty Years Since' distance of *Waverley*), and in her use of Lockwood as initial narrator.[26] Lockwood is a comic version of the typical Scott 'neutral' hero. Like the rather colourless young lowland Scots and Englishmen in the Waverley Novels, who wander beyond the Highland line in search of the picturesque and end up

---

[26]This aspect of Scott's influence on the novel is discussed by Ian Jack in his introduction to the World's Classics edition of the novel.

witnessing the tragedies of historical change, Lockwood is an emotional tourist who comes north to nurse his misanthropy and discovers emotional depths in himself and others that he had never suspected. He represents Emily Brontë's awareness that a bridge needs to be built between the sophisticated, urbanized world of her readers, and the imagined world of the Heights.

It is a bridge that is built suddenly and violently. Within a few pages of telling us, in fashionable-novel parlance, of his shy retreat from the 'most fascinating creature' who had returned his glances at the sea-coast, he is having his nightmare in the oak-closet, where another importuning girl is violently repulsed:

> As it spoke, I discerned, obscurely, a child's face looking through the window – Terror made me cruel; and, finding it useless to attempt shaking the creature off, I pulled its wrist on to the broken pane, and rubbed it to and fro till the blood ran down and soaked the bed-clothes: still it wailed, 'Let me in!' and maintained its tenacious gripe, almost maddening me with fear. (I, 3)

The terrifying thing about Lockwood's dream is not the child's face looking through the window, grim as that is; it is the violence and cruelty this arouses in Lockwood himself, of whom we expect no feelings stronger than a polite melancholy. In Scott's novels the movement north made by the protagonists of *Waverley, Rob Roy* or *Redgauntlet* is a movement from the civilized to the primitive, and is presented in terms of picturesque contrast. 'It is the strong contrast betwixt the civilized and cultivated mode of life on the one side of the Highland line,' he wrote of Rob Roy in his introduction to *Rob Roy*, 'and the wild and lawless adventures which were habitually undertaken and achieved by one who dwelt on the opposite side of that ideal boundary, which creates the interest attached to his name.' What in Scott is a geographical boundary, offering picturesque and ultimately safe experience of the 'wild and lawless', becomes in *Wuthering Heights* a psychological and moral boundary in crossing which the civilized self is profoundly shaken. It is the difference between a romantic outlaw like Rob Roy and Heathcliff. Lockwood's experiences at the Heights form a brilliant overture to a novel in which another retiring gentleman of civilized tastes, the much more sympathetically conceived Edgar Linton, is systematically destroyed by his exposure to the brutal authenticity of Heathcliff.

'Is Mr. Heathcliff a man?', Isabella Linton asks after her marriage. 'If so, is he mad? And if not, is he a devil?' (I, 13). In a sense the whole novel asks these questions, and its intricate narrative structure seems designed to prevent the reader settling for too quick or easy an answer. From the start we are presented with conflicting images of Heathcliff. There is the morose country farmer of the opening pages, and then in Nelly's narration we are taken back to the small dark orphan from Liverpool, the uncouth boy brutalized by Hindley, the degraded youth rejected by Catherine for Edgar Linton. The switch to the narrative present in chapter 10 reveals another side, an urbane landlord who comes to visit Lockwood and wins his gratitude by talking about 'some other subject than pills and draughts, blisters and leeches', and this prepares us (in Nelly's resumed narration) for the gentlemanly demon-lover who returns in the same chapter to destroy Catherine's marriage. Because Nelly has known Heathcliff as a child, her narrative goes some way to providing a psychological explanation for his later behaviour in his early sufferings at the hands of Hindley. But only some way: Hareton has also been brutalized, but does not respond as Heathcliff does, and there is besides a quality of demonic energy and cruelty in Heathcliff that cannot be explained in terms of psychological causation, at least so far as we are shown it in the novel. When he hangs Isabella's dog while eloping with her (I, 14), or brutally assaults the insensible Hindley after breaking into the Heights (II, 3), or repudiates Nelly's appeal to humanity at Catherine's death – ' "And that insipid, paltry creature attending her from *duty* and *humanity*. From *pity* and *charity*!" ' (I, 14) – we feel that a challenge is being mounted to the very categories of moral and social judgement in which the English novel has traditionally dealt.

Something similar is evident in the way Catherine and Heathcliff talk about and behave towards each other. Catherine's great declaration of her love for Heathcliff is justly celebrated:

> 'My love for Linton is like the foliage in the woods. Time will change it, I'm well aware, as winter changes the trees – my love for Heathcliff resembles the eternal rocks beneath – a source of little visible delight, but necessary. Nelly, I *am* Heathcliff – he's always, always in my mind – not as a pleasure, any more than I am always a pleasure to myself – but, as my own being. . .' (I, 9).

– but it strangely relegates the pleasing and the natural ('foliage in the woods'). Likewise, her warning description of Heathcliff to Isabella – ' "an unreclaimed creature, without refinement. . .an arid wilderness of furze and whinstone. . .a fierce, pitiless, wolfish man" ' (I, 10) – seems to acknowledge the irrelevance of such moral judgement to her own attraction to Heathcliff. And Heathcliff's behaviour at Catherine's deathbed shocks even the imperturbable Nelly: 'he gnashed at me, and foamed like a mad dog, and gathered her to him with greedy jealousy. I did not feel as if I were in the company of a creature of my own species. . .' (II, 1).

In Heathcliff, and in his love for Catherine, that 'necessary' relationship whose thwarting brings a whirlwind of destruction upon the houses of Earnshaw and Linton, we seem to be in the presence of a force which eludes description by the nineteenth-century novelist's ordinary language of manners and morals, just as it finally eludes sociological description in terms of social change or the class war. Something more elemental is at issue, which we glimpse at such moments as Heathcliff's account of looking in with Cathy at the Grange drawing-room, where Edgar and Isabella Linton are quarrelling over a dog – the children of the dark, bare-footed, staring in like night-animals on the children in the lighted room (I, 6). On one side of the pane of glass is the civilized world, where books are read and children are taught the renunciations that make civilization possible and breed its discontents. On the other is the encompassing darkness of primitive life, stretching away to Wuthering Heights and beyond to Penistone Crags and the rocks and wind and heath which give Heathcliff his name and define his identity. The novel imagines a necessary (in Blake's sense) interaction between the two, symbolized in the recurrent motif of a window being opened or broken, and its pattern is only complete when Lockwood's dream is echoed in Heathcliff's death in the oak-closet:

> I could not think him dead – but his face and throat were washed with rain; the bed-clothes dripped, and he was perfectly still. The lattice, flapping to and fro, had grazed one hand that rested on the sill – no blood trickled from the broken skin, and when I put my fingers to it, I could doubt no more – he was dead and stark! (II, 20)

There is a kind of reconciliation of opposites in the second generation. Young Cathy is both Linton and Earnshaw, and Hareton is a Heathcliff on whose nature nurture does stick. It is when she starts to educate him, and they both look up at Heathcliff and he sees that they have the eyes of Catherine Earnshaw (II, 19), that Heathcliff's destructive purpose starts to fail. The conflict works itself out and Hareton comes to inherit Wuthering Heights, the house that has his name over the door. But the power of the novel resides in the story of the first generation, and no synthesis seems possible there – as Nelly recognizes with instinctive tact when she returns the curl of Edgar's hair that Heathcliff had replaced with one of his own in the dead Catherine's locket: 'I twisted the two, and enclosed them together' (II, 2). The opposites remain opposed, and only force can unite them.

There is nothing quite like the conception of Heathcliff in Victorian fiction, although Hardy's Henchard in *The Mayor of Casterbridge* has at times a comparable elemental power. And yet *Wuthering Heights* also remains recognizably a Brontë novel. It shares with *Jane Eyre* and *Villette* the spiritual intensity and heightened feeling both for nature and for the hidden springs of the self, and that extraordinary combination of the commonplace and the visionary, which are the Brontës' unique contribution to the English novel.

4

Dickens

Dickens is the greatest Victorian novelist. His career started before, and ended after, the careers of all the novelists discussed so far in this study, and his genius was a major presence in the background of their work. To some contemporary subjects he came late: industrial life is only a lurid glare in the wings before *Hard Times* (1854), and he was never so interested in, or sympathetic to, provincial life as the Brontës or Elizabeth Gaskell. But the span of his novels offers a unique interpretation of the age and bears out the truth of Dr Leavis's assertion: 'The forty years of his writing life were years of portentous change, and, in the way only a great creative writer, sensitive to the full actuality of contemporary life, could, he registers changing England in the succession of his books with wonderful vividness.'[1] Dickens's artistic development is just as remarkable. His first novel, *The Pickwick Papers*, seems only half a step away from the world of Fielding and Goldsmith; the dark vision of the modern city in his last completed novel, *Our Mutual Friend*, where 'the set of humanity outward from the City is as a set of prisoners departing from gaol' (II, 15), is uncannily close to the alienated London of *The Secret Agent* or *The Waste Land*. A development so striking and yet so continuous, and one so central to our understanding of Victorian literature and civilization, needs to be seen in its own terms: no single category can hope to contain Dickens. He called himself The Inimitable, and he was; and the first task of criticism, before considering the sequence of his novels, is to try to come to terms with the unique imagination which conceived them.

Childhood is the obvious starting-point. Children and childhood are at the heart of Dickens's vision, both as a subject and as a way of seeing the world. When the first volume of Forster's *Life* appeared, with its revela-

---

Texts. All references are to the editions of Dickens's novels in the Penguin English Library, with the exception of those available in the Clarendon Dickens, reprinted in the World's Classics series, and in the Norton Critical Editions series. These are: in the Clarendon, *Oliver Twist* (ed. K. Tillotson, 1966), *Martin Chuzzlewit* (ed. M. Cardwell, 1982), *Dombey and Son* (ed. A. Horsman, 1974), *David Copperfield* (ed. N. Burgis, 1981), *Little Dorrit* (ed. H.P. Sucksmith, 1979), and *The Mystery of Edwin Drood* (ed. M. Cardwell, 1972); and in the Norton, *Bleak House* (ed. G.H. Ford and S. Monod, 1977) and *Hard Times* (ed. G.H. Ford and S. Monod, 1966).

[1] F.R. and Q.D. Leavis, *Lectures in America* (Chatto & Windus, 1969), p. 8.

tions that Dickens's father had been imprisoned for debt and the young Charles sent to work in a blacking-factory, one reviewer realized the creative significance of those early sufferings. 'It may seem putting the case too strongly,' Robert Buchanan wrote, 'but Charles Dickens, having crushed into his childish experience a whole world of sorrow and humorous insight, so loaded his soul that he never grew any older. . . .He saw all from a child's point of view – strange, odd, queer, puzzling.'[2] It is a critical commonplace that Dickens handles the child's point of view brilliantly, but the corollary is also true: Dickens succeeds with the child's perspective because that perspective came naturally to him and is indeed a dominant mode of vision in his novels. T.S. Eliot said of Blake that he 'saw man naked',[3] and the same could be said of Dickens. He saw many of his characters 'naked', as a child sees the adult world naked, with a startling clarity that penetrates the cushioning of habit and politeness which softens our sense of oddity and menace in the behaviour of others. There is a shocking directness about the way we experience the great Dickens characters; their inner being is not explored but projected outward, as it were, in those details that the eye registers, details which are anterior to (and which often remain anterior to) rational explanation or 'adult' analysis. Think of Pip's first encounter with Miss Havisham and Satis House and what we register through the child's startled vision: the bride who is also a witch, the rich dress and jewels on the withered form, the dark eyes moving in what seems to Pip a waxwork or a skeleton (8), and then the symbolizing context of the disused brewery in the garden and the rotting wedding-cake in the next room. These vividly perceived particulars alternately menace and enchant, reaching down into the diseased psychic life of Miss Havisham and out into the fantasy life of a society. The character's power to evoke these meanings is the product of the vividness with which she and her milieu are seen, and this in turn is directly related to the startling clarity of the child's vision and his inability to integrate the observed particulars into a larger, comprehensible whole: the normal adult allowances and explanations are not being made.[4] So too with speech in Dickens's novels. He knew, as the child intuitively knows, that there is a large element of suppressed soliloquy in adult conversation. He had an uncanny ear for the obsessive self-promotion and self-justification in human speech, and what is sometimes called his 'unrealistic' dialogue really comes from his understanding of the way speech so often expresses the melodrama of our inner lives.

In drawing attention to the affinities between Dickens's vision and the

---

[2]*St Paul's Magazine*, February 1872; quoted in Philip Collins, ed., *Dickens: The Critical Heritage* (Routledge & Kegan Paul, 1971), p. 579.

[3]*Selected Essays* (Faber, 1951), p. 319.

[4]I am indebted here to Roger Gard's fine essay on Dickens's use of the child's perspective in *David Copperfield*, in *Essays in Criticism* 15 (1965), pp. 313–25.

eye of childhood, I do not mean to suggest that he was a naive or primitive writer, or that he was unaware of this tendency in his imagination. *David Copperfield* shows that he knew the child is father not only of the man but of the artist, and in a chapter significantly entitled 'I Observe' he has the narrator provide a clue to the roots of his vision:

> I believe the power of observation in numbers of very young children to be quite wonderful for its closeness and accuracy. Indeed, I think that most grown men who are remarkable in this respect, may with greater propriety be said not to have lost the faculty, than to have acquired it; the rather, as I generally observe such men to retain a certain freshness, and gentleness, and capacity of being pleased, which are also an inheritance they have preserved from their childhood. (2)

If Dickens preserved undiminished the child's 'power of observation', he also had the childlike 'capacity of being pleased' by the kind of entertainment which appeals to children and the unsophisticated. He loved fairs and circuses and pantomime, and of course the festival of Christmas. His imagination was drawn to the large gestures and moral chiaroscuro of melodrama, and to all those popular forms in which emotion is freely displayed rather than implied. As the frequent references to fairy-tales and *The Arabian Nights* in his writings show, the mythic mode was deeply congenial to him, and the myth-making element in his imagination, the element which gives us Mr Pickwick, Fagin, Scrooge, Mrs Gamp, Micawber and so on, is clearly of fundamental importance. As Chesterton said, 'Dickens was a mythologist rather than a novelist; he was the last of the mythologists, and perhaps the greatest.'[5]

It is possible today to do justice to these elements in Dickens's art as it was not even 20 years ago, when Dr Leavis's 'great tradition' of moral realism was dominant in English criticism. George Eliot, a cornerstone of that tradition, said of Dickens that 'he scarcely ever passes from the humorous and external to the emotional and tragic, without becoming as transcendent in his unreality as he was a moment before in his artistic truthfulness.'[6] The inadequacy of that judgement no longer needs demonstrating: its premises relate to a kind of fiction Dickens was not trying to write and George Eliot was. The Dickens we read now is a great popular writer who found in the 'external' mode a richness of imaginative resource (including the 'emotional and tragic'), powers of wide communication combined with social analysis and generalization, not available to the same extent in the more normative realist-psychological tradition. Although he was, I believe, increasingly interested in the inner life of his characters during the second half of his career, from *Dombey* onwards, the development

[5]*Charles Dickens*(Methuen, 1906), p. 87.
[6]'The Natural History of German Life', in Thomas Pinney, ed., *The Essays of George Eliot* (Routledge & Kegan Paul, 1963), p. 271.

of his art should not be seen as a smooth progress from the 'immature' melodrama and picaresque of the early novels into more 'mature' and therefore, by implication, more nearly realistic later narratives. Rather, we need to think in terms of an increasing sophistication in Dickens's use of what, from the viewpoint of advanced Victorian realism, looked like primitive devices: melodrama, coincidence, myth, fairy-tale. Dickens saw these popular elements as important to his art, for they kept open certain channels of feeling and responsiveness – summed up in his use of words like 'fancy' and 'wonder' – which the literalistic, analytical strain in high Victorian culture threatened to block:

> It does not seem to me to be enough to say of any description that it is the exact truth. The exact truth must be there; but the merit or art in the narrator, is the manner of stating the truth. As to which thing in literature, it always seems to me that there is a world to be done. And in these times, when the tendency is to be frightfully literal and catalogue-like – to make the thing, in short, a sort of sum in reduction that any miserable creature can do in that way – I have an idea (really founded on the love of what I profess), that the very holding of popular literature through a kind of popular dark age, may depend on such fanciful treatment.[7]

It is here, to return to the central theme of this book, that the tendency of Dickens's imagination meets up with the age and his response to the age. Just as he deplored the 'frightfully literal and catalogue-like' tendency in the literature of his time, and set against it the fanciful expressiveness of his own art, so did he see in the life of his times a combination of forces, the complex legacy of evangelical religion and utilitarian rationalism, working in conjunction with the materialistic strain in Victorian commercial and industrial life, which was at war with the imagination and with those intuitive, feelingful, non-materialist modes of being which the imagination safeguards. Over and above the particulars of Dickens's social criticism, there is at the centre of his work a quintessentially Romantic, even Blakean, vision of Victorian England as a place where creative energy is imprisoned by institutions and by the 'mind-forged manacles' of the past. This vision, which takes shape and changes through the sequence of his novels, is already implicit in his first, *The Pickwick Papers* (1836–7).

From *Pickwick* to *Chuzzlewit*

Dickens's account of the origin of *Pickwick* is legendary. He tells in the 1847 Preface how he had been approached by Chapman and Hall and invited, on the strength of the literary sketches he was then writing for magazines and had just published as *Sketches by Boz* (1836), to write a

---

[7]John Forster, *The Life of Charles Dickens*, ed. J.W.T. Ley (Cecil Palmer, 1928), pp. 727–8. The passage quoted occurs at the end of Book 9, chapter 1.

monthly series of sporting sketches to accompany the illustrations of the comic artist Robert Seymour; and how he insisted that the plates should arise out of the text, and he be allowed to treat 'a freer range of English scenes and people' than the original idea of a 'Nimrod Club' allowed. 'My views being deferred to, I thought of Mr. Pickwick, and wrote the first number. . .' All Dickens's youthful confidence, and the abundance of his creative genius, are in that sentence. Yet the book did not come from nowhere. Like most first novels, *Pickwick* reveals indebtedness to its creator's reading: to *Don Quixote* in particular, Dickens's favourite novel, and to the eighteenth-century novelists who comfort David Copperfield in his childhood misery – Smollett, Fielding and Goldsmith. Dickens reversed the usual Cervantes formula by having a fat master and a thin servant, and the structure of the novel is a kind of tourist's version of the Smollett picaresque journey. The Pickwickians set off in pursuit of nothing more demanding than amusement and diversion (they are a 'Corresponding Society' rather than a club of sportsmen), and until the serious action of the novel begins with Mr Pickwick's trial for breach of promise of marriage, their aim is simply the tourist's desire to see new scenes and meet new people. The trial and Pickwick's imprisonment in the Fleet give a certain coherence and momentum, and a background seriousness, to the later scenes, but without transforming the basically episodic form. What was new in *Pickwick Papers* was not its form but the comic energy and irreverence with which a Smollettesque 'range of English scenes and people' was described, and the vitality of its language; and both these features can be traced directly to the introduction, in chapter 10, of Sam Weller, the cockney boots who becomes Mr Pickwick's manservant.

Sam is the agent of Mr Pickwick's, and the novel's transformation from slapstick into myth; without him *Pickwick Papers* might have remained on the level of waggish boisterousness found in the contemporary works it partly derives from, such as R.S. Surtees's *Jorrocks's Jaunts and Jollities* (1831–4). He is the necessary mediator between the holiday spirit of the Pickwickians and the realities from which they are escaping – necessary, because it is Sam's awareness of these realities which permits Dickens to develop in Mr Pickwick an innocence that is not merely ignorance, an idyllic virtue. As Steven Marcus says, *Pickwick Papers* 'celebrates the virtues of simplicity, innocence and directness in the relations of men', but 'it could not have done so successfully had it not incorporated some dramatic awareness that it is doing precisely this. Sam Weller *is* that awareness, and without it, without his constant commentary, we would not be convinced of the validity of the celebration.'[8] He is associated with the city, as Mr Pickwick (despite his Goswell St lodgings) is with the country; and it is when bowling through the autumn countryside in a stagecoach that Sam

[8]*Dickens: From Pickwick to Dombey* (Chatto & Windus, 1965), p. 35.

discloses his urchin childhood and his knowledge of ' "the dry arches of Waterloo Bridge. . . .I see some queer sights there. . . .Sights, sir. . .as 'ud penetrate your benevolent heart, and come out on the other side" ' (16). The moment nicely captures the mutuality on which their relationship is based. Sam's knowledge of poverty, injustice, the urban struggle for survival, complements Mr Pickwick's ignorance of these things, and his aphorisms have a macabre tinge expressive of the violence and cruelty absent from Pickwick's experience of life – e.g. ' "Business first, pleasure afterwards, as King Richard the Third said wen he stabbed the t'other king in the Tower, afore he smothered the babbies" ' (25). But Sam in his turn learns something from Mr Pickwick, who introduces him to the countryside and to Dingley Dell, and who provides an example of generous good faith which Sam has not encountered before. We feel that Sam is someone whose respect is not lightly earned, and this increases our respect for the man who wins it. Pickwick earns Sam's respect because he is capable of behaving independently of the ethical probabilities Sam has learned to live by.

If Sam's resilient worldliness helps to define and make credible Pickwick's benevolent unworldliness, then the comic vitality of the cockney idiom of Sam and his father Tony helps to precipitate, so to speak, the style of the novel. It is after the introduction of Sam that we become aware of the marvellous linguistic variety of *Pickwick Papers*. Sam establishes a standard of verbal suppleness and wit which reveals by contrast the rigidity, and therefore the comical falsity, of the various 'polite' styles in the book – the rhetoric of politicians and journalists, the cant of religious hypocrites, the bombast of the law, even the conventional sentimentalities of the Valentine card which Sam and his father explode between them in a hilarious chapter (33). The result is a wonderfully comic release of life and reality. Here is Serjeant Buzfuz:

'The plaintiff, gentlemen,' continued Serjeant Buzfuz, in a soft and melancholy voice, 'the plaintiff is a widow; yes, gentlemen, a widow. The late Mr Bardell, after enjoying, for many years, the esteem and confidence of his sovereign, as one of the guardians of his royal revenues, glided almost imperceptibly from the world, to seek elsewhere for that repose and peace which a custom-house can never afford.'

At this pathetic description of the decease of Mr Bardell, who had been knocked on the head with a quart-pot in a public-house cellar, the learned Serjeant's voice faltered, and he proceeded with emotion –

'Some time before his death, he had stamped his likeness upon a little boy. With this little boy, the only pledge of her departed exciseman, Mrs Bardell shrunk from the world, and courted the retirement and tranquillity of Goswell Street; and here she placed in her front parlour-window a written placard, bearing this inscription – "Apartments furnished for a single gentleman. Inquire within.". . . .Did it remain there long? No. The serpent was on the watch, the train was laid, the mine was preparing, the sapper and miner was at work. Before the bill had been in the parlour-window three days – three days – gentlemen – a Being, erect upon two legs, and bearing all the outward semblance of a man, and not of a monster, knocked at the door of Mrs Bardell's house. . . .This man was Pickwick – Pickwick the defendant.' (34)

At the time this was written Carlyle was observing how 'the structure of our Johnsonian English' was 'breaking up from its foundations, revolution *there* as visible as anywhere else.'[9] The trial-scene in *Pickwick* is Dickens's gleeful contribution to that break-up. He shows here how the grandeur of generality in Dr Johnson or Gibbon has degenerated to a pompous cliché-language of mechanical, inert periphrases ('glided almost imperceptibly from the world', 'stamped his likeness', 'the only pledge of her departed exciseman'). Buzfuz wins his case, but he meets his match in Sam:

> 'Now, attend, Mr Weller,' said Serjeant Buzfuz, dipping a large pen into the inkstand before him, for the purpose of frightening Sam with a show of taking down his answer. 'You were in the passage, and yet saw nothing of what was going forward. Have you a pair of eyes, Mr Weller?'
> 'Yes, I have a pair of eyes,' replied Sam, 'and that's just it. If they wos a pair o' patent double million magnifyin' gas microscopes of hextra power, p'raps I might be able to see through a flight o' stairs and a deal door; but bein' only eyes, you see, my wision's limited.' (34)

As this exchange shows, Sam Weller embodies the quality of irreverence that distinguishes the social vision of *Pickwick Papers*. Almost every profession, every exclusive club or pursuit, is mocked. Politics is the Blues and the Buffs and the Eatanswill election; journalism is the Tweedledum and Tweedledee antics of Pott and Slurk, the Eatanswill editors; the law is Dodson and Fogg, the corrupt solicitors, and Serjeant Buzfuz, or it is the listless Serjeant Snubbin, with his 'dull-looking boiled eye' (31); medicine is Bob Sawyer and Benjamin Allen, the dirty and dissipated medical students; literary society is Mrs Leo Hunter and her 'Ode to an Expiring Frog'; science is the search for the source of the Hampstead Ponds and Mr Pickwick's Theory of Tittlebats. In the end, as Orwell said, there is almost nothing Dickens admires except 'common decency'. His vision of the good life is that Valhalla of 'decency' in his books, Dingley Dell, the country home of Mr Wardle, where the Pickwickians go to celebrate a famous Christmas. Dingley Dell is a place where there is abundance of food, drink, and good fellowship (one anti-temperance statistician counted 295 references to alcoholic drinks in the novel),[10] where the old and the young can live in harmony, and the relations between the classes are unproblematic. It is an undemanding vision of the good life, yet quite central to Dickens's imagination of what the ideal relationship of men and

[9] *The Collected Letters of Thomas and Jane Welsh Carlyle*, ed. C.R. Sanders and K.J. Fielding (Durham, NC, Duke University Press, 1970-), VIII, p. 135.
[10] Cited in G.H. Ford, *Dickens and his Readers* (New York, Norton, 1965), p. 11.

women in society should and might be, and it irradiates *Pickwick Papers* with a warmth which is never felt with quite the same power in his novels again. 'The whole history of Dickens' novels', Angus Wilson has written, 'is the story of the attempt, often near to despair but never wholly forsaken, to retain something of the vision of *Pickwick Papers* against the inflow of the knowledge of evil's power.'[11]

Pickwick was the most popular book Dickens ever wrote: even after his death it continued to outsell any of his other works. To his contemporaries it was the most characteristic expression of his genius, and the yardstick by which his more sombre and complicated later works were measured and, as often as not, found wanting. Yet there is an essential continuity with those later works. The attack on the law looks forward to the Court of Chancery in *Bleak House*, where it figures as the focus of that novel's satire on the inherited injustices of social institutions. The debtor's prison reappears in the Marshalsea, the central symbol of *Little Dorrit*. The comic scepticism about social and political institutions, and the attendant distrust of the uniforms men wear to set them apart from their fellows, broadens into a radical social analysis, while the Pickwickian values of charity and good fellowship remain the standard by which individuals and institutions are judged in subsequent novels. What changes is not the moral framework but the form of his fiction, under the impact of Dickens's developing sense of his society and of himself.

'There are dark shadows on the earth,' the narrator remarks at the end of *Pickwick*, 'but its lights are stronger in the contrast' (57). Dark shadows predominate in his next novel, *Oliver Twist* (1837–9), which opens in the workhouse and ends with Fagin in the condemned cell. The fruitful balance of *Pickwick* has gone. The city is more cruel and menacing, the country more of an idealized – and unreal – retreat; rich and poor seem to inhabit different worlds, and to exist in mutual suspicion and hostility; the division between good and evil is stark and unhealed, amounting to an allegorical struggle between the Satanic figure of Fagin and Oliver, 'the principle of Good surviving through every adverse circumstance, and triumphing at last' (Preface). *Oliver Twist* is a novel of London, but it seems a different city. In *Pickwick* it is the city of the shabby genteel, of lawyer's clerks and medical students living in seedy digs, and also the London of the coachmen and the coaching-inns, a place where the young Sam Weller can be left to run about the streets and shift for himself and yet end up on the right side of the law as a gentleman's gentleman. The London of *Oliver* is dominated by the great citadels of the underworld – Jacob's Island and the St Giles Rookery known at the time as the 'Holy Land' – an underworld that seems more powerful and better organized than the forces of law and respectability; it is a place where the

[11]'Charles Dickens: A Haunting', in *The Dickens Critics*, ed. G.H. Ford and L. Lane (Ithaca, NY, Cornell, 1961), p. 382.

young Jack Dawkins gets sucked in to what seems an inevitable life of crime, and ends up getting transported as the Artful Dodger.

The Dodger apart, who provides a spirited comic performance at his trial (but unlike Sam, fails to discompose the 'beaks'), the comedy of *Oliver Twist* is different too; there is less of it, and what there is remains much more closely tied to the novel's satirical themes of greed and self-ishness – Bumble berating ' "them wicious paupers" ' or counting the spoons before proposing to Mrs Corney (27). And yet the novel is only partly satirical. The opening attack on the workhouse system and the Benthamite 'philosophers' responsible for the 1834 Poor Law Amendment Act gives way, when Oliver arrives in Fagin's den, to the struggle of good and evil; and while this serves Dickens's satirical point initially (the life of crime is shown to be more attractive to the penniless orphan than the charity provided by the state), it soon deflects it. The villain of the early chapters is the respectable 'gentleman in the white waistcoat' on the workhouse board who declares that Oliver will be hung, but the villains who are hung at the end are Sikes and Fagin, criminals but also victims of the society which tolerates the workhouse. The reason for this switch in direction is Dickens's increasing involvement with his child-hero: identification with the plight of the innately genteel orphan threatened by loss of caste overrides the book's more sober argument about the inhumanity of institutions. It is Oliver's nightmare of disinheritance that grips us – ' "I don't belong to them. I don't know them. Help! help!" ' (15) – willing him to escape Fagin's clutches and reach the middle-class home that is his spiritual birthright. Dickens was perhaps too close to the memory of his own similar experience in the blacking-factory to achieve artistic objectivity on this subject, although the novel is not the less powerful for that; indeed, it has been argued that nightmare and social denunciation reinforce each other in *Oliver Twist*, giving an unforgettably vivid picture of the underworld and its power to suck in and corrupt.[12]

Dickens's first two novels establish the imaginative poles of his early fiction. Both are journey novels and involve the central characters taking to the road, but there is really a considerable difference between the picaresque journey-as-tour of *Pickwick* and the Bunyanesque journey-as-pilgrimage of *The Parish Boy's Progress* (*Oliver*'s subtitle).[13] The one is a search for adventure, taking place in an unfolding present and involving incidental social criticism, ending in marriages all round and suburban retirement for Mr Pickwick. The other describes a child's flight from the City of Destruction and his quest for a secular version of the Heavenly City, and involves redemption of the past as well as life in the future, with

[12]See John Bayley, '*Oliver Twist*: "Things as they really are" ', in *Dickens and the Twentieth Century*, ed. J. Gross and G. Pearson (Routledge & Kegan Paul, 1962), pp. 49–64.

[13]I owe this useful distinction to George Ford's essay on 'Dickens and the Voices of Time' in *Dickens Centennial Essays*, ed. A. Nisbet and B. Nevius (Berkeley and Los Angeles, University of California Press, 1971), p. 58.

Oliver at the end standing before his lost mother's memorial tablet in the church. Rudimentary though it is, *Oliver Twist* gestures towards the *bildungsroman*, with its themes of memory and growth. Dickens's next novels alternate between the two forms. *Nicholas Nickleby* is his most Smollett-like book, opening out another wide social canvas and relishing its diversity, *The Old Curiosity Shop* is a pilgrimage away from the city, from energy and variety, towards the ultimate rest of a pastoral death. In one there is a vibrant sense of early Victorian England, in the other almost none.

These early novels are unabashedly melodramatic in mode, none more so than *Nicholas Nickleby* (1838–9). Dedicated to the Victorian actor Macready, and containing in the Crummles troupe Dickens's affectionately mocking tribute to the popular theatre of his day, *Nickleby* exploits to the full the rationale of melodrama so delightfully set out in the 'streaky bacon' analogy in chapter 17 of *Oliver Twist*, where the 'violent transitions and abrupt impulses of passion or feeling', the sudden shifts from comic to tragic and vice versa of melodrama, are justified as being true to life, however absurd as art. The main characters run to type: a poor but virtuous and genteel brother and sister in the leading roles, a villainous uncle who obstructs their progress at every turn, a beautiful heroine rescued in the nick of time from a mercenary marriage, charitable employers who materialize just in time to save the hero from poverty, a victimized simpleton who turns out to be the long-lost son of the villain. The action offers the coincidences and sudden reversals of fortune on which melodrama thrives, as well as such simple therapeutic confrontations of virtue and vice as Nicholas's thrashing of Squeers (13) or his last-gasp rescue of Madeline Bray from a death worse than fate at the hands of the miser Arthur Gride (54). For the reader willing to tolerate, or to skip, the main melodramatic elements, there is a rich undergrowth of comic characterization which can be savoured almost independently; and yet it ought also to be possible now to respond to the book's melodrama more positively, and recognize how appropriate it is to the portrayal of early Victorian life and how much in that life was congruent with its characteristic devices. The boom-and-bust swings of early nineteenth-century capitalism, and the wholesale uprootings and displacements of the industrial revolution, were likely to create a sense of the precariousness of urban living for which melodrama, with its extremes of prosperity and destitution, emphasis on chance and coincidence and ready access to emotions of anger and pathos, could provide both apt symbolism and release.[14] When to these are added the rôle-playing and social posturing of an age of class fluidity, it can be seen

[14]There is a very suggestive discussion of melodrama in *Nickleby* in Grahame Smith, *The Novel and Society* (Batsford, 1984), to which I am indebted here. Dr Smith argues that for Dickens 'the forms of existence characteristic of his period . . . lend themselves to melodramatic treatment because they carry the seeds of melodrama within them' (pp. 189–90).

that even the minor comic characters – Mrs Wititterly cultivating 'soul' in reading silver-fork novels, or Mr Mantalini affecting the dandy – are there not only for light relief but serve the novel's controlling vision of a society in which histrionic forms of behaviour are the norm.[15]

It is much harder now to recover the spirit in which the original audience read *The Old Curiosity Shop* (1840–1), the first of two weekly serials Dickens wrote for his short-lived periodical *Master Humphrey's Clock*. The central idea of a young girl and her grandfather wandering through the countryside held an appeal for the early Victorians – who, it is worth recalling, were just discovering something like the original text of *King Lear* in Macready's famous revival of 1838[16] – which it can hold for few readers today, and the novel now seems deeply flawed, split between the morbid pastoral of Nell's flight to death and the vitality of the London scenes and characters. Nell drifts inexorably towards death in the company of unmarried and sexless old men, and Dickens loads every rift of his subject with intimations of mortality – graveyards, decaying chapels, dead and dying children, a funereal sexton. Yet the book's embodiment of energy is equally extreme: the dwarf Quilp 'ate hard eggs, shell and all, devoured gigantic prawns with the heads and tails on, chewed tobacco and water-cresses at the same time and with extraordinary greediness, drank boiling tea without winking, bit his fork and spoon till they bent again. . .' (5). Quilp is Nell's necessary antithesis, a continual reminder of the forces of will and appetite that have been drained from her conception, and thus a comment on the enervated pastoral world in which she moves. 'Everything in our lives, whether of good or evil,' the narrator reflects, 'affects us most by contrast' (53), and in no other Dickens novel is the principle of contrast quite so fundamental to the design. The opening glimpse of Nell surrounded by the gothic trappings of the curiosity shop is emblematic of her subsequent pilgrimage through a landscape peopled largely by freaks and grotesques.

Like its successor in the *Clock*, the historical novel *Barnaby Rudge* (1841), *The Old Curiosity Shop* is nonetheless of some importance in Dickens's career, for it shows him trying to escape from the claims of the topical present to explore more 'Romantic' areas of experience. If he failed to do this successfully it is partly because his attitude to Romanticism was at this stage deeply ambiguous. The question of his relationship to Wordsworth is complex, but one can safely say that it took him a long time to disentangle, if indeed he ever did quite disentangle, the serious Wordsworthian inheritance in the treatment of memory, childhood and

---

[15]See here Michael Slater's valuable introduction to the Penguin edition of *Nickleby*, where he argues that 'theatricality and rôle-playing are the living heart of *Nicholas Nickleby*, giving it such artistic unity as it can be said to possess' (p. 15).

[16]See Paul Schlicke, 'A "Discipline of Feeling": Macready's *Lear* and *The Old Curiosity Shop*', *Dickensian* 76 (1980), pp. 79–90.

nature from its simulacrum in the sentimental parlour song of his youth, which for Dickens was always a source of comedy. As a consequence, parody always lies in wait for sentiment in the early novels. The chief, if unwitting parodist in the *Shop* is Dick Swiveller, with his ready repertoire of Tom Moore songs; and Dick's lyrical reflection on the 'death' of his hopes for Sophy Wackles –

'It has always been the same with me,' said Mr Swiveller, 'always. 'Twas ever thus – from childhood's hour I've seen my fondest hopes decay, I never loved a tree or flower but 'twas the first to fade away. I never nursed a dear Gazelle, to glad me with its soft black eye, but when it came to know me well, and love me, it was sure to marry a market-gardener.' (56)

– is its own devastating comment on the dilute Wordsworthianism of Nell's dying, just as his companionship with the Marchioness, the maid-of-all-work who nurses him back to health, is a touchstone of humanity in a novel where human nature often seems wrenched into gothic extremes.

When Dickens left for the United States in January 1842 he was not yet 30 and had written five long novels in as many years, a record of astonishing productivity. He went to America a youthful radical, full of hope; he returned, we may conjecture, a political sceptic, having found in the aggressive individualism of American public life a travesty of his own love of liberty. 'This is not the republic I came to see;' he wrote to Macready, 'this is not the republic of my imagination.'[17] One consequence of this disappointment was to make him aware how much his imagination was dependent on the old world, even on the legacy of its past with which he instinctively quarrelled, and something of this can be sensed in the evocation of rural and stagecoaching England in the serial novel he started to write on his return. *Martin Chuzzlewit* (1843–4) is a return to the picaresque form of *Nickleby*, with a peregrinating hero not much more developed than Nicholas and a comic servant, Mark Tapley, who seems a pale reflection of Sam Weller. These picaresque elements feel almost anachronistic now, and this is a sign both of the novel's fractured modernity (stagecoaching in the English scenes, railroads in America) and of its stirrings towards a different kind of organization. *Martin Chuzzlewit* is the first of Dickens's novels to have a professed 'theme' – selfishness – which attempts to unify what are in effect several novels contending within a single cover: there is the vestigial *bildungsroman* of Martin's 'great expectations' and his redemption through suffering in the swamp of the ironically named Eden; there is the counterpointing comic-satirical story of the rise and fall of Pecksniff as he manoeuvres for the favour and fortune of old Martin Chuzzlewit; there are the American chapters, virtually a self-contained episode; and there is the story of Anthony Chuzzlewit and

[17] *The Letters of Charles Dickens*, ed. M. House, G. Storey, and K. Tillotson (Oxford, Clarendon, 1965–), III, p. 156; letter of 22 March 1842.

Montague Tigg, beginning in satirical comedy and ending, after the murder of Tigg, in the quite different mode of the crime novel. The theme of selfishness can be stretched to cover these various centres of interest, but only at the cost of flattening out important differences of tone and treatment between them. When to these different elements is added the novel's two most memorable characters, Pecksniff and Mrs Gamp, whose vitality seems to exist for the most part independently of theme, it can be seen that *Martin Chuzzlewit* is very much a transitional novel in Dickens's career. It lacks especially a unified vision of society outwith the American chapters, which feel urgent and contemporary and satirically grasped as the stage-coach England of the rest of the book does not. *Martin Chuzzlewit* shows all the strengths and weaknesses of Dickens's early fiction: literally bursting with good things, and bursting beyond the power of the picaresque form to contain them, it gives a hint in the American scenes of the comprehensive social vision he was to move towards in subsequent novels.

From *Dombey* to *Dorrit*

Dombey and Son (1846–8), separated from its predecessor by the longest interval in Dickens's career to date, is the first novel of his maturity and the first in which, as Kathleen Tillotson has said, 'a pervasive uneasiness about contemporary society takes the place of an intermittent concern with specific social wrongs.'[18] Instead of the linear, picaresque universe of *Chuzzlewit*, we have in *Dombey* a 'round world of many circles within circles', in which, Dickens asks, 'do we make a weary journey from the high grade to the low, to find at last that they lie close together, that the two extremes touch, and that our journey's end is but our starting-place?' (34). The image of concentric circles aptly describes the movement of the book, which opens in the Dombey home with the birth of his son, and shows Mr Dombey's repressed and repressing attitude of mind radiating out to his business, to the educational system in which his son is reared, out even to 'the British possessions abroad' (10), for this is the first Dickens novel in which the reader is conscious of being at the heart of an empire. It is also the first to make a more or less systematic use of recurrent imagery to define character and theme. Mr Dombey is associated with rigidity, paralysis, ice and death; his dark and inhibiting nature is mirrored in his house:

> Mr Dombey's house was a large one, on the shady side of a tall, dark, dreadfully genteel street in the region between Portland Place and Bryanstone Square. It was a corner house, with great wide areas containing cellars frowned upon by barred windows, and leered at by crooked-eyed doors leading to

[18]Novels of the *Eighteen-Forties*, p. 157.

dustbins. It was a house of dismal state, with a circular back to it, containing a whole suit of drawing-rooms looking upon a gravelled yard, where two gaunt trees, with blackened trunks and branches, rattled rather than rustled, their leaves were so smoke-dried. (3)

Dombey presides here as 'the Head of the Home-Department' (3), and the novel locates the ills of society in the home – not now in the physical privations of the workhouse or the Yorkshire school, but in the blocked feeling of a prosperous middle-class household. At the birth of his son, the 'icy current' of his nature 'instead of being released by this influence, and running clear and free, had thawed for but an instant to admit its burden, and then frozen with it into one unyielding block' (5). Mr Dombey 'might have been hung up for sale at a Russian fair as a specimen of a frozen gentleman' at Paul's christening (5), and the parental frost is fatal in the end to the treasured son: 'The chill of Paul's christening had struck home, perhaps to some sensitive part of his nature, which could not recover itself in the cold shade of his father. . .' (8).

Against this imagery of frost and rigidity Dickens sets contrary images of flow and motion – 'the dark and unknown sea that rolls round all the world' which the dead mother drifts out to join at the end of the first chapter; the sea at Brighton whose waves Paul continually hears at Dr Blimber's Academy and which speak for the life of feeling and imagination which Dombey and Blimber deny. Dickens affirms the 'hopeful change' (20) brought by the new railways, now in motion and associated with the plump, apple-cheeked family of Mr Toodle the engine-driver, whose wife becomes Paul's nurse. Dombey's emotional paralysis is seen reaching out from the frozen and withered home to enforce a deadening respectability on society, and the novel portrays a struggle between these forces and the forces making for change and feeling and imagination.

To discuss the novel in these terms may make it seem abstract, but there is nothing abstract about the prose of the first 20 chapters, which is wonderfully concrete and fertile. The split between satire and sentiment, comedy and feeling, that sometimes mars the early novels has gone, subsumed in a compelling narrative flow where theme, image and what Bagehot called Dickens's 'endless fertility in laughter-causing detail' are united.[19] The difference can be readily seen by comparing Dotheboys Hall in *Nickleby* with Dr Blimber's Academy: Blimber is no less funny than Squeers and his régime no less harmful, although the man himself is kindly and well-meaning. But whereas Dotheboys Hall is an episode from which Nicholas passes on, Blimber's Academy is integral to the novel's vision, providing a comic educational version of Dombeyism and its violation of 'Nature':

[19]*Dickens: The Critical Heritage*, p. 395.

Doctor Blimber's establishment was a great hot-house, in which there was a forcing apparatus incessantly at work. All the boys blew before their time. Mental green-peas were produced at Christmas, and intellectual asparagus all the year round. Mathematical gooseberries (very sour ones too) were common at untimely seasons, and from mere sprouts of bushes, under Doctor Blimber's cultivation. Every description of Greek and Latin vegetable was got off the driest twigs of boys, under the frostiest circumstances. Nature was of no consequence at all. (11)

The terms of the social criticism here, with 'Nature' set against the artificiality of system, are quintessentially Romantic, and there is a new hospitality to Wordsworthianism in this novel. The sea, 'that old image of Eternity that I love so much' as Dickens described it,[20] figures prominently, and it is partly the 'immortal sea' of the 'Immortality Ode' –

> And see the children sport upon the shore
> And hear the mighty waters rolling evermore. (stanza 9)

– lines actualized in the book's closing image of the white-haired Mr Dombey playing on the seashore with his grandson. And the novel is Romantic in other senses too, in the new intimacy with which Dickens handles the child's point of view in Paul Dombey, and the new preoccupation with time and memory in his attempts to portray a change of heart in Mr Dombey. These are significant developments in his art and can be traced back to *A Christmas Carol* in 1843. Just as Scrooge's hard heart is pierced by the Ghost of Christmas Past taking him back to the scenes of his childhood, and the Ghosts of Christmas Present and Christmas Yet To Come teach him to live in 'the Past, the Present, and the Future' (IV), so Mr Dombey, left alone in the 'ghostly, memory-haunted twilight' (59) of his empty home, is forced to learn the lessons of time before he can recapture, through Florence and her children, a place in the present and the future.

To detect these new elements in *Dombey and Son* is not to argue that they are all handled with equal success. Many readers will feel that the waves have altogether too much to say in this novel, and will agree with the French critic Taine that Mr Dombey 'becomes the best of fathers, and spoils a fine novel'.[21] The important point is that Dickens had become interested in the processes of personal and social change, partly as a result of introspection. Throughout the 1840s he had been toying with the idea of writing an autobiography, began one in 1849, and then abandoned it to write *David Copperfield*, incorporating much of the material in that fictional autobiography. Both *Dombey* and *Copperfield* were written out of

---

[20] *The Letters of Charles Dickens*, ed. Walter Dexter (3 vols., Nonesuch, 1938), II, p. 218; letter of 11 June 1850.
[21] *Dickens: The Critical Heritage*, p. 341.

the field of force created by Dickens's awakening interest in his past. One consequence is the greatly increased sophistication in his treatment of childhood. Oliver Twist and Little Nell had been merely objects of pathos, symbols of suffering childhood in an adult world; Paul Dombey and David Copperfield are characters in their own right, and Dickens attempts to capture their way of seeing the world. Another consequence was the realization that human beings are to a considerable extent the product of the experiences that have shaped them, and that the individual's capacity for mental and emotional suffering was as real as their capacity for physical suffering. Dickens never ceased to castigate his society for its toleration of starvation, disease, ignorance and crime, but *Dombey and Son* shows his growing realization that these evils were often sanctioned by an attitude of mind among the respectable classes, an attitude which in their own spheres of home and school was psychologically crippling and neurosis-inducing. This perception required a new fictional form to express it.

A feeling for time and change links *Dombey* to *Copperfield* (1849–50). The first opens with a birth and a death, and nothing in its world stands still. Businesses flourish and decline, the railroad erupts like an earthquake in the London suburbs (6), and a new, rigorous sense of time, railway-time, is established, as inexorable as the railway itself or the loud ticking watches of Mr Dombey and the physician at his wife's deathbed (1). The sense of time in *Copperfield* is private, subjective, lyrical, focused in the consciousness of the narrator as he sets down the 'written memory' (48) of his life. Dickens's command of what Percy Lubbock aptly called 'the long rhythm of Copperfield's memory' makes possible the decisive shift from picaresque to *bildungsroman* in this novel.[22] The picaresque plot of fortune is still there in the story of the orphan boy who makes his way through the world to the point where, 'advanced in fame and fortune, my domestic joy. . .perfect' (63), he narrates the story of his life, but the story he tells is enriched and complicated by the processes of memory and by the essentially thematic organization of the material. No novel better illustrates Dickens's rare gift for being simultaneously popular and complexly suggestive. At the popular level *David Copperfield* is an early Victorian success-story enforcing the values of hard work, earnestness, prudence tempered by kindliness; its ostensible theme is the disciplining of David's 'undisciplined heart'. At the poetic level the novel tells, not exactly a different story, but a more humanly complex one. David may survive early hardship to become a successful author, but others are not so lucky: there is the death of David's mother at the hands of the Murdstones, the destruction of the Yarmouth home of Mr Peggotty and Little Em'ly by Steerforth and Steerforth's subsequent self-destruction, the betrayed affections of Betsey Trotwood, the crippled lives of Rosa Dartle and Steer-

[22] *The Craft of Fiction* (Cape, 1921), p. 129.

forth's mother, the death of Dora. We are made continually aware, in reading *David Copperfield*, of all the intractable tragic elements in life that cannot be understood in terms of the prudential morality of the disciplined heart. This undercurrent of loss and sadness serves to counterbalance the success-story element in the novel, and it is made an effective presence by the rhythm of the narrator's memory, continually returning us to the scenes and characters of his childhood and youth and revealing, through his intense emotional loyalty to them, how little the outgrown past has been truly outgrown:

> Can I say of her face [David reflects of his mother] – altered as I have reason to remember it, perished as I know it is – that it is gone, when here it comes before me at this instant, as distinct as any face that I may choose to look on in a crowded street? Can I say of her innocent and girlish beauty, that it faded, and was no more, when its breath falls on my cheek now, as it fell that night? Can I say she ever changed, when my remembrance brings her back to life, thus only; and, truer to its loving youth than I have been, or man ever is, still holds fast what it cherished then? (2)

For David, as for Tennyson in the contemporaneous *In Memoriam* (1850), there is an 'eternal landscape of the past' (lyric 46) which he can re-enter at will.

If memory unifies the tone of this novel, its structure owes much to Dickens's discovery and exploitation of the analogical possibilities of serial form. Because the monthly part had to carry something of the impress of the whole novel within it, serialization conduced to an art of parallelism and analogy. A large cast of characters could be linked together in relationship to some central theme or subject, and while that subject might be a simple and 'popular' one – growing-up in *David Copperfield*, the nature of parental responsibility in *Bleak House*, society as a prison in *Little Dorrit* – the orchestration of characters permitted it to be discussed, as it were, in a rich and various way. In *David Copperfield* the characters owe their existence not simply to the fact that they are amusing, or help to further the plot, as often seems the case in the early novels, but because they throw different lights on the central subject of growing-up in this society, and the attendant issues of love, marriage, parenthood, and career. We may not feel that David himself is explored to any significant depth, but depth is given to his representative story by the parallelism and contrast provided by the other young men making their way in the world – the homely, patient Traddles, prepared to wait for ever for his Sophy; the dashing Steerforth, embodiment of a dying dandyism which David must reject but cannot help admiring; Uriah Heep, exponent of the rising creed of sanctimonious self-help (" 'Be umble, Uriah,' says father to me, 'and you'll get on. . . .Be umble. . .and you'll do!' And really it ain't done bad!" [39]). Add to these Mr Micawber, who contributes his own delightfully subversive comic note to the subject of career and parenthood, and it can be seen that David's upward progress is set in a wide context of other possibilities, other ways of being, which implicitly comment upon, qualify, or affirm the particular choices he makes. So too with the treatment of marriage in the novel. A wide spectrum of marriages (most of them unhappy, it must be said) enable many diverse lights to be thrown on the question of where fulfilment in marriage lies. Is 'a loving heart. . .better and stronger than wisdom' (9), as David's father believes? A loving heart alone is not enough to protect Clara Copperfield and David from the destructive power of Mr Murdstone, or Em'ly from Steerforth. And yet the 'wisdom' which Agnes offers in marriage convinces few readers, so much does David seem naturally disposed to the Clara/Dora type of woman (and here memory shows him to be an emotional truant from the proffered ideal of the disciplined heart). The split between the two Claras – the girlish mother and the matronly Peggotty – runs through the book and is never healed. What David needs is not what he desires, and what he gets is something of a compromise: Phiz's final illustration shows David and Agnes sitting by the fireside, but with a portrait of Dora over the mantelpiece. So, although Dickens brings his novelist-hero to rest in marriage with Agnes, a marriage which offers the 'reward' of prudent domesticity, at the same time he manages to keep alive our sense of there being other moral and emotional possibilities, and to preserve, through the narrator's passionate memory, links with the imprudent, the wayward, the exiled and the defeated. At the popular, moralistic level *David Copperfield* tells of the successful disciplining of an undisciplined heart; at the deeper level it questions the notion of success and presents the quest for fulfilled and responsible living as a complex matter.

The mid-point of his *oeuvre*, and his own 'favourite child' among his books, *David Copperfield* can be seen as an act of fictional stocktaking on Dickens's part, an attempt to square his sensibility with that of his age, and to reconcile the sufferings of his childhood with his mature status as a famous author and Victorian family man. Having taken the world into his confidence via a confessional fiction Dickens had indirectly declared the private basis for his reformist involvement in the injustice, cruelty and social oppression of his age. Retreat into the past was followed by a characteristic rededication to the claims of the present. While writing *Copperfield* he founded a new weekly magazine, *Household Words*, in March 1850, and used it to air most of the social problems of the day – public health, legal and administrative reform, crime, education, factory conditions, and many more. These issues were especially prominent in the first five years of *Household Words*, and there is a particularly close topical relationship with the novels he wrote in those years, his most urgent and comprehensive satires: *Bleak House, Hard Times*, and *Little Dorrit*. It is as if the attempt to confront, in a fiction, the injustices of his own childhood had sharpened his awareness of the injustice in the world around him. The autobiographical impulse was continuous with, and complementary to, his reformist concern with society.

These twin preoccupations converge in *Bleak House* (1852–3). As every reader soon discovers, the novel is composed in two distinct narratives which offer different perspectives on the same world and approach it from different time-scales. One is written in a dramatic present tense and surveys society with a hawk-like omniscience and a topical urgency which recall in many ways the articles Dickens and his contributors were writing at this time in *Household Words*; the other, that of Esther Summerson, is an autobiographical narrative in the past tense after the manner of *David Copperfield*, private, introspective, concerned with the changing relations of a small group of characters as they came into contact with the larger world about them. One narrator knows everything, and presents the Court of Chancery and the slums of London in scornful terms, as present evils that must be reformed; the other is tentative and exploratory, hesitant in pronouncing judgement, feeling its ways through a baffling world and trying to make sense of it and do good at an individual level. One voice is apocalyptic and prophesies doom, the other is domestic and offers a modest hope for reform through individual charity and benevolence. The tension between these two narratives and the sheer imaginative delight Dickens takes in switching between and interrelating them make *Bleak House* hum with a linguistic energy unique even in Dickens, and also reveal how far he has come from the social vision of the early novels. Individual benevolence of the Pickwickian kind is still essential, but the Pickwick of *Bleak House*, John Jarndyce, is dwarfed by the scale of suffering, and the surreptitious half-crowns slipped to needy cases by the kindly Mr Snagsby seem almost comically insufficient. A question-mark hangs over the efficacy of individual action in a world where, the omniscient narrator suggests, 'Spontaneous Combustion' may be the fate awaiting society: 'Call the death by any name Your Highness will. . .it is the same death eternally – inborn, inbred, engendered in the corrupted humours of the vicious body itself, and that only – Spontaneous Combustion, and none other of all the deaths that can be died' (32). Esther, on the other hand, retains faith in ameliorative action: 'I thought it best to be as useful as I could, and to render what kind services I could, to those immediately about me; and to try to let that circle of duty gradually and naturally expand itself' (8). The dual narrative keeps open the question of who shall be proved right, the apocalyptic narrator or Esther with her gradually expanding circle of duty.

Bleak House is the greatest of all 'Condition of England' novels. Dickens's genius for what V.S. Pritchett calls 'comic social generalization' enabled him to create a vast panorama of contemporary society,[23] ranging

---

23'The Comic World of Dickens', in *The Dickens Critics*, p. 324.

from the fashionable world of Lady Dedlock, the Court of Chancery, and Parliament (Boodle and Buffy), to the outcasts of the slum Tom-all-Alone's, Jo the crossing-sweeper, and the impoverished brickmakers at St Alban's. 'What connexion can there be,' the omniscient narrator asks, 'between the place in Lincolnshire, the house in town, the Mercury in powder, and the whereabout of Jo the outlaw with his broom. . .' (16). The answer to that question is provided by the unfolding plot of the novel, which brings Esther at last to discover her aristocratic mother dead at the gates of the pauper cemetery where her father lies buried. The inter-connections are manifold, some melodramatic in the detective or sensation novel manner (and *Bleak House* is the first English detective novel) – who is Nemo? what is Lady Dedlock's Secret? who killed Mr Tulkinghorn? – others thematic in the analogical manner already discussed in the case of *Copperfield*. The unifying principle of this massive novel is not, as modern criticism has misleadingly suggested, the 'symbolism' of the fog (an atmospheric device figuring only in a few chapters), nor the Court of Chancery (the chief institutional focus of the novel's satire), but the large 'popular' theme of parenthood and responsibility. The world of *Bleak House* teems with orphans, and its epigraph might well be Mr Jarndyce's remark, in response to Harold Skimpole's description of Ada as a 'child of the universe', that ' "The universe. . .makes rather an indifferent parent, I am afraid" ' (6). The three young principals are all orphans, Esther, Ada, and Richard Carstone, as are Jo the crossing-sweeper and Guster, the Snagsbys' servant; others become orphans in the course of the novel, like the children of Neckett the bailiff, or might as well be orphans for all the care their parents provide, like Caddy Jellyby and her brothers and sisters. The corollary of this cast of orphans is the number of delinquent or neglectful parents in the novel: Esther's father and mother, Mrs Jellyby, Mrs Pardiggle, Mr Turveydrop, Harold Skimpole. The Court of Chancery symbolises the delinquency of the state in this regard, but other houses are also important to Dickens's definition of the condition of England – Chesney Wold, the beautifully evoked country-house of the childless Dedlocks, embodiment of a dying but still honourable way of life; Bleak House itself, which Mr Jarndyce has transformed from a ruin into a home for the orphans in Chancery; and Tom-all-Alone's, the pestiferous slum which no one is willing to transform. Esther is an appropriate guide through this universe of neglected children and 'indifferent parents', since she herself is a victim of the evils denounced by the narrator of the other narrative, scarred by the infection Jo brings from Tom-all-Alone's. A psychological victim too: her frequent expressions of amazement that others should care for or admire her, which seem coy to a modern reader, are Dickens's attempt to capture the profound insecurity of someone who has been told in childhood: ' "It would have been far better, little Esther, that you had had no birthday; that you had never been born!" ' (3). Her recovery from this crippling start, the sanity and charity she brings to the chaotic suffering in her world, reveal the power of the human spirit to transcend the determinism which the other narrative seems at times to endorse; and in the interaction between the two the complexity of the novel's social vision lies.

Bleak House is a key text in any consideration of Dickens's relationship to the life of his times, and it shows him to be at this stage open-minded about the forces of change at work in his society. The evils denounced are largely those inherited from the past, like the Chancery suit, and perpetuated by the sloth and self-interest of an establishment blind to the need for action and snobbishly resistant to receiving 'any impress from the moving age' (12). The 'moving age' itself, however, is viewed hopefully in the figure of Mr Rouncewell the Ironmaster, whose stately encounter with Sir Leicester Dedlock at Chesney Wold (28) is a symbolic confrontation of old world and new, south and north, feudal overlord and modern industrialist. Dickens's presentation of Rouncewell is not unequivocal, but on balance his sympathies lie with the new man and the possibility that his restless energy (' "we are always on the flight" ') will reinvigorate a moribund society. It is something of a shock, then, to move north in his next novel, *Hard Times* (1854), and discover that Dickens's sympathy for this contemporary figure has gone. In the transition from Mr Rouncewell to Mr Bounderby, Dickens's qualified admiration for the ironmaster who has risen from the ranks gives way to contempt for that 'Bully of humility', Bounderby, 'a man who could never sufficiently vaunt himself a self-made man' (I, 4), and who proves in the end to be a 'self-made Humbug' (III, 5). The idea that a new class of energetic self-made men will help to transform English society is abandoned. The social evils of *Hard Times* are no longer the legacy of the past but the creation of the new men of mid-Victorian England – bankers, industrialists, trade unionists, utilitarians. The moving age is seen to have created the bleak philosophy of Gradgrind and the soul-destroying monotony of Coketown, epitomized by the piston of the steam-engine which 'worked monotonously up and down like the head of an elephant in a state of melancholy madness' (I, 5).

Hard Times was followed by *Little Dorrit* (1855–7), a novel on the scale of *Bleak House* and organized along comparable lines, although without its versatility of style and ballast of social optimism. All roads in *Little Dorrit* lead to the Marshalsea Prison. The title-page illustration, showing Little Dorrit caught in a shaft of light as she returns to the darkness of the prison, is a fitting emblem for the novel, not only because imprisonment is the central theme but because its design is founded on the alternation of dark and light and on other binary oppositions – 'Poverty' and 'Riches', for example, the titles of the two 'Books' into which it is divided. In the opening chapter, 'Sun and Shadow', we move from the 'staring' brightness of Marseilles in summer to the darkness of the city prison, where Rigaud, in Phiz's illustration, is perched at the grating looking up to the light; and throughout the novel the darkness of terrestrial life is contrasted with a light above or beyond it, to which the central characters, Arthur Clennam and Amy Dorrit, aspire. There is a continual awareness in *Little Dorrit* of a dimension beyond the imprisonment of social life, and this makes it both more and less than a satirical anatomy of contemporary society. The satire is powerfully there, and imprisonment provides a very comprehensive metaphor for what is wrong: the stifling, nepotistic bureaucracy of the Circumlocution Office; the swindling of Mr Merdle, himself the prisoner of his vast concerns, 'clasping his wrists as if he were taking himself into custody' (I, 33); the willed immobility of 'Society' and the imprisoning propriety of Mrs General; the incarceration of the poor and unemployed in Bleeding Heart Yard. But it can be argued that satire is secondary to other concerns, and that *Little Dorrit* is more 'a novel of individuals',[24] more of a *bildungsroman* even, than the satirical anatomy promised by Dickens's original title, 'Nobody's Fault'.

The *bildungsroman* in *Little Dorrit* centres in Arthur Clennam, a middle-aged man returned to England after many years abroad, and seeking renewal of what seems a wasted life. His attempts to fulfil his father's dying wish to right an obscure family wrong, the mainspring of the novel's involved and tedious plot, becomes a search for continuity with his own past, and this he can find neither in his grim Calvinistic mother, ' "shut up from all pleasant change" ' (I, 15) in his childhood home, nor in his former sweetheart, the delightfully garrulous Flora Finching, a Dora Copperfield returned in middle age to shatter the consolations of memory. Clennam's personal crisis has been well defined and explored before the Circumlocution Office makes its first appearance in chapter 10, and it seems to colour the book's social vision: everywhere he looks English institutions and English manners seem trapped in the past, like the city of Rome visited by the Dorrits in their prosperity where 'everything seemed to be trying to stand still for ever on the ruins of something else' (II, 7). The prison of the past is inescapable: it captures Mr Dorrit again when, given the illusory freedom of 'Riches', he breaks down at Mrs Merdle's Roman banquet and regales the company with the scenic delights of the Marshalsea (II, 19); and it claims Clennam, imprisoned as a kind of scapegoat for the sins of society after the crash of Merdle. In this most religious of his books, something like redemption comes for Clennam when Little Dorrit visits him in the Marshalsea, bringing a New Testament spirit of love and healing to counter the Old Testament punitiveness of his mother; and Mrs Clennam is redeemed too by Little Dorrit's forgiveness, which leads to her 'resurrection' from her wheelchair at the end.[25] Dark and light come

[24]As Kathleen Tillotson argues, tracing the book's evolution from the more narrowly topical 'Nobody's Fault', in *Dickens at Work* (Methuen, 1968 edn), p. 232.

[25]See the fine discussion of the religious elements in *Little Dorrit* in Dennis Walder, *Dickens and Religion* (Allen & Unwin, 1981).

together to underline the Christian paradox of Clennam's salvation in the Marshalsea: 'As they sat side by side, in the shadow of the wall, the shadow fell like light upon him' (II, 29). Elsewhere the religious dimension remains a background rather than a framework: it is there in the tranquil summer twilight which follows on Mrs Clennam's resurrection, when 'great shoots of light streamed among the early stars, like signs of the blessed later covenant of peace and hope that changed the crown of thorns into a glory' (II, 31); or in the large perspectives of time and eternity which frame the action and confer a measure of dignity on even the weakest lives – 'The two brothers were before their Father; far beyond the twilight judgements of this world; high above its mists and obscurities' (II, 19).

Little Dorrit can be seen, then, as a transitional work in Dickens's career, still concerned to expose and denounce the ills of society, but more concerned with the psychological and spiritual meanings of imprisonment: the Marshalsea, after all, had long ceased to be a prison by the time the novel was written. In the figure of Clennam, the middle-aged failure for whom the past is a burden, Dickens seems to be revising the consolations of *Copperfield*, as Flora revises Dora; and the autobiographical basis for this revision can be studied in Dickens's letters, 'Memoranda Book', and in the relevant chapters of Forster's *Life*. The following year, 1858, the acute restlessness he confessed to while writing the novel, and the personal unhappiness and need that lay behind it, finally broke through the respectable surface of his life: he separated from his wife, to take up a liaison of some sort with a young actress, Ellen Ternan; he began the series of public readings from his books that continued off and on until his death (and hastened it, some observers thought); and he broke with the publishers of *Household Words*, and started a new journal, *All the Year Round*, in 1859. These linked developments have an important bearing on the concerns of his later fiction. First, the topical, reformist urge in his journalism, already weakening in *Household Words* after about 1855, continues to wane in *All the Year Round*, and Dickens's own contributions, collected in *The Uncommercial Traveller*, are much quieter and more introspective. Then, and in keeping with this trend, there is a notably increased inwardness in the novels in this final phase: themes of disguise and secrecy, doubling relations between respectable and unrespectable characters, and a developing interest in exploring the hidden depths of personality, become prominent concerns – not surprisingly perhaps in a novelist whose private life was drifting further away from Victorian domestic norms at the very time when he was more than ever in the public gaze as a consequence of the readings (although this did not prevent him from seriously proposing *Household Harmony* as a name for his new periodical!). Last, the significance of the readings themselves should not be overlooked: Dickens was re-reading his own work to select suitable passages, and it is no accident that there should be an element of revision, a sophisticated reworking of earlier themes and motifs, in late novels like *Great Expectations* and *Our Mutual Friend*. All these factors need to be borne in mind when considering the direction Dickens's fiction was to take in his final decade.

The Last Novels

Dickens wrote two novels for his new periodical, *A Tale of Two Cities* (1859), his second historical novel, and *Great Expectations* (1860–1), his second *bildungsroman*. The latter has some claim to be considered, if not his masterpiece (for Dickens wrote several), then his most characteristic work, the quintessential expression of his vision of life. Chesterton thought that all his novels could be called 'Great Expectations', and the logic of Dickens's development can be seen as a persistent drive inwards to the personal myth which is also a social myth, an increasingly radical understanding of the orphan's pilgrimage and its concomitant elements of cruel and kind step-parents, social disinheritance and social acceptance, the prison and the hearth, the outcast and the gentleman. *Great Expectations* is the novel in which this cluster of imaginative preoccupations is comprehended at last with a classical lucidity; it is a work of revision – the revision of former attitudes, being a story of worldly failure rather than success, told with irony rather than nostalgia – and also of re-vision, in which the characteristic Dickensian way of seeing the world is significantly amended. This combination of attributes in a work which also shows an almost perfect fit between plot, form, and theme, makes *Great Expectations* a centrally important work in the Dickens canon.

The opening scene is unforgettable. The emblematic starkness and loneliness of the child standing beside the graves of his parents and five little brothers, the convict who erupts from among the graves like a vengeful father, turning Pip upside down and emptying his pockets (he will later turn him upside down by filling his pockets) – the entire novel unrolls naturally and inevitably, it seems, from these first pages. There is an element of comic relish in the writing, though; not all the stops are pulled out in the description of Magwitch, as they were with Fagin or Mr Murdstone. This 'man who had been soaked in water, and smothered in mud, and lamed by stones, and cut by flints, and stung by nettles, and torn by briars; who limped, and shivered, and glared and growled' seems scarcely human to Pip. Yet in the very exaggeration of Dickens's prose we can read the signs of Magwitch's humanity, and in the course of the novel Pip will have to see again, to revise, his first horrified vision of the convict. The irony which plays lightly over the first chapter hints at what is held in reserve.

Pip's story stands in ironic relation to that of David Copperfield, reversing or subverting the motifs of the earlier novel. There is no childhood idyll with a pretty, loving mother, only Mrs Joe, thrashings with 'Tickler' and violent dosings with tar-water, which make Pip 'conscious of going about, smelling like a new fence' (2). No genteel birthright either, such as Oliver and David are given. They climb out of crime or social degradation into the sunlight of secure respectability; Pip is never secure and his orphan's progress is circular, returning him at last to the convict and a vision of the ultimate interrelatedness of all human life. In a sense he always knows this, for his guilty conscience, the omnipresent 'taint of prison and crime' (32) he can never shake off in his upward rise, is a subconscious recognition of the ties which bind together the social opposites of his world, as the mystery plot does also. In discovering the sources of his great expectations, Pip discovers the tangled roots from which the artificial class divisions of nineteenth-century society have grown. The social and the personal, the anatomy of society and the *bildungsroman*, are blended in the perfectly unforced symbolism of the novel.

It is notable that Dickens does not present Pip's progress as a simple fall from rustic innocence to urban disenchantment, nor does he take the entirely hostile view of Pip's attempt to become a 'gentleman' that most twentieth-century critics do. Life on the marshes is shown to be violent, backward and stultifying, and Pip's discontent with it precedes his visit to Satis House in chapter 8; only the companionship of Joe makes it tolerable. This is not the idyllic rurality of *Adam Bede* (published, and read by Dickens, in 1859) but a mean backwater, whose inhabitants are given suitably uncouth names: Hubble, Wopsle, Pumblechook, Gargery.[26] London may be disenchanting but the companionship and freedom Pip finds there are invigorating; he enjoys his first meal in Herbert's rooms, 'with no old people by, and with London all around us' (22), and Herbert is the first friend of his own age and intelligence he makes. He picks up some bad habits there but also some good ones, like civilized manners and the rudiments of taste, and he never forfeits our sympathy because, unlike David Copperfield, he is hard on himself in retrospect. This is the one Dickens novel to portray convincingly a character who learns and changes.

Pip can change because he learns what David Copperfield arguably never learns, to unweave the spell of childhood vision and fantasy. For much of the novel he remembers Magwitch as the not quite human figure of the opening chapters, a man who makes clicking noises in his throat like a clock, who eats like a dog and fights like a wild beast. Miss Havisham too is barely human, a fairy godmother, a waxwork and skeleton come to life. In the last third of the novel he moves beyond the horrified or enchanted vision of childhood to see these characters again with the sad eyes of unillusioned adulthood, as fellow-sufferers and fellow-victims, sharers in

---

[26] I owe this and the following point to Q.D. Leavis's important reading of the novel in F.R. and Q.D. Leavis, *Dickens the Novelist* (Chatto & Windus, 1970). For a study which attempts to rehabilitate the gentlemanly idea in this and other Victorian novels, see my *The Idea of the Gentleman in the Victorian Novel* (Allen & Unwin, 1981).

the commonalty of human fallibility. So Pip can hold the old convict's hand after his recapture and later at his trial:

> For now, my repugnance to him had all melted away, and in the hunted
> wounded shackled creature who held my hand in his, I only saw a man who
> had meant to be my benefactor, and who had felt affectionately, gratefully, and
> generously, towards me with great constancy through a series of years. I only
> saw in him a much better man than I had been to Joe. (54)

With Miss Havisham, too, the 'repugnance' of childhood vision is over-come when, the source of his expectations finally revealed, he can see her again not as a witch but as an old woman who needs forgiveness, as he himself needs to be forgiven (49).

In the sad sobriety of these moments of un-enchantment it is possible to see evidence of Dickens's recognition that the confident mimicry of exter-nal traits and mannerisms on which his art had been raised (and which, I argued earlier, has significant affinities with the child's vision) was no longer sufficient, or solely sufficient. 'Where We Stopped Growing' is the title of an 1853 essay in which Dickens confessed that 'There are real people and places that we have never outgrown. . .which we always regard with the eye and mind of childhood'.[27] *Great Expectations* shows that to 'stop growing' may be destructive, and that healthy growth may require seeing beyond 'the eye and mind of childhood'. Pip's re-vision of his childhood nightmares and fantasies is analogous to Dickens's revision of his characteristic themes and imaginative mode, and this may account for the sadness of *Great Expectations* and its relative lack of the characteristic Dickensian exuberance. A supreme work of the imagination itself, it also questions the power of imagination to weave destructive spells, and opts for the unweaving of spells, for the plain utterance that alone can express the sense of human fallibility and loneliness that is the book's controlling vision and tone.

Dickens wrote two endings for *Great Expectations*. In the first, Pip and Estella meet again in a London street and part, sadder and wiser; in the second, published ending, written at the instigation of Bulwer-Lytton (and possibly the latter's one enduring contribution to English fiction) they are united in the ruined garden of Satis House and Pip sees 'no shadow of another parting from her'. The second ending is not unambiguous, but the first is clearly truer to the mood and imagery of the novel. Estella is asso-ciated from the first with the cold stars of an inhospitable universe, coming 'along the dark passage like a star' and eluding Pip when they play in the disused brewery ('Estella was walking away from me even then'); he sees her 'pass among the extinguished fires, and ascend some light iron stairs, and go out by a gallery high overhead, as if she were going out into the sky' (8) – the same sky glimpsed by Pip on his way to Satis House: 'And then I

[27]*Miscellaneous Papers*, 'The Biographical Edition' (Chapman & Hall, 1908), p. 361.

looked at the stars, and considered how awful it would be for a man to turn his face up to them as he froze to death, and see no help or pity in all the glittering multitude' (7). That Dickens should have been prepared to alter an ending so consonant with the book's vision of human loneliness reveals how ambivalent he had come to feel about the happy ending. His art was pulling in directions which put the comic and romantic resolution of its themes under increasing strain, and yet he also felt his obligation as a great popular entertainer to 'try to sweeten the lives and fancies of others' even if he himself were soured.[28] This strain is felt only at the end of *Great Expectations*, but it runs throughout his last completed novel, *Our Mutual Friend* (1864–5), and threatens to break it in two.

After the 'secret prose' of *Great Expectations*, as Graham Greene has called it, 'that sense of a mind speaking to itself with no one there to listen',[29] the prose of *Our Mutual Friend* is a polyphony. ' "He do the Police in different voices" ', Betty Higden says of Sloppy's readings from the news-paper (I, 16), and the same could be said of Dickens in this novel. His is a prose of 'different voices' corresponding to different fictional modes, some recapitulating previous styles, others reaching into new areas, all resisting easy synthesis and manifesting Dickens's virtuosic delight in shaping his material at will (one thinks of the late works of other great masters like Shakespeare or Beethoven). The Boffin sub-plot, for example, seems to be a return to the bravura mode of *Nickleby* and *Chuzzlewit*, with its one-legged comic villain, Silas Wegg, and Mr Boffin's impersonation of the traditional hand-rubbing, side-hugging miser of melodrama. As an expo-sure of the corrupting power of money it is strangely old-fashioned beside the *nouveaux riches* satirized in the 'Society' chapters, the Veneerings and Podsnaps, who belong recognizably to the 1860s and a later stage of Victorian capitalism, where economic activity is covert and a respectable front indispensable. These are satirized in the dramatic present tense of comparable passages in *Bleak House* and *Little Dorrit*, but with an edge of bitter irony that reveals how much Dickens despises these hollow men of his day. In marked contrast to the highly wrought satire on the superficial-ity of Society is the attempted inwardness in the presentation of John Harmon, the 'living-dead man' (II, 13) who is the mutual friend of the book's title and may owe something to the 'supposed dead, but not so' formula of the sensation novel, and Bradley Headstone, the respectable schoolmaster turned murderer. Different again is Dickens's handling of Mortimer Lightwood and Eugene Wrayburn, the redeemable gentlemen-renegades from Society, where he almost seems to be moving into the terri-tory left vacant by Thackeray's death in 1863, and attempting a type of cynical, sophisticated, educated young man of the world not hitherto sympathetically handled in his fiction.

---

[28]*Letters from Charles Dickens to Angela Burdett-Coutts*, ed. Edgar Johnson (Cape, 1953), p. 370; letter of 8 April 1860.
[29]'The Young Dickens', *Collected Essays* (Bodley Head, 1969), p. 104.

The novel's social patterning is rich and complicated, and in conjunction with the symbolism of the Harmon dust-mounds serves a vision of mid-Victorian England similar to that of pre-Victorian England in *Great Expectations* (which is set back in time to the 1820s), a vision of ultimate interdependence in a world where there is no such thing as 'clean' money. Yet *Our Mutual Friend* is more than a satire on ' "money, money, money, and what money can make of life" ' (III, 4), important as that subject is; it is also a novel about the mysteries of the human personality, about surfaces and depths, and about deception and disguise – psychological concerns which threaten to pull away from the sociological subject. There is Eugene Wrayburn's indecisive pursuit of Lizzie Hexam, the multiple disguises assumed by John Harmon, Boffin's impersonation, the treachery of the Lammles, Fledgeby's use of Riah as a front for his money-lending business, the conflict between passion and respectability in Bradley Headstone. Some of these are integrated with the social satire, but others, such as the powerful study of Bradley Headstone, seem largely irrelevant to it, pursued by a Dickens now compulsively drawn to the psychology of the outcast. It is here that the strain in the novel's form is most acutely felt.

There are two characters through whom Dickens's interest in secrecy and disguise is chiefly expressed, John Harmon and Bradley Headstone. Harmon was clearly intended as the chief vehicle for the exploration of this subject, but the story of his presumed death and resurrection runs aground in a welter of petty complexities which requires an awkward chapter of explication (II, 13) to set right. Nor is his role as the engineer of Bella Wilfer's education at the hands of Mr Boffin any happier. In Bradley Headstone, however, the nominal villain, the experience of alienation and thwarted desire is explored with a tragic power entirely absent from the Harmon plot. ' "No man knows till the time comes," ' Bradley tells Lizzie Hexam, ' "what depths are within him" ' (II, 15), and the depths evoked in his sexual jealousy and social humiliation make the Bella–Harmon love affair seem a very shallow business indeed. It is not just that the romantic resolution of the Harmon plot runs against the darker tenor of the novel, it positively simplifies the issues: the coy domesticity of their marriage is a betrayal of the depth and complexity of feeling elsewhere in the novel, its easy accommodation of wealth a betrayal of earlier insights into the origins and consequences of riches. The happy ending represented by Bella's conversion and marriage seems almost perfunctory, a gesture in the direction of the comic form which can no longer express what is creatively vital in Dickens's vision. Its facile optimism fails to engage with the dark force of his real inspiration in the book – the great images of despair and confusion in the London landscape, the harsh energy of the satire, the depths stirred up in Bradley Headstone by his hopeless passion, and his tormented wanderings ending in violent death.

The deeper current of Dickens's art was moving towards the portrayal of troubled and self-divided consciousness, and this continues in his last novel, *The Mystery of Edwin Drood* (1870), unfinished at his death. The broad social canvas of previous novels has narrowed to a single cathedral town, Cloisterham (Rochester), and at its centre is John Jasper, a character like Bradley Headstone whose depths are at war with his surface, respectable choir-master in the cathedral but also an opium-addict and, it seems likely, a murderer. *Drood* is both a valediction and a new beginning. It returns to the town where the Pickwickians had had their first adventure, and finds that 'All things in it are of the past' (3); but it discovers new life in the mystery-form of the sensation novel, then in vogue, which Dickens characteristically was going to adapt, according to his daughter Kate, not 'for the intricate working out of his plot alone' but because he wished to display 'his strange insight into the tragic secrets of the human heart'.[30] Her words are a fitting epitaph for this last, unfinished phase of Dickens's remarkable pilgrimage.

---

[30]Quoted by Margaret Cardwell in her introduction to the World's Classics edition of the novel (Oxford, OUP, 1982), pp. xiii–xiv.

5

The Novel in the Age of Equipoise: Wilkie Collins, Trollope, George Eliot

At one point in *Our Mutual Friend* Charley Hexam, the young pupil-teacher on the make, repudiates the interest Eugene Wrayburn is taking in his sister Lizzie's education because it is a slight to his 'respectability' at a time ' "when I am raising myself in the scale of society by my own exertions and Mr Headstone's aid" ' (II, 6). The sense of society as a 'scale' and the prospect of 'raising' oneself on it are mid-Victorian assumptions, implying a new-found stability in the social order. In April 1865 Lord Palmerston, the then Prime Minister, gave a prizegiving speech at the South London Industrial Exhibition in which he told an artisan audience that they were fortunate to be living under a consitutional monarchy, 'and of such a monarchy an aristocracy of wealth and an aristocracy of rank are essential ingredients'. No 'impassable barriers' separated these from the rest of the nation, as in less fortunate countries, and his hearers should take comfort from the example of those who had risen from humble beginnings:

> And so I say to you – you are competitors for prizes. You may not all become Lord Chancellors or Archbishops; you may not become members of the Cabinet; but depend upon it, you will, by systematic industry, raise yourselves in the social system of your country – you will acquire honour and respect for yourselves and for your families.[1]

Both the occasion and the underlying assumptions of Palmerston's speech reveal a confidence in the stability of a hierarchical social order which would not have been felt so forcibly, if at all, 20 years earlier, and would have seemed unduly complacent 20 years later. That an aristocratic Prime Minister could speak to a predominantly working-class audience of the benefits of monarchy and aristocracy suggests how much the mood of the

Texts: Reference to Wilkie Collins's *The Woman in White* and *The Moonstone* are to the editions in the World's Classics series; those to *Armadale* are to the first book edition (1866). References to Trollope's *The Warden, Barchester Towers, Framley Parsonage, The Last Chronicle of Barset,* and *Phineas Finn* are to the editions in the Penguin English Library; other references are to editions in the World's Classics series. All references to George Eliot's novels are to the editions in the Penguin English Library.

[1] Quoted by Geoffrey Best in *Mid-Victorian Britain 1851–75* (Weidenfeld & Nicolson, 1971), pp. 234–6.

country had changed since the days of Chartism and the Anti-Corn-Law League. The change can be dated from the collapse of Chartism in 1848 and the orgy of national self-congratulation aroused by the Great Exhibition of 1851, and stretches for something like two decades, until the Second Reform Bill of 1867 and possibly a little later. Whether we call these the Palmerston years, or use W.L. Burn's phrase the 'Age of Equipoise', it seems very difficult, as one recent historian has said, 'not to believe in some kind of calm through at least the years 1850–65'.[2]

'Equipoise' is a useful word because it suggests a dynamic rather than static equilibrium, a balancing of forces. If the balance was underpinned in those decades by the unmistakable evidence of Britain's growing industrial prosperity and influence, then it also reflected, or so at least middle- and upper-class observers thought, the strength and adaptability of Britain's political institutions and aristocratic leadership. There was some relief mixed up in the self-congratulation, for aristocratic leadership had been under challenge in the 1840s from the industrial middle classes as much as from the Chartists. That challenge had been met, most dramatically by the repeal of the corn laws in 1846, and Palmerston was speaking here in its aftermath, in the knowledge that the order to which he belonged had, by adaptation when it mattered, consolidated its influence and prestige. His words implicitly invoke two of the concepts which modern historians have found indispensable in understanding mid-Victorian Britain, concepts particularly associated with the writings of Walter Bagehot, whose *The English Constitution* (1867) is the political classic of its time. One is the notion of 'deference', the respect traditionally paid to the squire and the duke in a country where the rights and responsibilities of landed ownership had until recently been supreme. The other is what Bagehot called 'the system of *removable inequalities*, where many people are inferior to and worse off than others, but in which each may *in theory* hope to be on a level with the highest below the throne'.[3] So Palmerston can tell the workingman to 'raise' himself in the 'social system of [his] country'; he may not become a General or an Archbishop, but upward mobility is both possible and desirable.

These ideas are very much in the air at this time, and they reflect a change in the social and intellectual climate. Samuel Smiles's *Self-Help* was published in 1859, and its author's own history illustrates the shift as well as anyone: an active radical in the 40s, Smiles came to preach a message of self-improvement essentially similar to Palmerston's in his speech. The final chapter of *Self-Help* is entitled 'Character: The True Gentleman', and the progressive democratization of the gentlemanly ideal is an important factor in the mid-Victorian balance, offering at least the

[2]Best, *Mid-Victorian Britain*, p. 228. See also W.L. Burn, *The Age of Equipoise* (Allen & Unwin, 1964).

[3]'Sterne and Thackeray', in *Literary Studies* (2 vols., Dent, 1911) II, pp. 125–6.

promise of a moral meeting-ground beyond the divisions of class. Fitz-james Stephen noted in 1862 'a constantly increasing disposition to insist more upon the moral and less upon the social element of the word' gentle-man.[4] The apocalyptic tone of Carlyle was out; he had descended to rant in *Latter-Day Pamphlets* (1850), and the hysterical 'Shooting Niagara: and after?' (1867) was widely seen as an intemperate and eccentric contribution to the political debate surrounding the Second Reform Bill. The Condi-tion-of-England question had given way to more patient and thoughtful examination of existing institutions and their underlying principles. In addition to *The English Constitution* and Matthew Arnold's, *Culture and Anarchy* (1869), the period saw the publication of J.S. Mill's classic essay *on Liberty* (1859) and his *Considerations on Representative Government* (1861). In the developing debate about reform in the 1860s the question was no longer 'Will the social fabric survive?', but 'How has it survived these changes so well?', and 'How far and how fast should parliamentary reform go?'. A confident gradualism had taken over from earlier fears of revolution and apocalypse.

These changes in the climate of opinion are reflected in the novel. Dickens did not share the optimism of Palmerston or Samuel Smiles, but his last two completed novels deal with themes of self-improvement and class mobility in ways that suggest the topicality of the self-help ideology, as does the carpenter-hero of *Adam Bede* (1859). Similarly, the mid-Victorian *bildungsroman* is less emotionally intense than *Jane Eyre* or *Villette* but more intellectually ambitious and self-conscious, as in George Eliot's *Mill on the Floss* (1860) and Meredith's high-stepping *Ordeal of Richard Feverel* (1859). The dominant mode of mid-Victorian fiction is domestic realism, a realism grown philosophically confident in the novels of George Eliot, who in chapter 17 of *Adam Bede* gave a classic declaration of art's necessary commitment to the real:

> Paint us an angel, if you can, with a floating violet robe, and a face paled by the celestial light. . .but do not impose on us any aesthetic rules which shall banish from the region of Art those old women scraping carrots with their work-worn hands, those heavy clowns taking holiday in a dingy pot-house, those rounded backs and stupid weather-beaten faces that have bent over the spade and done the rough work of the world. . . .It is so needful we should remember their existence, else we may happen to leave them quite out of our religion and philosophy, and frame lofty theories which only fit a world of extremes. Therefore let Art always remind us of them; therefore let us always have men ready to give the loving pains of a life to the faithful representing of commonplace things – men who see beauty in these commonplace things, and delight in showing how kindly the light of heaven falls on them.

Such faith in the validity of realism is itself a manifestation of the

4'Gentlemen', *Cornhill Magazine* V (1862), p. 330.

confidence of the times; the belief that reality is stable and knowable and that a consensus can be reached between writer and readers about how to describe and interpret it reveals an assurance not found in, for example, Thackeray's use of the omniscient narrator, which is continually invaded by his scepticism. It was on the basis of this confident contract between writer and reader that George Eliot and Trollope set out to map the past and present respectively of English provincial life, of Middlemarch and Barchester, for this is the heyday of the provincial novel, a time when the changes in regional life wrought by the railways and industrialization were making the Victorians aware of what they were losing. A time of institutional curiosity also: Trollope's Parliamentary novels were written for a public interested in the political process itself. Their subject is the choices, adjustments, compromises and alliances that men have to make in Parliament, and the discussion of these in the society drawing-room, the gentleman's club and the country-house. Their context is the premiership of Palmerston (1855–65) whose life Trollope wrote, and the reform debates which followed it; and the writings of Bagehot and Mill. It is not to these sober, down-to-earth matters that I wish to turn first, however, but to another side of mid-Victorian fiction which must seem their antithesis, although it is as characteristic of this period as the novels of Trollope and George Eliot; and that is the so-called 'sensation novel'.

Wilkie Collins and the Sensation Novel

'You know that my novels are not sensational', Trollope wrote to George Eliot in 1863. 'In Rachel Ray I have attempted to confine myself absolutely to the commonest details of commonplace life among the most ordinary people, allowing myself no incident that would be even remarkable in every day life. I have shorn my fiction of all romance.'[5] The twin poles of mid-Victorian fiction are the realistic novel of 'commonplace life' to which Trollope aspired, and the 'sensational' novel, a vogue started by the success of Wilkie Collins's *The Woman in White* in 1860. On the face of it no two kinds of fiction could seem more different from each other than Trollope's lightly plotted comedies of manners and Collins's extravagantly plotted melodramas, and yet they shared a common concern with domestic relationships, a common devotion to the matter-of-fact in execution if not conception, and a common readership among the middle classes. A subscriber to the *Cornhill Magazine* in 1865, for example, could have followed in the same issue the instalments of Elizabeth Gaskell's *Wives and Daughters*, 'An Every-Day Story' of provincial life in the 1820s, and Wilkie Collins's dark, violent *Armadale*. The first seems almost plotless, so unobtrusively is its tale of family relationships built up, and so

---

[5] *The Letters of Anthony Trollope*, ed. N. John Hall (2 vols., Stanford, Stanford UP, 1983) I, p. 238; letter of 18 October 1863, sending a copy of his novel *Rachel Ray* to George Eliot.

completely is incident subordinated to the revelation and development of character. It deals with the relations of two families in a Midlands village, the Gibsons and the Hamleys, and the unspectacular events which change their lives – remarriage, deaths, the successes and failures of children, the unlooked-for disappointments and renewals of ordinary life. When the novel does touch on sensational matter, in Osborne Hamley's secret marriage to a French nursery-maid, there is nothing sensational or melodramatic in Gaskell's treatment: the character is humanized and made the agent of the humanizing of others, by bringing a grandson to brighten the old squire's life. *Armadale* is sensational from start to finish. It has been rightly described as 'one of the most over-plotted novels in English literature',[6] and defies brief summary, but its central action involves the friendship of two men called Allan Armadale, one 'light' and carefree and wealthy, the colourless young hero of conventional fiction, the other 'dark', thoughtful, haunted and forced to suppress his true identity by the prophecy that he will be the agent of the other's destruction, which almost comes to pass through the intervention of one of the most memorable villainesses in Victorian fiction, Lydia Gwilt. The difference between the two novels, and between the two genres, can be seen by comparing the governess figure in each book. Hyacinth Kirkpatrick, the ex-governess Mr Gibson marries, is a pretty but shallow and snobbish woman, rendered peevish by a lifetime's struggle with genteel poverty, disposed to make his home comfortable but only on her own terms: she denies him the toasted cheese he loves because ' "it's such a strong-smelling, coarse kind of thing" ' (11). Their relationship is a masterly study in the small, grating incompatibilities of second marriage, where each partner is too set in their ways to adjust to the other. With Lydia Gwilt in *Armadale* we move from the subtle comic art that can intimate domestic discontent through a disagreement about cheese to the broad brush of melodrama and the lurid world of laudanum drops and the poison-bottle. The red-haired Lydia is tall, beautiful and sexually attractive, with 'full, rich, and sensual' lips (III, 10) and, as Collins hissingly puts it, 'a subtle suggestiveness in her silence, and a sexual sorcery in her smile' (IV, 7). A convicted criminal, she confesses frankly to her diary how she plans to use her sexuality to trap the young heir and then murder him. The misery caused by Mrs Kirkpatrick may be altogether more probable and lifelike, but the melodramatic Miss Gwilt still communicates a convincing moral *frisson* which is a reminder of human potentialities the novel of domestic realism tended to overlook.

We have supped full with horrors since, of course, and the interest the Victorian sensation novel holds today lies less in its power to shock than in the way it shadows and subverts the sunlit world of domestic realism. In the 1860s, when Trollope was aspiring to a fiction shorn of all romance,

[6]Winifred Hughes, *The Maniac in the Cellar: Sensation Novels of the 1860s* (Princeton, NJ, Princeton UP, 1980), p. 155.

gothic romance was making a spectacular return in novels like Collins's *Woman in White* (1859–60), *No Name* (1862), *Armadale* (1864–6), and *The Moonstone* (1868), in Mrs Henry Wood's *East Lynne* (1861), Mary Elizabeth Braddon's *Lady Audley's Secret* (1862) and *Aurora Floyd* (1863), and Charles Reade's *Hard Cash* (1863) and *Griffith Gaunt* (1865–6). Although these have features peculiar to their time, such as a preoccupation with the domestic 'crimes' of bigamy and adultery, and the presence in several of the detective police, they belong in the wider view to the strain of gothic in English fiction which the novel of manners never quite succeeded in banishing. Jane Austen's *Northanger Abbey* (1818) was only a temporary victory. Henry Tilney may rebuke Catherine Morland's suspicions that his father is a Bluebeard with a confident appeal to common sense – ' "Remember the country and the age in which we live. Remember that we are English, that we are Christians. . . .Does our education prepare us for such atrocities? Do our laws connive at them?" ' (24) – but 30 years later in *Jane Eyre* the discovery of a secretly imprisoned wife is the turning-point of the novel. Charlotte Brontë breathed new life into gothic by bringing it home from Italy to an English gentleman's country residence, and this innovation, as developed by the sensation novelists, gave a new impetus to 'the literature of horrors', in Henry James's view: 'Instead of the terrors of *Udolpho*, we were treated to the terrors of the cheerful country-house and the busy London lodgings. And there is no doubt that these were infinitely the more terrible.'[7]

'Wild and yet domestic', Dickens's comment on the opening chapters of *The Moonstone*,[8] aptly sums up the yoking together of romance and realism in the sensation novel. Scrupulously matter-of-fact in its working-out of initially improbable plot premises, the genre's speciality is the infiltration of the everyday by exotic, bizarre, or criminal secrets. Lady Audley's secret is bigamy and insanity, and the revelation that this pretty, golden-haired, model wife has murdered her first husband and is prepared to poison her second. Lady Isabel Vane in *East Lynne*, tricked into adultery by an aristocratic villain, returns after her presumed death disfigured and disguised to become the governess to her own children. Dickens's *Mystery of Edwin Drood* opens with an English cathedral town surfacing in the opium-den dreams of a respectable choir-master. *The Woman in White* is the best of the genre not because it is any less melodramatic than the others – indeed we need to stop using melodrama as a pejorative critical term in discussing these novels – but because it is more successfully constructed, and because its melodrama is convincingly integrated with characterization and setting.

[7]'Miss Braddon', in *Wilkie Collins: The Critcal Heritage*, ed. Norman Page (Routledge & Kegan Paul, 1974), pp. 122–3.

[8]*The Letters of Charles Dickens*, ed. W. Dexter (3 vols., Nonesuch, 1938) III, p. 534; letter of 30 June 1867.

Wilkie Collins (1824–89) was a protégé of Dickens who may well have influenced his master. *The Woman in White* was serialized in *All the Year Round* and anticipates the preoccupation with disguise and secrecy, with the figure of the white woman and the dead-yet-alive character, in *Great Expectations* and *Our Mutual Friend*. *The Moonstone* has long been recognized as a likely influence on *Edwin Drood*.[9] For his part Collins may well have been inspired by the Lady Dedlock plot in *Bleak House* to raise the novel-with-a-secret to the new heights of technical and psychological sophistication he achieved in *The Woman in White*. The central idea was more sensational than anything in *Bleak House*, although it had a 'factual' basis in a volume of French trials Collins picked up on a Paris bookstall. An heiress is tricked by her husband and his villainous accomplice into a private lunatic asylum, where she is substituted for a woman who resembles her – her half-sister as it turns out – and whose death leaves the heiress officially 'dead'. (The popularity of false imprisonment in these novels – it figures centrally in Reade's *Hard Cash* and *It Is Never Too Late To Mend* – is a good example of the way the sensation novelist adapted an old gothic device, the dungeon, to modern unease.) The nucleus of melodrama in *The Woman in White* is given credibility by Collins's skill in approaching and disclosing it through various different narrators. Dickens had used two narrative voices in *Bleak House*, Collins uses no fewer than ten (11 if one includes 'The Narrative of the Tombstone' recording Lady Glyde's presumed death); his stated aim was to present the story as it might unfold in a court of law, 'to trace the course of one complete series of events, by making the persons who have been most closely connected with them, at each successive stage, relate their own experience, word for word' ('Preamble'). The sometimes improbable dovetailing of narratives which this involves is offset by the way Collins varies the kind and length of his documents (diaries and letters mainly, but interspersed with the testimony of servants, a doctor, even the tombstone), and by his skill in giving each speaker an individual character and an individual voice. The effect is to throw the interest on to the way of telling as much as on to what is told.

It is this narrative self-consciousness which makes Collins an innovator, rather than his sensational material itself. Compared (say) to Mrs Henry Wood, he brought a sophisticated approach to melodrama. *East Lynne* is certainly sensational enough; it offers murder, adultery, (unwitting) bigamy, even the arrest of a corpse for debt! But the book's moral premises are the simplistic ones of popular melodrama. The hero is a middle-class paragon; the villain is the typical heartless rake; Lady Isabel's sufferings as governess to her own children and mute witness to her husband's new domestic happiness are milked for all the pathos they can yield, and more, yet they only confirm the inviolability of the code she has transgressed,

[9]See Sue Lonoff, 'Charles Dickens and Wilkie Collins', *Nineteenth-Century Fiction* 35 (1980), pp. 150–70.

and lest we miss the moral the author is at hand to supply it: 'Oh, reader, believe me! Lady – wife – mother! should you ever be tempted to abandon your home, so will you awaken! Whatever trials may be the lot of your married life. . .*resolve* to bear them. . .'[10] Collins is never so explicit, and rarely so unambiguous as this; without condoning the crime, he suggests that the criminal is more complex and closer to home than stage melodrama allows us to think. So *The Woman in White* offers two villains. Sir Percival Glyde is obviously the bad baronet of popular melodrama, but there is nothing obvious about Count Fosco, his accomplice. A large man, larger than life, Fosco seems the antithesis of Glyde: soft-spoken where the other is loud, gentle where he is violent, considerate towards dependents and chivalrous to women, over whom he exercises a strange power, Fosco has a quality of unpredictability one finds in the great fictional characters. Unlike Dickens's Pecksniff, whom he resembles in his vanity and florid eloquence, Fosco is given those little redeeming touches which make a character unsettling and difficult to judge – his love of pastry, his tender handling of the white mice he takes everywhere with him, the admiration for Marian Halcombe which stays his hand against her at the end. He embodies in his own person the moral relativism and denial of platitude about criminals which he expounds in a memorable scene in the boathouse at Blackwater Park: ' "Crimes cause their own detection, do they? And murder will out (another moral epigram), will it? Ask Coroners who sit at inquests in large towns if that is true, Lady Glyde. Ask secretaries of life-assurance companies if that is true, Miss Halcombe. Read your own public journals" ' (No. 14; II, 3).

As with the criminals, so with the two heroines in the novel: the pairing of contrasted characters establishes a totality of suggestion that is subversive of conventional norms. Laura Fairlie, later Lady Glyde, is the fairhaired heroine of romance, the Victorian ideal of woman as passive and in need of protection; her sister Marian is the antithesis of this type, as Fosco is of Glyde: she is dark-skinned, ugly, 'masculine', but also intelligent, witty, resourceful and brave. Together, and in the *ménage à trois* they form with the hero, Walter Hartwright, they suggest something of the dissociation of sensibility at the root of Victorian sexuality.[11] Marian Halcombe implicitly criticizes, even as she also complements, the sweetly spiritual ideal of womanhood the novel endorses at the level of romantic plot-making; the beautiful figure below her ugly face, the warmth and vigour of her personality, Fosco's admiration – these intimate a subterranean sexual vitality which the official image could not accommodate, to its loss.

It is Collins's feeling for the unusual in human nature that makes *The Woman in White* a classic, and rescues it from the common charge that in

[10]*East Lynne* (Dent, 1984), ch. 29.
[11]As Harvey Peter Sucksmith suggests in his introduction to the Oxford English Novels edition of *The Woman in White* (OUP, 1975), p. xviii.

the sensation novel character is subordinated to plot. The novel certainly has an elaborate plot and its fair share of sensational incidents. Who can forget Walter Hartwright's first meeting with the woman in white on moonlit Hampstead Heath, or the heroine's reappearance by the side of her own gravestone? The gradual revelation of menace in the behaviour of Sir Percival and Fosco is skilfully done, too, disclosed through successive entries in Marian's diary. But this balance of psychological and sensational interest is lacking in Collins's other novels, where either the sense of menace is less, as in *The Moonstone*, or excessive plotting tends to swamp character, as in *Armadale*. The latter's over-plotting stems from his attempt to provide a working-out of Allan Armadale's prophetic dream which would keep both 'natural' and 'supernatural' explanations open, but such gestures towards the idea of Fate seem less thrilling now than the entirely terrestrial villainy of Lydia Gwilt. The prominence given to this red-haired siren in the second half of the novel, her mimicry of respectability combined with the contempt for the young hero and his sweetheart which she confides to her diary (a contempt which Collins's perfunctory handling of these characters seems to endorse), make *Armadale* the most cynical and daring of his novels, and the one which attracted the most adverse comment from contemporary reviewers.

In contrast to *Armadale* the sensationalism of *The Moonstone* is muted. There is no villainess, not even the usual unconventional heroine. One of Collins's sources was a famous contemporary crime committed within a middle-class home, the Road murder, but he softened the violence, changing murder to theft, and the bloodstains on an incriminating nightgown to paint stains.[12] In *The Moonstone* the sensation novel modulates into the detective novel, where the process of detection rather than sensational event is the chief interest of the narrative. Several elements later to become the staple of mystery and detective fiction are here brought together: a secluded country-house menaced by mysterious foreigners; a dinner-party ending in the theft of the diamond, putting the whole household under suspicion; the advent of an interesting but fallible detective, Sergeant Cuff, who fails to unearth the culprit; a series of false trails followed by the least expected of denouements, in which the hero is discovered to have taken the jewel in a trance induced by opium. The story is ingenious, and ingeniously told by a number of narrators, but none of them is as memorable as Marian Halcombe or Lydia Gwilt or Count Fosco, and what they relate lacks the wildness and menace of the previous novels. Despite the Hindoo mysteries of Imperial India which open and close the novel, the air of mystery in *The Moonstone* evaporates with the elaborate explanation of the theft; such *frissons* as it has to offer are felt on the periphery rather than at the centre, in (for example) the love of the

[12]See Anthea Trodd, 'The Policeman and the Lady: Significant Encounters in Mid-Victorian Fiction', *Victorian Studies* 27 (1984), pp. 435–60.

crippled servant girl, Rosanna Spearman, for Franklin Blake and her suicide in the sinister Shivering Sand.

The Moonstone may seem not quite sensational enough to sustain its length and the at times somewhat laboured joinery of its construction; and in this it is perhaps typical of the genre as a whole. The laugh that Jane Eyre hears on the third story of Thornfield Hall, 'distinct, formal mirthless' (11), is more chilling than volumes of Miss Braddon or Mrs Henry Wood. Dickens's woman in white, Miss Havisham, touches the psychic life of a whole society; Collins's, powerful creation though she is, remains a woman in white. These comparisons are unfair, since manifestly Collins was not a Dickens or a Charlotte Brontë, and they should not be allowed to obscure the real, if limited, interest of the genre. This is twofold. 'Its primitive, troublesome vision collided sharply with that of the reigning domestic novel – which was never quite the same again', Winifred Hughes concludes in her study of the sensation novel.[13] It aired the contemporary sexual and psychological discontents of middle-class Victorian life, if only in the limited form of criminal behaviour. And by giving new and vigorous life to the element of plot in fiction, to an aesthetic which showed character at the mercy of incident and not vice versa as in the domestic novel, it provided a resource for a later novelist like Hardy, for whom that aesthetic was also a metaphysic. We shall return to this legacy of the sensation novel in the final chapter.

Anthony Trollope

Of all the Victorian novelists, Anthony Trollope (1815–82) seems furthest from the concerns of the sensation novel. Murder is infrequent in his fiction, and when it happens, as in the murder of Mr Bonteen in *Phineas Redux*, the mystery about the murderer is quickly dispelled and attention shifts to the reactions of the man falsely accused of the murder. When he introduces an element of mystery, as in the theft of the diamonds in *The Eustace Diamonds*, it is done partly in parody of the central event of Wilkie Collins's *The Moonstone* and is made wholly subordinate to the portrayal of the adventuress-heroine, Lizzie Eustace. Although he wrote in his *Autobiography* that a good novel should be 'at the same time realistic and sensational. . .and both in the highest degree' (12), it is a formula that better fits Dickens or Hardy than Trollope himself. Plot is nearly always secondary to character in his best work. Yet Trollope began his career with a novel as violent as any by Wilkie Collins or Charles Reade. *The Macdermotts of Ballycloran* (1847) contains the murder of an excise officer, a particularly gruesome account of the revenge taken on a local lawyer, in which his foot is hacked off with an axe, and the death by hanging of the

[13]Hughes, *Maniac in the Cellar*, p. 37.

central character. The book is also unsparing in its portrayal of the grinding relentlessness of poverty in rural Ireland, a highly topical subject in the 1840s. For a novelist often dismissed as a comfortable conformist, the chief merit of whose work is supposed to be, in Henry James's phrase, 'a complete appreciation of the usual', [14] this first novel is in many ways unusual – unusual in choosing a Catholic rather than Ascendancy family for its subject, and in portraying the local priest as a good man, and unusual in the quality of sympathy it brings to the characterization of Thady Macdermott in his struggles with family debt and inarticulate feelings of love for his seduced sister.

I begin with *The Macdermotts of Ballycloran* because it points to two important but often neglected facts about Trollope's work: that he was not only, or not simply, the bread-and-butter realist and mild recorder of the unspectacular everyday that his reputation, confirmed by a reading of the later chapters of the *Autobiography*, would suggest; and that he could imagine the subtle interrelations of mid-Victorian life so well because he was to some extent an outsider. It is worth remembering, when considering Trollope's portrayal of the rituals and institutions of English society, that he spent almost 16 years of his adult life in Ireland, was happy and tasted success in his Post Office career there, and wrote several of his early novels in, and two of them about, that country. Ireland, as Robert Tracy says, helped to make him an English novelist. 'When Trollope turned to novels of English life with *The Warden*, he adapted his methods of social analysis to the new subject and again wrote at least partly as an outsider.'[15] Indeed, doubly an outsider, since the *Autobiography* reveals how miserable he had been at Harrow and Winchester, where, dirty and impoverished as a result of his father's debt and his mother's neglect, he was made to feel a 'Pariah'. Trollope saw the rituals of English social life with the eye of someone who had in his youth been almost excluded from them, and he saw the great institutions of Victorian England from the perspective, initially, of an Ireland experiencing famine and unrest in the 1840s. Approaching these institutions as a partial outsider, he was able to bring to their depiction an awareness both of their stability and of the changes with which, in an age of change, they were threatened. This is especially true of the Barchester novels with which he made his reputation.

The charm of Barchester is not that it is a Never-Never Land, like the world of P.G. Wodehouse, but that it is a place threatened by, yet *coping with* change. This is surely the source of the comic reassurance offered by *Barchester Towers*. The modern world invades sleepy Barchester in the form of railways, newspapers, the new bishop from London with his

---

[14] *Partial Portraits* (Macmillan, 1888), pp. 100–1.

[15] ' "The Unnatural Ruin": Trollope and Nineteenth-Century Irish Fiction', *Nineteenth-Century Fiction* 37 (1982–3), pp. 358–82; p. 381. Trollope lived in Ireland from 1841 to 1851, and from 1853, apart from trips abroad, until he came back to settle in England in 1859.

low-church wife and aggressively evangelical chaplain, Obadiah Slope. In the early chapters we are made continually aware that society in Trollope, as the Victorian critic R.H. Hutton said, is 'a great web of which London is the centre, and some kind of London life for the most part the motive-power'.[16] We are firmly in the world of the 1850s. Yet the novel is ultimately reassuring because, against all the odds, the threat of change is beaten off. Mr Slope is defeated and retreats to London, and the pastoral values of rural Barsetshire, epitomized by the old squire Wilfred Thorne and his sister, win the day at the social battle of the Ullathorne Sports.

The series takes its characters from the first Barsetshire novel, *The Warden* (1855). Trollope tells in his *Autobiography* how in 1851 he had been sent to examine rural deliveries in the West of England: 'In the course of this job I visited Salisbury, and whilst wandering there on a mid-summer evening round the purlieus of the cathedral I conceived the story of *The Warden*, – from whence came that series of novels of which Barchester, with its bishops, deans, and archdeacon, was the central site' (5). It seems an idyllic moment, and it can easily lull us into forgetting that *The Warden* is an intensely topical, and even in its way partisan novel. Mr Harding is an elderly clergyman who has been appointed to the clerical sinecure of the wardenship of Hiram's Hospital, a medieval charity for old men, by his friend the bishop. A good and honest man, he never questions his right to the annual salary of £800 until a local reformer, John Bold, who also happens to be the suitor of Mr Harding's younger daughter, makes a public issue of it. Why should the warden have £800 a year out of John Hiram's estate, while the 12 old men have each only one shilling and fourpence a day? The issue is taken up by the *Jupiter* newspaper (*The Times*) and by other reformers such as Dr Pessimist Anticant (Carlyle) and Mr Popular Sentiment (Dickens), and battle is joined between the reformers and the conservatives, led by Mr Harding's son-in-law, Archdeacon Grantly. Caught between these loud and warring factions, Mr Harding decides to resign. In words that capture the fineness and firmness of his moral scruple, Trollope writes of him that 'he was not so anxious to prove himself right, as to be so' (3).

It is a slight story, 'simply the history of an old man's conscience' Henry James called it,[17] yet in its working out deeply characteristic of Trollope and of the distinctive note he was to contribute to Victorian fiction. For in essence *The Warden* is an anti-reform novel, written at a time when the Church of England was under attack for its failure to reform itself and adjust its ways to the demands of the new industrial society. *The Times*, Trollope's *Jupiter*, was an especially persistent critic of the Established

---

[16]'From Miss Austen to Mr Trollope', *Spectator*, 16 December 1882; reprinted in Donald Smalley (ed.), *Trollope: The Critical Heritage* (Routledge & Kegan Paul, 1969), p. 511.

[17]*Partial Portraits*, p. 113.

Church at this period.[18] The novel paints its picture of the charming ways of the provincial and country clergy in the shadow of the knowledge that these ways are ceasing to be relevant to the needs of Victorian England. It is this knowledge which gives the book its slight air of elegy, of special pleading for a losing cause. But it also gave Trollope his opportunity; in the bad fit between the grand view of reforming rhetoric and the intricacy of the individual case he found a subject which released his creative genius. *The Warden* is something in the nature of a personal and artistic manifesto. The thinly veiled attacks on Carlyle, Dickens and *The Times* are a declaration of a different ethic and aesthetic; against the moral imperialism of the reforming temper, in life and in letters, Trollope set the quiet-voiced realism that was to become his hallmark. What looks a clear-cut case from the newspaper office or the reformer's study proves not to be so simple on the ground in Barchester – and typically, the editor of the *Jupiter* never visits the town. The best defence of Mr Harding's sinecure is not Archdeacon Grantly's, that he is entitled to it by law – which he may or may not be – but that he performs the duties of warden well and from the heart, providing the old men in his care with something that no salary can buy, 'that treasure so inestimable in declining years, a true and kind friend to listen to their sorrows, watch over their sickness, and administer comfort as regards this world, and the world to come' (4). This is the heart of the matter, and no theoretical settlement of rights can affect it, except for the worse, as the old men discover when Mr Harding leaves. Trollope always found the individual case more interesting than the general principle or theory, and the more individual the case the better. Hard cases may make bad law, but they make good novels, and *The Warden* is one of his best.

The theme of reform is continued and developed in *Barchester Towers* (1857), where it is given a more broadly comic treatment. The efforts of the Proudie faction to remould high-church Barchester in their low-church image touched on another topical subject because of the many low-church preferments made by Palmerston since 1855, but the *odium theologicum* inherent in the subject is skilfully avoided by Trollope, who makes the ground of contention not the differences in belief themselves but the offensiveness with which Mrs Proudie and Mr Slope go about challenging time-honoured Barchester practices. Slope's attack on music and ceremony in his cathedral sermon (I, 6), his rudeness in telling Mr Harding that 'new men' are ' "carting away the useless rubbish of past centuries" ' (I, 12), leave the reader in little doubt about where Trollope's sympathies lie, and the interest in the novel lies less in whether the Proudie faction will be defeated, but how. And defeated they are, but not by Archdeacon Grantly. By a delicious comic irony, the effective

---

[18] *The Times*'s campaign against clerical abuse and the Church's failure to adapt to modern conditions, and the relevance of these issues to *The Warden*, is discussed in my introduction to the Penguin edition of the novel (Harmondsworth, 1984).

champions of old Barchester turn out to be the son and daughter of the absentee cleric Dr Vesey Stanhope, whose residence 'on the shores of the Lake of Como, adding to that unique collection of butterflies for which he is so famous' (I, 6) is flagrant even by pre-reform standards. His bohemian son Bertie, and beautiful crippled daughter the Signora Neroni, bring a spirit of well-bred anarchy to Barchester with which the Proudie faction cannot cope. The turning-point is the havoc they create at Mrs Proudie's reception, with Bertie first outraging the bishop with his questions (' "Is there much to do here, at Barchester?" ') and then moving the recumbent signora on her sofa through Mrs Proudie's lace train – 'Gathers were heard to go, stitches to crack, plaits to fly open, flounces were seen to fall, and breadths to expose themselves – a long ruin of rent lace disfigured the carpet, and still clung to the vile wheel on which the sofa moved' (I, 11).

The resistance to the incomers begun at the Proudie reception in the first volume is completed in the counterbalancing scene in the third, the comic-feudal Ullathorne Sports, the final 'battle' of the novel where Mrs Proudie is discomfited and Mr Slope humiliated. This is a doubly appropriate comic reversal – that it should happen on the occasion of Miss Thorne's absurd attempts to revive a medieval jousting tournament, and in the area of Barsetshire seemingly most ripe for Mr Slope's rubbish-cart of progress. The action of the novel thus rolls back the tide of change, moving from London to Barchester and out to pastoral Ullathorne, where the childless Miss Thorne presides over the resurrection of Barchester tradition by bringing together Mr Harding's daughter and the new high-church dean, Mr Arabin. And Arabin's desire to marry Eleanor is another reversal, since in his youth he had been influenced by John Henry Newman and had aspired to a stern and solitary apostleship, and now finds himself in early middle age longing 'for the allotted share of worldly bliss, which a wife, and children, and happy home could give him, for that usual amount of comfort which he had ventured to reject as unnecessary for him. . .' (II, 1). Arabin's discovery about himself points to what is most individual in Trollope's vision in these early novels. In an age of reform, *The Warden* and *Barchester Towers* question the moral absolutism of the reforming temper; they speak up for the comic truth that we need the 'usual amount of comfort', and that accepting the human fallibility involved in that need may be the beginning of wisdom. We should not lay claim to higher standards than we can humanly live by. This emphasis is very out of step with the high Victorian drive towards idealism and renunciation, and is a reminder of how much in Trollope has its roots in the eighteenth rather than the nineteenth century.

The six Barsetshire novels fall naturally into three pairs. The first two are concerned with the politics of the cathedral close and the conflict between old ways and new men (and women). *Doctor Thorne* (1858) and *Framley Parsonage* (1860–1) move out into the hinterland of Barsetshire and deal in more muted fashion with another conflict, that between the small gentry and their values and the larger Whig landowners, lightly underscored by the political divisions between East Barset (Tory) and West Barset (Whig). *The Small House at Allington* (1862–4) and *The Last Chronicle of Barset* (1866–7) complete the series by seeing the now familiar landscape in a more searching light, revealing the vulnerability of 'small house' values in the modern world, and the clerical poverty which coexists in Barsetshire with the prosperity of Archdeacon Grantly and his friends. Considered as a whole the six novels show how well the recurring people and scenes of the chronicle form suited Trollope's imagination; he could settle down to a particular group of characters, possess them and their world with increasing confidence and subtlety, and arrive in the course of the series at some surprising insights and conclusions.

Framley Parsonage, with illustrations by Millais, was the lead serial in the first issue of the *Cornhill Magazine*: Trollope had arrived. It has been seen by many as the pivotal novel in the Barsetshire series, but that distinction surely belongs to its successor, *The Small House at Allington*, also serialized in the *Cornhill* and illustrated by Millais. Although Trollope did not at first include it among the Chronicles of Barsetshire, and although it lacks the social range of the others and (like *Doctor Thorne*) has no clerical matter, this unhappy love-story signals an important shift in his perception of Barsetshire. *The Small House* is a Victorian *Sense and Sensibility*, the story of two sisters and their widowed mother living in the country. Both have to endure love trials, but while the elder is careful in managing her affections, Lily Dale falls deeply and, as it proves, irretrievably in love with a London civil servant, Adolphus Crosbie, becomes engaged to him, and is then betrayed as he deserts her for the attractions of rank and marriage to Lady Alexandrina De Courcy. As with Mark Roberts in *Framley*, aristocratic society proves the undoing of Crosbie, but he falls into worse than debt by succumbing to Lady Alexandrina; and the loss for Lily and her family is too painful to allow the romantic resolution which has hitherto been applied in these novels. Through this love-affair and its attendant pastoral symbolism, and in the loneliness and childlessness of nearly all the Allington characters, Trollope intimates the enfeeblement of 'small house' gentry society and its values, their vulnerability to challenge from outside. The 'spice of obstinacy about Miss Dale' (2) is handled with a psychological subtlety that is new in his work. Is Lily a 'prig', as Trollope called her (*Autobiography*, 10), for hugging her loss to her, sentimentally disinheriting herself from life by persisting in loyalty to the memory of her love for a man she comes to see is worthless? Or is she the romantic maid of constant sorrow the Victorians loved, and loved all the more (as Trollope shrewdly realized) because she will not marry her devoted suitor, Johnny Eames? Or is she a study in a proud and private temperament, living in the spirit of Emily Dickinson's lines – 'The soul selects her own society, Then shuts the door. . .'? Trollope does not decide for us, and it is a measure of the artistic tact for which he does not always get credit that no two readers are likely to agree about how to interpret Lily Dale.

Lily reappears in *The Last Chronicle of Barset*, carrying her 'spice of obstinacy' and her suffering into a novel centrally concerned with the much more obstinate and more greatly suffering figure of Josiah Crawley, the perpetual curate of Hogglestock. Trollope considered this his finest novel, and Crawley is certainly his most powerful creation. Introduced in *Framley Parsonage* as a man of spiritual authority, capable of chastening the worldly-inclined Mark Roberts, but poor, proud and bitter, he comes under a cloud at the start of *The Last Chronicle*, suspected of having stolen a cheque for £20. 'He was a man who when seen could hardly be forgotten. The deep angry remonstrant eyes, the shaggy eyebrows. . .the repressed indignation of the habitual frown, the long nose and large powerful mouth, the deep furrows on the cheek, and the general look of thought and suffering, all combined to make the appearance of the man remarkable. . . .No one ever on seeing Mr Crawley took him to be a happy man, or a weak man, or an ignorant man, or a wise man' (18). For the first time in the series we see the comforts of clerical Barchester from the other side of the fence, through the figure of an impossible man who has been cruelly wronged, a better Hebrew scholar than the Dean of Barchester yet still a perpetual curate on £130 a year, toiling not in the leafy lanes of the county but among the labouring poor of bleak Hogglestock. Trollope stops short of tragedy, but the clearing of Crawley's name and his final acceptance into the ranks of 'gentlemen' by Archdeacon Grantly (83) do not settle the uncomfortable questions this novel asks about the justice of Church establishments and the worth of that comfortable freemasonry of gentlemen which should have sustained Crawley in his hour of need but did not. Trollope comes to these questions not through any increased radicalism of attitude, but through the accumulated density of a world now so thoroughly known and familiar that he can afford to surprise us, and perhaps even himself – as he does in the magnificent scene where the dirty and dishevelled Crawley routs Mrs Proudie in her stronghold at the bishop's palace (18). Like Archdeacon Grantly and the Proudies, and later Plantagenet and Glencora Palliser, Josiah Crawley is a triumph of patient characterization. The portrait of his stubborn, painful integrity – 'It's dogged as does it' is the wisdom he learns from an old brickmaker in Hogglestock (61) – is enriched by the perspectives provided by Lily Dale on the one hand, continuing in her lonely decision to remain single, and on the other by the serenity of Mr Harding, whose peaceful death at the end breathes a tranquillity absent from Barchester now.

Plantagenet Palliser makes his first appearance, as a dry, blue book politician, in *The Small House at Allington*, which was followed by the first of the so-called Palliser or Parliamentary novels, *Can You Forgive Her?* (1864–5). Trollope's political novels grew naturally out of the later Barsetshire and are six in number, the others being *Phineas Finn* (1867–9), *The Eustace Diamonds* (1871–3), *Phineas Redux* (1873–4), *The Prime Minister* (1875–6), and *The Duke's Children* (1879–80). These are not political novels in the sense that Disraeli's are political novels, romantic tales of young patrician heroes grappling with their conviction of destiny in a time of falling ministries and intellectual ferment. Trollope's are novels of a political middle age, where the room for effective action is very limited. In keeping with his description of himself as 'an advanced, but still a conservative liberal' (*Autobiography*, 16), his sympathies go out to those mildly reforming politicians in the Liberal party who are trying to hold the line between dangerous Radicals on their own side and the tergiversations of an unscrupulous Tory leadership desperate for office at almost any price. Plantagenet Palliser has no grand scheme for political change: his only 'cause' is decimal coinage, and that is portrayed as a ridiculous hobbyhorse. It is for what he is, a public-spirited landed magnate, and not for anything that he might do, that he is important to Trollope.

'If I wrote politics for my own sake, I must put in love and intrigue, social incidents, with perhaps a dash of sport, for the sake of my readers': Trollope's definition of his task in the *Autobiography* (17) has led to a view of these novels as not really political at all, but merely novels of manners against a political background. In fact, as John Halperin demonstrates in his excellent *Trollope and Politics*, such a separation of 'love' from 'politics' is artificial: they are intertwined by what Trollope saw as the fundamental reality of life for the aspiring politician – money. Those with money, like Plantagenet Palliser, can afford to be independent and vote with their consciences; those without it must be subservient to party discipline for the pickings of office, and therefore involved in continual moral and political compromises, and in the no less compromising search for the one sure refuge in a precarious career, a wealthy wife. As Phineas Finn acknowledges at the end of *Phineas Redux*, public life is probably a 'mistake' for those without means:

> 'For a poor man I think that it is, in this country. A man of fortune may be independent; and because he has the power of independence those who are higher than he will not expect him to be subservient. A man who takes to parliamentary office for a living may live by it, but he will have but a dog's life of it.' (79)

Hence the motor of plot in the first four Palliser novels is a character's search for the partner with money. In *Can You Forgive Her?* this is the 'wild man' George Vavasor, who wants to marry his cousin Alice to use her money to get into Parliament. In the *Phineas* novels it is the 'Irish member', Phineas Finn, who is in love at different times with three eligible and influential women, and is loved in turn by two of them. In *The Eustace Diamonds* Lizzie Eustace is sought after for her money and social position by Frank Greystock and Lord Fawn, both young, poor, aspiring politicians.

Phineas is the most sympathetically conceived of these adventurers, if adventurer he can be called. An Irish Tom Jones, handsome and warm-hearted, he owes his entrée to English political society to the love of Lady Laura Standish, who 'was related to almost everybody who was anybody among the high Whigs' (5). She provides him with the family rotten borough when he loses his Irish seat, and uses her influence to get him a government post at the Treasury. But when she marries the wealthy but dour Scots laird Robert Kennedy, hoping thereby to have a larger say in political life, it causes Phineas little heartache to turn his attentions to another society lady with political connections, Violet Effingham. These amorous intrigues run parallel to the political intrigues in a House of Commons beginning to be engaged with the issue of parliamentary reform – the very issue which exercised Parliament at the time of the 1867 Reform Bill debates, when Trollope was writing the novel. There are lively portraits of the political leaders: Disraeli can be glimpsed in Daubeny, Gladstone in Gresham, John Bright in the radical manufacturer Turnbull; and Trollope is excellent at portraying the party managers and hacks like Barrington Erle, who 'hated the very name of independence in Parliament, and when he was told of any man, that that man intended to look to measures and not to men, he regarded that man as being both unstable as water and dishonest as the wind' (2). Phineas is not over-burdened with political convictions, but even he squirms with pain at having to vote against his conscience on the issue of rotten boroughs (47). He rises faster than his performance in Parliament warrants, and falls as fast when on a visit to Ireland he commits himself to the cause of Irish tenant-right. Again love and politics intertwine: Phineas votes for Ireland and honesty in both, resigning from government and marrying his home-town sweetheart, despite the tempting offer of Madame Max Goesler's hand and fortune. His reward is to become Inspector of the Poor Houses in Cork, a far cry from the Palace of Westminster.

Between the two *Phineas* novels fell the shadow of Trollope's bitter experience at the Beverley election in 1868, when he came bottom of the poll as Liberal candidate in a constituency subsequently disfranchised for bribery. *Phineas Redux* is a much darker book than its predecessor. There is disillusionment in many of the narrator's reflections, such as his obser-vation on Phineas's return to Parliament that he 'was again in possession of that privilege for which he had never ceased to sigh since the moment in which he lost it. A drunkard or a gambler may be weaned from his ways, but not a politician' (13). The behaviour of politicians here invites the most cynical of interpretations. The Tories take up the cause of Church

Disestablishment, in denial of all their traditions, to stay in office. A corrupt MP is acquitted in the courts after a commission convicts him of bribery, and nobody minds except 'some poor innocents here and there about the country who had been induced to believe that bribery and corruption were in truth to be banished from the purlieus of Westminster' (44). An innocent man, Phineas Finn, is nearly convicted of murder, and emerges from his trial disillusioned with political life: ' "What does it matter who sits in Parliament? The fight goes on just the same. The same falsehoods are acted. The same mock truths are spoken. The same wrong reasons are given" ' (68). Like *Phineas Finn*, *Phineas Redux* ends with a resignation and a marriage. Phineas resigns his seat, refuses Mr Gresham's offer of a Treasury post, makes the wealthy match he has always sought; and yet this time he resigns with conviction rather than regret, 'because the chicaneries of office had become distasteful to him' (78). It is an important turning-point in the series.

Trollope was ambivalent about politics, revering the institution of Parliament while increasingly deploring much that went on there. The reverence he held on to despite deepening pessimism came to be focused in the figure of Plantagenet Palliser, who emerges as Trollope's ideal statesman in the later novels. He stands in relation to his uncle, the old Duke of Omnium, who dies in *Phineas Redux*, as the Victorian gentleman to the Regency grandee: where his uncle is idle and pleasure-loving, yet a man who 'had looked like a duke, and known how to set a high price on his own presence' (24), Plantagenet is hard-working and abstemious, and looks like an anxious civil servant. He is indifferent to the appurtenances of rank; he would rather serve his country as Chancellor of the Exchequer than be Duke of Omnium, and when he becomes Duke he prefers to live in Matching, his country gentleman's home, than at Gatherum Castle. His growth in stature to the noble statesman (if incompletely successful Premier) of *The Prime Minister* is Trollope's vindication of the principle of government by hereditary aristocracy, first set out in *Can You Forgive Her?*:

> Mr. Palliser was one of those politicians in possessing whom England has perhaps more reason to be proud than of any other of her resources, and who, as a body, give to her that exquisite combination of conservatism and progress which is her present strength and best security for the future. He could afford to learn to be a statesman, and had the industry wanted for such training. He was born in the purple, noble himself, and heir to the highest rank as well as one of the greatest fortunes of the country, already very rich, surrounded by all the temptations of luxury and pleasure; and yet he devoted himself to work with the grinding energy of a young penniless barrister labouring for a penniless wife, and did so without any motive more selfish than that of being counted in the roll of the public servants of England. . . . It is the trust which such men inspire which makes them so serviceable; – trust not only in their

labour, – for any man rising from the mass of the people may be equally laborious; nor yet simply in their honesty and patriotism. The confidence is given to their labour, honesty, and patriotism joined to such a personal stake in the country as gives them a weight and ballast which no politician in England can possess without it. (24)

What brings this paragon to life is Trollope's brilliant handling of his marriage to Lady Glencora. It is not portrayed as a perfectly happy marriage: in the first novel she is shown hungering for the handsome wastrel her relatives prevent her marrying, and there remain needs in her nature which her husband can never understand or satisfy. He for his part is always likely to be embarrassed by her tendency to be impulsive and indiscreet. Yet the respect that slowly grows between them, the way they complement each other's qualities so that we see depths of feeling and integrity beneath his staidness and her flightiness, make this one of the few convincing marriages in Victorian fiction. And in his typically modest way, Trollope knew the rare quality of achievement they represent: 'I do not think it probable that my name will remain among those who in the next century will be known as the writers of English prose fiction; – but if it does, that permanence of success will probably rest on the character of Plantagenet Palliser, Lady Glencora, and the Rev. Mr. Crawley' (*Autobiography*, 20).

Because they allowed his characteristic gifts most room to develop and reveal themselves, the Barsetshire and Palliser novels must be accounted his central achievement. But there are a dozen other novels as good in their own way, and one, *The Way We Live Now*, which I shall touch on in the next chapter, considered by many to be his masterpiece. If we try to define what is most characteristic in Trollope's art, we shall find ourselves talking sooner or later about three qualities in his work. First, his grasp of character: there is a good deal of conventional characterization in Trollope, inevitable in a novelist who wrote so much and relied so heavily on the romantic entanglements of love and property, but where his imagination was deeply engaged one finds an intimacy of portraiture as penetrating as anything in Victorian fiction. Second, there is the combination in his work of a mature understanding of society as a great network of institutions, rituals, codes, with an intense sympathy for the frequent loneliness of the individual within society, and especially for the exiles and misfits, those who for whatever reason have stepped beyond the accepted boundaries of their caste or social group. One thinks of Mr Crawley tramping the muddy lanes of Hogglestock, of the swindler Melmotte in his downfall in *The Way We Live Now*, or even Bishop Proudie coming to terms with the isolation his wife has created around him, and after her death 'praying that God might save him from being glad that his wife was dead' (*Last Chronicle*, 67). And finally there is his irony, a very un-

Victorian irony in many ways, directed typically at the tendency – to which the Victorians were especially prone – to lay claim to higher standards of conduct than could be sustained in ordinary living. The novelist who made his name in *The Warden* with a book criticizing an importunate reformer, always retained a 'kindly but ironic perception', as Hugh Sykes Davies put it, 'of the gap between what we are, and what we ought to be, wish to be, or believe ourselves to be.'[19]

George Eliot

George Eliot (1819–80) and Trollope were good friends, and as novelists they have much in common. Both made their reputations as chroniclers of provincial England, both were avowedly realistic in their aims (it was to George Eliot that Trollope declared his ambition to write a fiction 'shorn. . .of all romance'), both held a fundamentally melioristic view of human society and history – indeed George Eliot was credited in her lifetime with coining the word 'meliorism' to define the belief that the world can be improved by human effort.[20] About each other's work they were warmly respectful, Trollope placing her novels second after Thackeray's among novelists of his day but confessing to their difficulty and lack of 'ease' (*Autobiography*, 13), George Eliot acknowledging the importance of Trollope's influence in encouraging her to write *Middlemarch*, but acquiescing in the common view of him as 'a Church of England man, clinging to whatever is, *on the whole*, and without fine distinctions, honest, lovely and of good report'.[21] But there are also many differences between them, and two in particular of far-reaching importance. George Eliot was a novelist of the past, whereas Trollope dealt almost exclusively with the present; and she was a formidable intellectual, as he was not. It could not be said of Trollope or any other Victorian novelist, what Basil Willey said of George Eliot, that his development was a 'paradigm' of the 'most decided trend' of English intellectual life in the nineteenth century, but this is certainly her distinction. 'Starting from evangelical Christianity, the curve passes through doubt to a reinterpreted Christ and a religion of humanity: beginning with God, it ends in Duty.'[22]

George Eliot came to novel-writing late, after many years on the frontier of Victorian intellectual life. The story has often been told. It begins in Coventry with the young and outwardly evangelical Mary Ann Evans reading Charles Hennell's *Inquiry Concerning the Origin of Christianity* (1838), in which she encountered, and was at once convinced by, an

[19] *Trollope* (Writers and their Work, No. 118, Longman, 1960), p. 32.

[20] See James Sully, *Pessimism: A History and a Criticism* (Henry S. King, 1877), p. 399.

[21] *The George Eliot Letters*, ed. G.S. Haight (9 vols., New Haven, Yale UP, 1954–78) IV, pp. 81–2; letter of 16 April 1863. See also M. Sadleir, *Trollope: A Commentary* (Constable, 1927), p. 367*n*.

[22] *Nineteenth-Century Studies* (Harmondsworth, Penguin, 1964), p. 215.

interpretation of the Gospels that required, in Hennell's words, 'no devia-
tion from the known laws of nature' for their explanation, nor 'more than
the operation of human motives and feelings, acted upon by the peculiar
circumstances of the age and country whence the religion originated'.[23]
The effect of reading Hennell was to replace in her mind the supernatural
Jesus of Christianity with the natural Jesus of history, but characteristically she did not rest in this negative position. Her reading of David
Friedrich Strauss's *Das Leben Jesu* (1835–6), which she translated into
English as *The Life of Jesus* (1846), introduced her to a seminal work of the
German 'Higher Criticism'. Strauss argued that although Jesus was not
divine his life and ministry were profoundly expressive, as symbol and
'myth', of certain universal human truths, needs, and hopes. The process
of reconstruction was completed when, after moving to London and
becoming assitant editor of *The Westiminster Review* in 1851, she read and
translated Ludwig Feuerbach's *The Essence of Christianity* (1854).
Feuerbach provided the ethical redirection her essentially religious nature
needed. He saw religion as the projection of an entirely human need for a
perfect and transcendent being: the true 'essence' of Christianity was the
divinity of the human, not the humanity of the divine, and what could be
rescued from the wreck of supernatural theism was a 'Religion of Humanity', founded on the bonds of feeling and sympathy between human
beings. The essence of Feuerbach is summed up in George Eliot's comment: 'Heaven help us! said the old religions – the new one, from its very
lack of that faith, will teach us all the more to help one another.'[24] This
'new' religion gave her an object of reverence, Humanity, and a creed,
belief in the power of awakened sympathy to create fellowship, which her
novels would proceed to illustrate, but also to test. She wrote in 1874 that
her books 'have for their main bearing a conclusion. . .without which I
could not have cared to write any representation of human life – namely,
that the fellowship between man and man which has been the principle of
development, social and moral, is not dependent on conceptions of what is
not man: and that the idea of God, so far as it has been a high spiritual
influence, is the ideal of a goodness entirely human (i.e. an exaltation of the
human).'[25]

'It was not science itself', Noel Annan has written, 'but science interpreted *as history*, which upset the orthodox cosmology.'[26] George Eliot
understood and accepted the implications of that intellectual revolution
more completely than any other English novelist of his time. Fundamental to all her writings are the notions of sequence and development, at work
in the history of society, of religion, of matter. She praised one writer in a

[23]Quoted by Willey, *Nineteenth-Century Studies*, p. 220.
[24]*Letters* II, p. 82; letter of 22 January 1852.
[25]*Letters* VI, p. 98; letter of 10 December 1874.
[26]*Ideas and Beliefs of the Victorians* (Sylvan Press 1949), p. 151.

review for his 'recognition of the presence of undeviating law in the material and moral world – of that invariability of sequence which is acknowledged to be the basis of physical science, but which is still perversely ignored in our social organization, our ethics and our religion'. And in the same review of 1851 she made her first recorded reference to the founder of Positivism, Auguste Comte, and wrote that 'the teaching of positive truth is the grand means of expelling error.'[27] George Eliot was clearly a positivist of sorts, in the sense that she accepted the scientific rather than supernatural explanation of the universe, and tried in her novels to incorporate it in a progressive and affirmatory vision of human history, society and morals. But she came to positivism before she read Comte's grandiose systematization, and hers was a very English and Wordsworthian version: a faith in progress qualified by reverence for the past and a great tenderness for the human need and longing which had been expressed through, and consoled by, religious forms which could no longer be held to be supernaturally true. There is no more revealing detail in her biography than the image we have of her groaning over the translation of Strauss's *Leben Jesu* – a work that was to act like a depth-charge in the lives of many Victorian half-believers – 'dissecting the beautiful story of the crucifixion', as a friend wrote, and turning for consolation to 'an ivory image of Christ on the Cross above her desk'.[28] She disliked the label 'freethinker' and soon moved away from any spirit of antagonism to dogmatic Christianity, writing in 1859: 'I have no longer any antagonism towards any faith in which human sorrow and human longing for purity have expressed themselves; on the contrary, I have a sympathy with it that predominates over all argumentative tendencies.'[29] At once intellectually advanced and emotionally conservative, striving always to reconstruct, to rescue the human truths enshrined in past forms and reconcile them with the inevitable development toward newer forms, she represents the 'conservative-reforming intellect' ('Amos Barton', 1) of her time at its most responsible.

When this has been said, however, and it is inevitably the first thing that is said about George Eliot, it must sometimes trouble the reader coming to her novels for the first time to know quite how this 'advanced' intellectual activity meets up with the nostalgic evocation of pre-Victorian village life he or she will find in, for example, *Adam Bede* or *Silas Marner*; and the same reader will look in vain in her novels for any treatment of a religious crisis comparable to her own. She left to a later generation of novelists, to Hardy and Mrs Humphry Ward, the novel of religious doubt she was uniquely qualified to write. Indeed, it is a striking feature of all her novels

[27]'The Progress of Intellect', in *Essays of George Eliot*, ed. T. Pinney (Routledge & Kegan Paul, 1963), pp. 31, 29.
[28]Walter Allen, *George Eliot* (Weidenfeld & Nicolson, 1965), p. 49.
[29]*Letters* III, p. 231; letter of 6 December 1859.

apart from her last, *Daniel Deronda*, that they are set in a period before the intellectual upheavals of the Victorian age. Her favoured time is around 1830, between Catholic Emancipation in 1829 and the Reform Bill of 1832, but before the rise of the Oxford Movement and the impact of geology and biblical criticism in the 1830s. The first question to be asked, then, in considering George Eliot as a Victorian novelist is why the Victorian age itself is largely absent from the subject-matter of her fiction.

Part of the answer is a combination of nostalgia for the past with a natural imaginative gravitation to the world of her childhood, but more important are the ideas of history and society set out in her review-essay of 1856, 'The Natural History of German Life'. She begins there by criticizing the unrealistic portrayal of the working classes in contemporary art and literature: 'our social novels profess to represent the people as they are, and the unreality of their representations is a grave evil'. There has been no 'natural history' of the English people comparable to the study of the German peasantry undertaken by the sociologist Heinrich von Riehl in the volumes under review. Riehl had not only observed the peasant more closely, he had brought to the exploration of peasant culture a 'thoroughly philosophical kind' of '*social-political-conservatism*':

> He sees in European society *incarnate history*, and any attempt to disengage it from its historical elements must, he believes, be simply destructive of social vitality. What has grown up historically can only die out historically, by the gradual operation of necessary laws. The external conditions which society has inherited from the past are but the manifestation of inherited internal conditions in the human beings who compose it; the internal conditions and the external are related to each other as the organism and its medium, and development can take place only by the gradual consentaneous development of both.[30]

There is much in this passage and in the review as a whole that is deeply characteristic of George Eliot, and anticipatory of her novels. Here, to reverse Professor Annan's terms, is history interpreted as science. Words like 'law', 'organism', 'medium', 'development', a phrase such as 'natural history' itself, portray the study of society as a scientific activity, and there is a strong implicit analogy throughout the review between the sociologist and the novelist. He too is a 'natural historian' exploring the '*incarnate history*' of society, perceiving 'the gradual operation of necessary laws', tracing the influence of external upon internal in individual lives. And if the novelist is a natural historian, then his medium is history and he must choose a period sufficiently distanced from the present to enable 'the gradual operation of necessary laws' to be perceived. Distance and objectivity will enable the novelist to achieve the realism of presentation which is his equivalent of the sociologist's observations, and is necessary to

[30]*Essays*, pp. 270, 287.

create the sympathetic understanding that is the moral end of art – for 'the greatest benefit we owe to the artist, whether painter, poet, or novelist, is the extension of our sympathies' (p. 270).

George Eliot's aim to write a 'natural history' of English life drove her back to the time of her own childhood and beyond, where the web of society, to use one of her favourite metaphors, could be held securely in memory. The result is a curious double perspective. 'She has walked between two epochs', Sidney Colvin said in his review of *Middlemarch*, 'upon the confines of two worlds, and has described the old in terms of the new. To the old world belong the elements of her experience, to the new world the elements of her reflection on experience'. Hence 'there is the most pointed contrast between the matter of these English tales and the manner of their telling. The matter is antiquated in our recollections, the manner seems to anticipate the future of our thoughts.'[31] This contrast between the pre-Reform Bill world she writes about and the modernity of her reflections upon it makes for a different fictional treatment of the past than in other Victorian novelists. Elizabeth Gaskell, like Thackeray also in one of his moods, is concerned with the links that bind past and present, with the continuity of memory. In novels like *Cranford* and *Cousin Phillis* she portrays the forces of change at work in the recent past that will transform the communities she writes about, and bring them into the present where she and her readers are living. In *Adam Bede*, with its 60-year time-gap, we are more aware of a disjunction between two worlds. Past relates to present by contrast and analogy – the 1832 Reform Bill in *Felix Holt* and *Middlemarch* paralleling their first readers' recent experience of the 1867 Reform Bill is another example – rather than through the threads of continuity traced by Gaskell or Thackeray. The gap between worlds is bridged but not closed by the authorial commentary, which moves, sometimes fluently, sometimes uneasily, between the different responses of irony, nostalgia and 'scientific' detachment.

Irony and nostalgia jostle on the first page of her first story, 'The Sad Fortunes of the Rev. Amos Barton' in *Scenes of Clerical Life* (1858). 'Shepperton Church was a very different-looking building five-and-twenty years ago', it begins, and the narrator goes on to confess ambivalence about the improvements that have taken place since. The 'well-regulated mind' approves, but 'imagination does a little Toryism by the sly, revelling in regret that dear, old, brown, crumbling, picturesque inefficiency is everywhere giving place to spick-and-span new-painted, new-varnished efficiency. . .'. The irony tells against a too-confident faith in progress and, less securely perhaps, against conservative nostalgia ('a little Toryism by the sly'). There is a double irony here, for it is the new man, the evangelical clergyman Amos Barton, who sets these improvements in motion, before

---

[31]*George Eliot: The Critical Heritage*, ed. David Carroll (Routledge & Kegan Paul, 1971), p. 332.

his 'sad fortunes' take him away from Shepperton; and he is most in need of the tolerance of the old ways. Barton is an utterly unremarkable man, a point George Eliot makes repeatedly in the story: 'a man whose virtues were not heroic, and who had no undetected crime within his breast; who had not the slightest mystery hanging about him, but was palpably and unmistakably commonplace; who was not even in love, but had had that complaint favourably many years ago' (5). For, 'I wish to stir your sympathy with commonplace troubles – to win your tears for real sorrow: sorrow such as may live next door to you – such as walks neither in rags nor in velvet, but in very ordinary decent apparel' (7). He is plain, awkward, ill-educated, ineffective, and, like Trollope's Mr Crawley, desperately poor on a salary of £80 a year, with six children to support. The one redeeming touch in his life is his beautiful wife Milly and her love for him, and when she dies, and he has to vacate his living, he is desolate. But his sorrows create the sympathy among his parishioners that his preaching has failed to do, and they rally round him and are sorry to see him go – 'his recent troubles had called out their better sympathies, and that is always a source of love. Amos failed to touch the spring of goodness by his sermons, but he touched it effectually by his sorrows; and there was now a real bond between him and his flock' (10). This simple story expresses George Eliot's 'religion of humanity' at its plainest – the human need and sympathy that were for her the Feuerbachian 'essence of Christianity'. 'Amos Barton' is not a very well-constructed work, too leisurely at the start and too rushed at the end, but it is told with a spare and compassionate realism that is strangely moving.

'Janet's Repentance' is a more ambitious story on a similar theme, also set around 1830 and concerned with an evangelical clergyman in a provincial town, but with the main elements reversed: Milby is not picturesque like Shepperton, but ignorant and backward, whereas Edgar Tryan is everything that Amos Barton is not – handsome, charismatic and a gentleman. It is a noticeably more accomplished piece of writing, better-paced and clearly focused on the central moral action of the Rev. Tryan's rescue of Janet Dempster from the despair and incipient alcoholism that her loveless marriage has brought her to. The story of Janet's conversion would edify even the most devout reader, but again the Feuerbachian message is made clear: the 'essence' of her rescue is the human love and pity shown by Tryan, working within the evangelical forms. She cannot feel the 'Divine Pity. . .it kept aloof from her, it poured no balm into her wounds, it stretched out no hand to bear up her weak resolve. . .' (15). It is only when Tryan stretches out a human hand, gives of himself by confessing to his own guilty past, that the channels of feeling open: 'The tale of the Divine Pity was never yet believed from lips that were not felt to be moved by human pity' (18). All this is impressively done, and yet the spare power of 'Amos Barton' is lacking. 'Janet's Repentance' gives the air of hedging its metaphysical bets a little too calculatingly; there are too many ambiguous references to the 'Divine Presence', 'Divine sympathy', 'Infinite Love', and 'the strange light from the golden sky' which falls on Mr Tryan's hair and 'makes it look almost like an auréole' (3) indicates that we are being given a modern saint's life. It is revealing to compare the funerals that end the two books. That of Milly in 'Amos Barton' takes place 'while the Christmas snow lay thick upon the graves', and is unconsoling; they go home and 'the broad snow-reflected daylight was in all the rooms; the Vicarage again seemed part of the common working-day world, and Amos, for the first time, felt that he was alone. . .' (9). Mr Tryan is buried surrounded by intimations of immortality – it is spring, the cloudy weather clears and the sun shines, the clergyman speaks of the Resurrection and the Life, the crocuses bloom, and Janet walks 'in the presence of unseen witnesses – of the Divine love that had rescued her' (28). Given George Eliot's stated beliefs, the ending of 'Amos Barton' is not only more logical, but more honest and more moving.

These two novellas point to diverging tendencies in George Eliot's art, the one to an unadorned realism attempting the sympathetic presentation of middling characters, the other to a yearning identification with those characters who transcend the real by their exceptional gifts of sympathy and self-sacrifice. Although her philosophy committed her to the real she could not rest in it, as Trollope could; there was always a stirring beyond to more ideal forms of life, and she was intensely susceptible to the appeal of self-denying conduct. 'All self-sacrifice is good', she once wrote,[32] a statement one cannot imagine Trollope or Thackeray making. Thus her aesthetic of realism is always potentially a divided aesthetic, as U.C. Knoepflmacher says: 'Throughout her career, George Eliot's desire to be faithful to the conditions of actual existence clashed with her efforts to transcend or dignify the meanness of those conditions'.[33] The problem of fact and value inherent in literary realism is never settled in her work, and the desire to affirm value in fact keeps breaking in, either in the form of characters like Will Ladislaw in *Middlemarch*, who is made miraculously exempt from the forces of environment which bear so heavily on the others, or in the stirrings towards millenarianist romance which she surrendered to in *Daniel Deronda*. There is always an element of idealism in the realism she professed and practised. She saw no theoretical contradiction in this, following G.H. Lewes in his belief that 'Realism is. . .the basis of all Art, and its antithesis is not Idealism, but Falsism.'[34] But the contradiction is there nonetheless, and it is especially apparent in her first full-length novel.

[32]*Letters* I, p. 268; letter of 11 June 1848.

[33]*George Eliot's Early Novels: The Limits of Realism* (Berkeley & Los Angeles, University of California Press, 1968), pp. 34–5.

[34]'Realism in Art: Recent German Fiction', *Westminster Review* 70 (1858), p. 493.

Adam Bede (1859) is a professedly realistic novel, George Eliot's attempt to do for the English countryman in fiction what Riehl had done for the German peasant in his pioneering work of sociology. But a reader looking for the English peasant as he is portrayed in her review of Riehl, with his 'slow gaze', 'heavy slouching walk', 'coarse laugh', and 'tipsy revelry' (p. 269), will soon be disappointed. *Adam Bede* is set among a respectable class of village artisans and tenant-farmers, and there is a corresponding elevation of treatment. The famous analogy with Dutch painting in chapter 17 is appropriate not because it underlines anything especially down-to-earth in George Eliot's art, but because it points to a reverent, glowing quality in her rendering of ordinary life, and to the pictorial, even picturesque, element in the early chapters. The community of Hayslope is built up almost tableau by tableau, like a series of Victorian genre-paintings – 'The Workshop', 'The Preaching', 'The Rector', 'The Dairy', 'Church'. The principal characters and their idiom have a similar air of heightened typicality. The Adam Bede we meet in the opening chapter, broad of chest and straight of back, surveying his work with 'the air of a soldier standing at ease' and singing 'Awake, my soul, and with the sun/Thy daily stage of duty run. . .', is not just any workman, but the incarnation of the best attributes of the workman; he does not merely embody duty, he sings about it too, lest we miss the point. This is a special kind of realism, which rather like the *Lyrical Ballads* published the year before the novel's opening date of 1799 (and mentioned by Arthur Donnithorne in chapter 5) celebrates the moral qualities of a simple way of life in the process of describing it. Likewise, the colourful idiom of Mrs Poyser, the sharp-tongued farmer's wife, which is grounded in the discipline of farming, expresses the moral value which for George Eliot resides in the decency and worked-for plenty of the Hall Farm. So when she speaks to her Methodist niece in defence of Mr Irwine, the tolerant rector of the parish, and says of his appearance in the pulpit that

> 'it's like looking at a full crop of wheat, or a pasture with a fine dairy o' cows in it; it makes you think the world's comfortable-like. But as for such creaturs as you Methodisses run after, I'd as soon go to look at a lot o' bare-ribbed runts on a common. Fine folks they are to tell what's right, as look as if they's never tasted nothing better than bacon-sword and sour-cake i' their lives.' (8)

– the association between the rector's 'comfortable' preaching and the fruits of good husbandry is not just Mrs Poyser's characteristic way of speaking, it also evokes a whole scheme of values in the novel. The pastoral fecundity of the Hall Farm is a touchstone by which the angularities of Methodism, its tendency to self-denial and even masochism, are judged. Dinah Morris has to learn to come to terms with the natural rhythms for which Mrs Poyser is the spokeswoman, and in doing so she has to learn some of Mr Irwine's tact and moderation in matters of religion. It is significant that at the end she has given up preaching and her figure is 'fuller'.

In his essay 'The Pastoral of Intellect', John Bayley has an astute comment on the kind of characterization Adam Bede or Mrs Poyser represent: 'It is a process, above all, of making things and people lovingly characteristic of themselves, but the very minuteness and care in the externalization reveals all too clearly its origins in the pictured world of historical idea, of pondered subject. . . .Carpenters do not chat so as to reveal the workings of their calling to one another. . .'.[35] Lovingly characteristic of themselves is exactly what the rustics in *Adam Bede* or *Silas Marner* are; they express George Eliot's idea of what their relationship to their environment should or might be, and in this, as Bayley suggests, they betray their origins in an act of historical idealization, 'historic pastoral' he calls it. What purports to be an exercise in realism turns out to be a realistic version of pastoral, in which the values of a pre-Victorian, pre-industrial England are held up for our approval and for our solace. Significantly, although the action is placed on a symbolic turning-point, 1799, there is little sense in the body of the novel of how society was turning on that point. The indicators of social change are there (Methodism, the presence of an industrial town at Stoniton) but the engine of social change is lacking; or rather the engine is moving in reverse, bringing Methodism back from the industrial town to blend with the unchanging countryside; just as Silas Marner's redemption is indicated by the gradual shedding of his urban, Dissenting past, and by his adoption of village ways – church, pipe-smoking and all. Change is present, but only in the narrator's consciousness, as she reminds us of the passing of 'Old Leisure' (52) or tells us how irreplaceable men like Adam Bede are (19). The imagination of *Adam Bede* is indeed doing 'a little Toryism by the sly': its deepest impulse seems to be the wishing away of the industrial revolution.

There is another side to the novel, however, the moral and psychological exploration of the love affair between Arthur Donnithorne and Hetty Sorrel, the squire's heir and the dairymaid, and its consequences. George Eliot speaks a good deal in her letters and narrative asides about sympathy, but there is little sympathy on hand for Hetty. As her name implies, the pretty but vain and shallow Hetty is a weed in the pastoral garden, and it hardly increases one's respect for the cosy ruralities of Hayslope to see how ruthlessly she is rooted out of the community, and how unsparing is the nemesis visited on her and Arthur. Because she is pretty and empty-headed, Hetty brings out a punitive streak in George Eliot's moralism, which is all the more jarring because of the caressing tones in which it sometimes expresses itself: 'How pretty the little puss looks in that odd dress! It would be the easiest folly in the world to fall in love with her. . .'

---

[35]*Critical Essays on George Eliot*, ed. Barbara Hardy (Routledge & Kegan Paul, 1970), pp. 201, 203.

(15), and so on. The story of Hetty and Arthur grows out of the pastoral world and its politics of deference, but Ian Gregor is surely right to see it as belonging in the end to a diferent mode, to a world of tragic destiny where, in the words of Mr Irwine, ' "Consequences are unpitying. Our deeds carry their terrible consequences, quite apart from any fluctuations that went before – consequences that are hardly ever confined to ourselves." ' (16)[36] It is true that Adam and Dinah are sucked into Hetty's fate, Adam through his love for her, Dinah through the comfort she brings to her cousin in the condemned cell, but these two are restored to Hayslope at the end, and the last book is given over to the restoration and celebration of the rural community in the harvest supper (53) followed by their marriage. The tragic losers are Hetty and Arthur, exiles from the pastoral world in which the teeth of fate are safely drawn and consequences are not unpitying.

With her next novel, *The Mill on the Floss* (1860), George Eliot moved beyond the static simplicities of pastoral, coming forward in time from the pre-industrial world of *Adam Bede* to the period of her own childhood and youth in the 1820s and 30s. The pastoral landscape of Dorlcote Mill, where the heroine Maggie Tulliver grows up, is seen in relation to the modern trading town of St Oggs, home of her prudent, bourgeois relations the Dodsons. The interaction between the two ways of life and the two families, the one pre-industrial, impulsive, warm, the other 'modern' and calculating, is the central subject of the novel, linking the *bildungsroman* of Maggie Tulliver to the larger forces of history and change symbolized by the River Floss. It is well known that George Eliot put a good deal of her divided feelings about her own childhood into the story of Maggie and Tom, on the one hand celebrating the Wordsworthian 'natural piety' of the deep-rooted bonds of feeling associated with place and family, on the other shrewdly exposing the male arbitrariness with which the older brother treats his emotionally hungry sister. Again, irony and nostalgia move across the gap between the narrator and the past. One readily sees why Proust should have been so moved by the recollected emotional and sensuous fullness of the opening chapters, but the 'golden gates of their childhood' which close on Maggie and Tom at the end of Book 2 close also on a scene of conflict and, for Maggie, of unfulfilled yearning. Her 'need of being loved, the strongest need in poor Maggie's nature' (I, 5), is continually thwarted by Tom and her Dodson aunts; an emotional pattern of impulsive rebellion followed by self-reproach is established in childhood and repeats itself in adulthood. The child who pushes 'poor little pink-and-white Lucy into the cow-trodden mud' (I, 10) grows into the young woman who runs – or rather drifts – off with Lucy's admirer, Stephen Guest, only to return full of remorse to ask for forgiveness. Fallible,

---

[36]'The Two Worlds of *Adam Bede*', in I. Gregor and B. Nicholas, *The Moral and the Story* (Faber, 1962), pp. 13–32.

impetuous and warm-hearted, Maggie is the most human of heroines, and also, in her way, a tragic figure in a novel which reaches for the full tragic effect. The narrator says of the spurt of jealousy that leads to Maggie pushing Lucy into the pond, that 'There were passions at war in Maggie at that moment to have made a tragedy, if tragedies were made by passion only' (I, 10); elsewhere she observes that 'Mr Tulliver had a destiny as well as Oedipus' (I, 13); and the novel ends with the drowning of Maggie and Tom.

Such intimations of tragic destiny in a novel purporting to deal with ordinary individuals in a provincial setting make *The Mill on the Floss* a work of considerable significance in the history of Victorian fiction. Broadly speaking, and with important exceptions like *Wuthering Heights*, the English novel had not hitherto been tragic in its *form*. For reasons that have to do with the novel's historical evolution from drama and epic, and its tendency to deal with the ordinary and the typical rather than the exceptional individual, it has been sceptical of the heroic (think of *Don Quixote* or *Vanity Fair*), and when it has dealt with a greatly suffering individual, like Richardson's Clarissa Harlowe, has tended to relate their suffering to a larger vision of Providence, or to an ultimately reassuring comic restoration of balance (*Adam Bede* and *The Last Chronicle of Barset* are the examples nearest to hand). The novelist's attitude to suffering has always been a little like that of the 'Old Masters' praised in W.H. Auden's '*Musée des Beaux Arts*', who understand

> Its human position; how it take place
> While someone else is eating or opening a window or just walking
>   dully along . . .

The sense of other things going on deprives the tragic protagonist of the exclusive attention he receives in classical tragedy. George Eliot's innovation was to try to do justice to 'that element of tragedy which lies in the very fact of frequency' (*Middlemarch*, 20) and in ordinary living. 'The pride and obstinacy of millers, and other insignificant people, whom you pass unnoticingly on the road every day, have their tragedy too; but it is of that unwept, hidden sort, that goes on from generation to generation, and leaves no record' (*Mill*, III, 1). This involves a different, more muted kind of tragic effect. The older model of the heroic protagonist boldly confronting fate will no longer do. 'For us,' Walter Pater wrote in 1867, 'necessity is not, as of old, a sort of mythological personage without us, with whom we can do warfare. It is rather a magic web woven through and through us. . .penetrating us with a network, subtler than our subtlest nerves, yet bearing in it the central forces of the world. Can art represent men and women in these bewildering toils so as to give the spirit at least an equivalent for the sense of freedom?'[37] George Eliot saw no easy answer to

[37]'Winkelman', *The Renaissance* (1873; Collins, 1961), p. 218.

that question. The liberating spectacle of the Brontë heroine struggling successfully against a demeaning society gives way, in her work, to the much more evenly balanced struggle of characters like Maggie, aspiring 'above the mental level of the generation before them, to which they have been nevertheless tied by the strongest fibres of their hearts' (IV, 1). Like Pater's web, the forces of the environment are now written in the consciousness of individuals, by heredity and accumulated association, limiting their ability to break free and making that break, when it comes, a painful self-rending.

The Mill on the Floss can be seen as transitional between the old and the newer forms of tragedy. The heroic death of Maggie and Tom on the river breaks decisively with the compromise comic form of most Victorian fiction, and offers the liberation of spirit associated with traditional tragedy. But it also simplifies and even contradicts Maggie's tragic predicament at the end of the novel, which is the modern one of stalemate; she has appeared to violate communally evolved values which she herself shares, and can neither make good her escape nor repair the damage. Although it would be a misplaced emphasis to see the prudential morality of St Oggs as in any sense a 'good', the kind of tragic effect George Eliot was moving towards with Maggie Tulliver was the Hegelian conflict of valid claims discussed in her 1856 essay on 'The Antigone and Its Moral':

> [The] struggle between Antigone and Creon represents that struggle between elemental tendencies and established laws by which the outer life of man is gradually and painfully being brought into harmony with his inward needs. Until this harmony is perfected, we shall never be able to attain a great right without also doing a wrong. Reformers, martyrs, revolutionists, are never fighting against evil only; they are also placing themselves in opposition to a good – to a valid principle which cannot be infringed without harm.[38]

So Maggie Tulliver can be seen as a 'martyr' in the conflict with the 'established laws' of her society, laws which deny her the education and the field of action open to her brother, but which are also inscribed within her, as she shows when she cannot carry through her elopement with Stephen Guest. He argues for the supremacy of the 'natural law' of instinct, she counters with an assertion of the 'sacred ties' of the past: ' "If the past is not to bind us, where can duty lie? We should have no law but the inclination of the moment" ' (VI, 14). The trouble with this denouement is that the elopement with the conventionally handsome Stephen bears little relationship to the terms of Maggie's dilemma, as these have been defined in the first two-thirds of the novel. A similar objection may be made to the drowning of Maggie and Tom at the end: it substitutes the pathos of death for the difficult task of repairing what seems by then an almost irreparable breach between brother and sister. We have to wait

[38]*Essays*, p. 264.

until *Middlemarch* for a novel which adequately expresses the muted modern sense of tragedy.

The first phase of George Eliot's career culminates in the short and almost flawless moral fable, *Silas Marner* (1861). This Wordsworthian story of the redemption of a lonely weaver by his love for a foundling child is, as George Eliot told her publisher, 'a sort of legendary tale'.[39] With its spinning-wheels and bags of gold and timeless English village, its sense of the mysterious 'dealings' of Providence which reward Silas with the golden-haired Eppie and leave her natural father, the local squire, childless, *Silas Marner* belongs to the mode of myth and fairy-tale. It is George Eliot's most successful pastoral novel partly because it recognizes and delights in the 'legendary' quality of pastoral and does not try to yoke it to history, as *Adam Bede* does. History, however, dominates the second phase of her career, the phase that begins with *Romola* (1862–3). This historical novel, set in a meticulously detailed Renaissance Florence, and featuring historical personages such as Savonarola and Machiavelli, is, by a familiar paradox, the least historically interesting of her novels as well as the most heavy-going, although there is a link with her more characteristic themes in Romola's development out of disillusionment into a kind of secular sainthood at the end. The experience of attempting a fully historical fiction was valuable for George Eliot, and its fruits can be seen in the heightened historical awareness she brought to the First Reform Bill era in her next two novels. The first of these is *Felix Holt, The Radical* (1866), which contrasts the idealistic moral radicalism of Felix, a self-educated working-man, with the opportunistic political radicalism of the worldly Harold Transome, and comes down too easily but predictably (given George Eliot's own susceptibility to ethical idealism) on the side of Felix – although not without showing in the tragic figure of Mrs Transome a feeling for the complexities of human nature absent from the Felix plot. The second is *Middlemarch* (1871–2).

Middlemarch is George Eliot's masterpiece and one of the greatest of Victorian novels, if not indeed the greatest of all. This 'Study of Provincial Life', dealing with a number of interlinking characters living in a Midlands town (Coventry mostly) in the period 1829–32, is her most ambitious and successful attempt to create the impression of '*incarnate history*' she had praised in Riehl. The movement from a country or village to an urban location, and one of reasonable size, is significant and – for this reader at any rate – almost wholly a gain, since it meant a shift from the pastoral landscape of memory, with all its temptation to nostalgic idealizations, to the townscape of history. Middlemarch is a modern town of 1830, with its industry, banking system, local politicians, lawyers and doctors, a place where a 'subtle movement' of class relationships is going

[39] *Letters* III, p. 382; letter of 24 February 1861.

on, 'constantly shifting the boundaries of social intercourse, and begetting new consciousness of interdependence' (10) – a complex 'medium', then, for the explorations of the novelist as natural historian/scientist. If 'there is no private life which has not been determined by a wider public life' (*Felix Holt*, 3), what better place for examining the interaction of the two than a town in the middle of England, in the middle of the agitation surrounding the First Reform Bill, itself a middle stage in the 'march' of progress to the supposedly enlightened legislation of the Second? The historical analogy between 1832 and 1867 keeps irony and sympathy in a steady focus: the reader of 1872 is invited to look back 40 years to the genesis of the society he is living in, and any tendency he may have to condescend to these struggling and fallible characters is checked by the inescapability of change in George Eliot's universe – in 40 years time his own generation will be similarly vulnerable to the condescension of children and grandchildren.

Private life and public life are brought together by the concern so many of the characters show with reform, whether in the political, the scientific or the intellectual spheres. The Prelude suggests that the St Theresa figure of the greatly aspiring woman seeking an 'epic' life will be central, and also that her modern fate is likely to be one of failure, 'for these later-born Theresas were helped by no coherent social faith and order which could perform the function of knowledge for the ardently willing soul. Their ardour alternated between a vague ideal and the common yearning of womanhood; so that the one was disapproved as extravagance, and the other condemned as a lapse.' Thus is hinted the decline of the Christian world-vision and the special problem the modern St Theresa, Dorothea Brooke, faces in being a woman. Hers is the chief of the four plots on which *Middlemarch* is built, and in three of them the desire of characters to improve the world, or to add to the world's store of knowledge, is prominent. There is Dorothea herself, continually seeking to know how she can serve her fellow-beings, and continually checked and thwarted. There is the story of Tertius Lydgate, the young doctor with aristocratic connections, who comes to Middlemarch fired with the conviction that the medical profession might be 'the finest in the world; presenting the most perfect interchange between science and art; offering the most direct alliance between intellectual conquest and the social good' (15). Similarly concerned with intellectual conquest but, to Dorothea's dismay, indifferent to 'social good', is her husband Casaubon, the elderly pedant who has devoted his life to the search for a 'Key to All Mythologies', as Lydgate proposes to devote his to the search for the 'primitive tissue' of human physiology. Both fail, for reasons that are in differing degrees temperamental and historical. There is the story of the evangelical banker Nicholas Bulstrode, who seeks to salve his guilty conscience by doing good works in Middlemarch, in particular setting up a new fever hospital with Lydgate as the medical attendant. And fourthly there is the plot concerning the Garth family and Fred Vincy, the story of Fred's love for the plain but spirited Mary Garth, and his search for a vocation in life which she will approve. These characters, and the Rev. Camden Farebrother, who loves Mary and generously stands aside so Fred can have her, act as a foil to the greater aspirations of the others. They remind us that an honest and unselfish life is possible in Middlemarch, despite the many forces in the town conspiring to reduce all its inhabitants to the same middling standard.

The main characters are forced to live in a climate of gossip. The remarkable social density of *Middlemarch* owes much to George Eliot's command of the many different voices that make up public opinion in the town. There is the 'county' view of Mrs Cadwallader, with her robust and witty attitude to Dorothea's marriage with 'our Lowick Cicero', as she calls Casaubon: ' "She says, he is a great soul. – A great bladder for dried peas to rattle in!" ' (6). Yet she is not allowed the last word; her placing tones are themselves placed by the larger ironic vision of the narrator, who says of Mrs Cadwallader: 'Her life was rurally simple, quite free from secrets either foul, dangerous, or otherwise important. . .' (6). When Lydgate is introduced at Mr Brooke's dinner-party in chapter 10, it is through the conversation of Lady Chettam ('I like a medical man more on a footing with the servants') and Standish the lawyer, who have ominously lower expectations of the medical profession than Lydgate himself. The local shopkeepers, doctors and lawyers on the Infirmary board make the decision about the hospital chaplain into a virtual declaration of political and denominational allegiances, and for the first time Lydgate feels 'the hampering threadlike pressure of small social conditions, and their frustrating complexity' (18). His vote for Tyke rather than his friend Farebrother binds him to Bulstrode in the eyes of the town, with painful consequences. Lower down the social scale it is in the Green Dragon public-house that the rumours about Bulstrode's shady past start, quickly gathering to a head in the public meeting where he is asked to leave and takes the innocent Lydgate out – and down – with him (71).

The web is George Eliot's favourite metaphor for the complex inter-relations of community which the narrator-scientist seeks to probe and unravel (15). So closely woven is this web that the scope for 'epic' action is very limited: Middlemarch is the most testing medium in her novels for the characteristic George Eliot idealist, a role shared by Dorothea and Lydgate. In the hopes they have conceived for their lives, both are disappointed, Dorothea because her 'spiritual grandeur' is 'ill-matched with the meanness of opportunity' open to women in this society (Prelude), and 'there is no creature whose inward being is so strong that it is not greatly determined by what lies outside it' (Finale). Lydgate's is the more tragic case because he enters the lists fully equipped, it seems, to do battle with the unreformed world of pre-Victorian medicine. The issue is more in doubt, and more dependent on 'character' than environment. So the narrator says of him, in contrast to the sentence from the Finale quoted above, 'It always remains true that if we had been greater, circumstance would have been less strong against us' (58). What makes his story so powerful is the intellectual grasp George Eliot brought to the imagination of his scientific ambitions, and her sense of the way these are entwined with Lydgate's masculinity. The intellectual sympathy is of itself remarkable, and many readers have sensed a resonance of affinity between George Eliot's description of Lydgate's research and her own procedure as a psychological and social anatomist:

> He for his part had tossed away all cheap inventions where ignorance finds itself able and at ease: he was enamoured of that arduous invention which is the very eye of research, provisionally framing its object and correcting it to more and more exactness of relation; he wanted to pierce the obscurity of those minute processes which prepare human misery and joy, those invisible thoroughfares which are the first lurking-places of anguish, mania, and crime, that delicate poise and transition which determine the growth of happy or unhappy consciousness. (16)

But even more remarkable than such penetrating sympathy with intellectual processes is the way they are incarnated in a figure who is convincingly masculine, with powerful emotional susceptibilities and, beneath his 'spots of commonness', great physical tenderness: 'he was an emotional creature, with a flesh-and-blood sense of fellowship which withstood all the abstractions of special study. He cared not only for "cases", but for John and Elizabeth, especially Elizabeth' (15). His instinctive tenderness surfaces at two crucial points in his story. One is the moment of his proposal to Rosamond, when he is surprised into a declaration by the sight of her tears:

> There could have been no more complete answer than that silence, and Lydgate, forgetting everything else, completely mastered by the outrush of tenderness at the sudden belief that this sweet young creature depended on him for her joy, actually put his arms round her, folding her gently and protectingly – he was used to being gentle with the weak and suffering – and kissed each of the two large tears. This was a strange way of arriving at an understanding, but it was a short way. (31)

The other moment is the bitter one when Bulstrode seems to stagger when rising from the public meeting at which he has been accused, and Lydgate instinctively rises to help him from the room, knowing that the action will confirm everyone's suspicion that he is in league with Bulstrode (71). In both cases the quality in Lydgate which makes him such a fine doctor contributes to his downfall. The logic of that downfall has been often and rightly praised, and there is perhaps nothing in Victorian fiction – or

English fiction for that matter – to match the slow deterioration of Lydgate's marriage under the pressure of debt and the growing sense of incompatibility between two people who still, at some level, love each other.

'Each is a tale of matrimonial infelicity,' Henry James said of 'the balanced contrast between the two histories' of Lydgate and Dorothea, 'but the conditions in each are so different and the circumstances so broadly opposed that the mind passes from one to the other with that supreme sense of the vastness and variety of human life, under aspects apparently similar, which it belongs only to the greatest novels to produce'.[40] The critic cannot hope to demonstrate that greatness in a short space; the best he can do is to point. This critic would point, for example, to chapter 42, where Casaubon comes face to face with the prospect of his own death, and Dorothea overcomes her opposition and frustration and goes out to meet him on the dark landing. To chapter 52, where Farebrother, himself attracted to Mary Garth, goes to plead Fred Vincy's case with her. To chapter 58, where Rosamond goes horse-riding against her husband's wishes and loses her baby, and Lydgate comes to realize the 'terrible tenacity of this mild creature' and his powerlessness over her. To chapter 74, where Mrs Bulstrode learns of her husband's disgrace, and silently renouncing the pleasure and finery of her life, puts on a 'plain black gown' and goes down to support him. To Dorothea's crisis in chapter 80, when she spends the night struggling with jealousy and disappointment at what she thinks is a love-affair between Will Ladislaw and Lydgate's wife, but resolves in the morning to silence her pain and go to help Rosamond. Most of these scenes are moments of recognition and renunciation, when a character confronts the inevitable conditions of his or her life, and is forced to renounce habit or expectation in favour of the claims of compassionate sympathy. They are sad moments, as all renunciation of energy is sad, yet also moments of subdued moral grandeur, which show the power of quite ordinary people to transcend selfishness and find meaning and value in compassion for others. To read them is rather like receiving the impression made on Dorothea after her night of crisis, when she opens the curtains to see figures moving on the road outside her gates and feels 'the largeness of the world and the manifold wakings of men to labour and endurance' (80). And lest this makes the novel seem too sombre, one would also want to point to comic scenes, such as Mr Brooke's experience on the hustings (51), and to the comic irony that plays over the portrayal of Mr Casaubon. His letter proposing marriage (5) is as good in its way as Mr Collins in *Pride and Prejudice*, and Jane Austen would not have disowned such well-turned irony as the description of Mr Brooke as a man 'of acquiescent temper, miscellaneous opinions, and

[40]*Critical Heritage*, p. 357.

uncertain vote' (1), or the observation of Mr Casaubon that 'he determined to abandon himself to the stream of feeling, and perhaps was surprised to find what an exceedingly shallow rill it was. . .he concluded that the poets had much exaggerated the force of masculine passion' (7).

If Henry James was right to praise the 'vastness and variety of human life' in *Middlemarch*, was he also right to call it 'a treasure-house of details, but. . .an indifferent whole' (p. 353)? Certainly the novel lacks the kind of form James himself was to aspire to, the concentration of a fully drama-tized point of view, and perhaps it is none the worse for that. And almost as certainly modern criticism has woven too tight a mesh in arguing for the comprehensive unifying power of imagery, theme and structural paral-lelism. These elements are there, and they do unify up to a point, but there is much in the novel they do not touch. Like most of the great Victorian novels, *Middlemarch* has a redundancy of matter and life over form: that is the condition of their greatness. But it does have one important factor making for unity of tone and perspective. Like *Vanity Fair*, the novel is held together by the authority of the narrator's voice. It is this voice, by turns awkward, shrewd, arch, ironic and profound, continually mediating between the action the fictional characters are involved in and the moral life of the reader, instructing us in the difficulties and the necessity of moral conduct, asking us to feel what we know, that gives *Middlemarch* its characteristic tone of elevated pathos:

> Her finely-touched spirit still had its fine issues, though they were not widely visible. Her full nature, like that river of which Cyrus broke the strength, spent itself in channels which had no great name on the earth. But the effect of her being on those around her was incalculably diffusive: for the grow-ing good of the world is partly dependent on unhistoric acts; and that things are not so ill with you and me as they might have been, is half owing to the number who lived faithfully a hidden life, and rest in unvisited tombs. (Finale)

These are noble words. They express 'that religious and moral sympathy with the historical life of man' which George Eliot felt to be 'the larger half of culture'.[41] That, and her sense of the ineluctability of moral conse-quences, was the source of her profound appeal to her contemporaries. One understands why the founders of the London Library should have made an exception for her books when some of them wanted to ban fiction from the shelves. As Walter Allen has said, 'It was on the thoroughness and cautiousness of her investigations into the problems of conduct as they face the free spirit, who must be responsible to himself in the absence of traditional and religious sanctions felt as binding, that George Eliot's great moral authority in the nineteenth century rested.'[42]

The words are sad, but is the novel they close tragic? Yes and no. There

[41]*Letters* IV, p. 97; letter of 8 August 1863.
[42]*George Eliot*, p. 93.

is the tragic downfall of Lydgate, but the fates of Casaubon and Bulstrode are more pathetic than tragic, and that of Dorothea, though 'unhistoric' in act, is still one of domestic happiness and 'fine issues'. As George Eliot told her publisher when completing the novel, there was to be 'no unredeemed tragedy in the solution of the story'.[43] In this desire to balance the tragic stress with a hope for 'the growing good of the world' she remains a novelist of her age – the age of equipoise.

[43]*Letters* V, p. 296; letter of 4 August 1872.

6

Continuity and Change in the Later Victorian Novel: George Eliot, Meredith, James, Stevenson

In his 1873 review of *Middlemarch*, Henry James concluded that 'It sets a limit. . .to the development of the old-fashioned English novel'.[1] His words were prophetic. *Middlemarch* is almost the last of the great panoramic novels of the Victorian period. Of novels contemporary with it, only Trollope's *The Way We Live Now* (1874–5) has a comparable range; but despite the topicality of its theme and title Trollope's satire on the rise of the speculator Melmotte is in some respects rather traditional, looking back to Dickens's attacks on Merdle in *Little Dorrit* and on share speculation in *Our Mutual Friend*, and to the treatment of the interplay between aristocracy and new wealth in Thackeray's *The Newcomes*. In form of publication, too, *The Way We Live Now* looked backward: it was the last novel to be serialized in the old Dickens–Thackeray pattern of 20 monthly parts, and lost money for the publishers. The age of the novel as domestic epic, as social panorama or satirical anatomy, was passing.

With hindsight we can see that this contraction of scale was inevitable, brought about by a number of interrelated developments: changes in the reading public, an increasingly problematic sense of the writer's relation to the later Victorian age and to his audience, the aesthetic stimulus of foreign writing, in particular the new realism of Flaubert, Turgenev and Zola. Every artistic form has a dynamic of internal change, and after George Eliot and Trollope this was pulling in the direction of shorter, more specialized, more 'artistic' novels. This development was obscured, and to some extent obstructed, by the continuing dominance of the three-decker through the power of the circulating libraries. James, who had complained of the 'diffuseness' of *Middlemarch*, was moved to protest

Texts: All references to Meredith's novels are to the Memorial Edition (29 vols., 1909–12). The text of *The Ordeal of Richard Feverel* in this edition is available as a World's Classics paperback. Quotations from Henry James's *The Portrait of a Lady* and *The Princess Casamassima* are taken from the first editions, and not from the revised New York editions which are usually the texts reprinted; for *The Spoils of Poynton* the World's Classics edition has been used. In the case of Stevenson, the Penguin English Library editions of *Dr Jekyll and Mr Hyde and Other Stories* and *Weir of Hermiston and Other Stories* have been used, and the World's Classics edition for *The Master of Ballantrae*. All other quotations from his works not specified in the notes are taken from the Vailima Edition (26 vols., Heinemann, 1922–3).

[1]*George Eliot: Critical Heritage*, p. 359.

against 'the tyranny of the three volumes' in his 1874 review of Hardy's *Far From the Madding Crowd*: it 'gives us an uncomfortable sense of being a simple "tale", pulled and stretched to make the conventional three volumes'. He found that 'Almost all novels are greatly too long, and the being too long becomes with each passing year a more serious offence'; and he prophesied that novels would be 'defeated in the struggle for existence unless they lighten their baggage very considerably and do battle in a more scientific equipment.'[2]

This is a common perception and a frequent complaint among novelists of James's generation. 'It is fine to see how the old three volume tradition is being broken through', George Gissing wrote in 1885. 'One volume is becoming commonest of all. It is the new school.'[3] In fact it took another ten years for the single volume to oust the three-decker, almost too late for Gissing himself, who chafed continually against the length of the traditional form but still managed to produce his best work within it. The inexorable financial logic of the three-decker is the subject of the novel – itself a three-decker – which many consider Gissing's finest, *New Grub Street* (1891), where the struggling writer Edwin Reardon gives voice to his sense of helplessness before the power of the circulating libraries:

> 'For anyone in my position,' said Reardon, 'how is it possible to abandon the three volumes? It is a question of payment. An author of moderate repute may live on a yearly three-volume novel – I mean the man who is obliged to sell his book out and out, and who gets from one to two hundred pounds for it. But he would have to produce four one-volume novels to obtain the same income; and I doubt whether he could get so many published within the twelve months. And here comes in the benefit of the libraries; from the commercial point of view the libraries are indispensable. Do you suppose the public would support the present number of novelists if each book had to be purchased? A sudden change to that system would throw three-fourths of the novelists out of work.'[4]

Yet that sudden change was just around the corner. It had been prepared for by George Moore's dramatic public campaign against Mudie's, when after they banned his novels *A Modern Lover* (1883) and *A Mummer's Wife* (1885), he published his famous pamphlet attacking the libraries' prudishness, *Literature at Nurse, or Circulating Morals* (1885). The cry of censorship gave publicity to the problem, but it was the decision of Moore's publisher, Henry Vizetelly, to issue *A Mummer's Wife* and subsequent works in a single volume, six-shilling first edition that pointed the way forward. The new format started to catch on, and this fact, in conjunction with the declining profitability of the three-decker, the growth of free

---

[2] *The House of Fiction*, ed. Leon Edel (Hart-Davis, 1957), pp. 270–1.
[3] Quoted in Guinevere L. Griest, *Mudie's Circulating Library and the Victorian Novel* (Bloomington, Indiana UP, 1970), pp. 98–9.
[4] *New Grub Street* (Harmondsworth, Penguin, 1968), ch. 15, p. 236.

libraries, and a narrowing time-gap between first edition and cheap reprint, brought the libraries to a momentous decision. In 1894 Mudie's and Smith's issued statements announcing, in effect, that they would cease to pay an economic price for three-volume novels. One hundred and eighty-four of these were published in 1894, 52 in 1895, in 1897 only four.[5] By the end of the century the three-volume novel, the staple form of Victorian fiction, was dead.

If its demise was sudden, it was also long overdue, and the protracted existence of this inwardly dying but commercially dominant form through the 1880s and early 1890s helps to explain something of the transitional character of much later Victorian fiction, the sense one has in reading Hardy, Gissing and even some of Henry James, of a continuing quarrel with the tradition, of an incomplete modernism struggling through the conventions inherited from an older form. And there was loss as well as gain in its passing. Behind those features of the classic Victorian novel which later writers wished to sacrifice in the interests of concentration and what Gissing called a 'dramatic mode of presentment'[6] – leisurely narration, profuseness of detail and proliferation of character, a garrulous omniscience – there was an expansiveness bred of a confidence in the novelist's relationship to his or her reader and to the world, and a confidence in the novelist's power to interpret the world, both of which the circulating-library reflected and, with all its faults, helped to foster. By the 1870s that confidence was slipping. The decline of the three-decker is bound up with this development, with a growing uncertainty about the nature of the reading public and of the society, and a corresponding weakening of the novelist's societal grasp. These issues will be explored in the next section.

The major novelists of this transitional phase of English fiction are Henry James and Thomas Hardy, although the slightly older figure of George Meredith is also important. James and Hardy were both influenced by George Eliot, developing that inheritance in different directions. Broadly speaking, James was interested in George Eliot the psychological novelist, the creator of Dorothea Brooke, Gwendolen Harleth and Henleigh Grandcourt, Hardy in George Eliot the agnostic intellectual and novelist of provincial life. One can exaggerate the differences (Hardy and James were both deeply interested in the 'woman question', for example, as was almost every other novelist of the time) but the two writers stand at opposite poles of fictional possibility, and for this reason I have chosen to divide discussion of the later Victorian novel around the distinction which their separate achievements point to. James, a great critic as well as a great novelist, deeply versed in French realism but sceptical of Zola's naturalism, and passionately interested in the form of fiction, is the natural link

[5] I am indebted here to Griest, *Mudie's Circulating Library*, from which these figures are taken (p. 208).
[6] Quoted Griest, p. 100.

between the Meredithian psychological romance and comedy of manners and Stevenson's sophisticated exploitations of genre, while at the same time offering in his middle-period novels a fascinating renegotiation of the high Victorian tradition. Hardy is much closer to native roots but also more hospitable to Naturalism, or to those aspects of the movement which could be adapted to the provincial novel's characteristic concerns with class, social mobility and religious belief. His work thus forms a bridge between the more traditional kind of provincial novel being written at this time by Richard Jefferies and William Hale White ('Mark Rutherford'), and the modern naturalistic novel of Moore and Gissing. As these various names suggest, this is a rich and diverse phase of Victorian fiction, and it is necessary now to consider how, and in what ways, it reflects changes in the Victorian age itself.

The Novel and Society in the 1870s and 1880s

'We have lived through a period of change – ', J.A. Froude wrote in 1882, 'change spiritual, change moral, social, and political. The foundations of our most serious convictions have been broken up; and the disintegration of opinion is so rapid that wise men and foolish are equally ignorant where the close of this waning century will find us. We are embarked in a current which bears us forward independent of our own wills, and indifferent whether we submit or resist. . .'[7] What is new about the mood of the last quarter of the nineteenth century is not so much the perception of change, to which the Victorians had become accustomed, but the sense of being on the wrong side of change, drifting on the current rather than controlling it. From the early 1870s a note of declining confidence can be detected in Victorian society. The death of Palmerston in 1865 had marked for many contemporaries the end of an era, the rise to power of Bismarck and the proclamation of the German Empire in 1871 the start of another, less favourable to Britain's commercial and imperial dominance. The industrial challenge from Germany and the United States, the influx of cheap wheat from the newly opened American West, and the improvements in shipping and refrigeration that made the importing of foreign food profitable, all helped to bring about the 'Great Depression' in British agriculture and manufacturing industry, which most historians date from 1873. The decline was only relative, it is true, and comfort could be found in the growing African empire. The 'scramble for Africa', a phrase coined by *The Times* in 1884, is a feature of the 1880s, a decade which also saw a new awareness of a dark continent closer to home, the destitute poor of London and other great cities. The 'Condition of England' question, dormant to

7'Preface', *Short Studies on Great Subjects: Fourth Series* (Longman's, Green, 1883).

some extent since the 1840s, surfaced again in the 1880s with a new urgency. Andrew Mearns's pamphlet, *The Bitter Cry of Outcast London* (1883), is the first of a number of works drawing attention to the plight of the urban poor at this time, culminating in the publication of the first volume of Charles Booth's pioneering sociological study, *Life and Labour of the People in London*, in 1889. These social investigators drew extensively and ironically on the language of exploration from the imperial discovery of Africa – William Booth's *In Darkest England and the Way Out*, for example, was published in the same year, 1890, as H.M. Stanley's *In Darkest Africa*.[8]

Politically, the 1880s were dominated by the problem of Ireland, which entered an acute phase with Gladstone's attempt to enact a Home Rule Bill in 1886, and by the scare of socialism, inflamed by the Trafalgar Square riots of 1886 and 1887. Intellectually and culturally, Froude's 'disintegration of opinion' is evident everywhere. This is the age of the competing 'isms' – Naturalism, Aestheticism, Impressionism, Agnosticism, Pessimism – as the mid-Victorian consensus started to fracture. Pater's *The Renaissance*, the first coherent work of 'aesthetic criticism', appeared in 1873; the first great exhibition of Impressionist paintings was held in Paris in 1874; translations of Zola's novels started to appear from 1885 onwards. The changing climate is illustrated by two celebrated court cases of the time, the libel action which the artist J.M. Whistler brought against Ruskin in 1878 for derogatory comments on his painting in *Fors Clavigera*, and the trial ten years later of Henry Vizetelly, Zola's English publisher, under the Obscene Publications Act. Whistler won his case and one-farthing damages (the legal expenses ruined him), Vizetelly lost, and in 1889 was tried again and sentence to imprisonment; but more important than the verdicts were the rifts which these cases exposed in late Victorian artistic and literary opinion. Whistler's trial was, in effect, the trial of Aestheticism and 'Art for Art's Sake', Vizetelly's the trial of Naturalism (or 'Realism' as it was confusingly referred to at the time); and although Aestheticism and Naturalism are theoretically divergent movements, both had common cause in challenging the dominant moral aesthetic of high Victorian culture, the aesthetic of Ruskin and George Eliot. Whistler's witty conduct of his case (Ruskin did not appear) helped to break Ruskin's hold on the Victorian art world, and with it the hold of the Ruskinian ideal that the artist should be responsible to society. The Vizetelly trials lack this element of symbolic drama, but again the background to the case is the polarization of opinion between those, like George Moore, Gissing and Hardy, who were prepared to welcome French Naturalism, and those who followed Andrew Lang and George Saintsbury in attacking Zola and

[8]See, for discussion of these 'social explorers', Peter Keating (ed.), *Into Unknown England 1866-1913: Selections from the Social Explorers* (Manchester, Mancehster UP, 1976).

vigorously promoting a new school of 'Romance' centred round the rising star of Robert Louis Stevenson.[9]

It is not surprising that writers of an older generation felt this to be a time of crisis. A note of apocalypse runs through Ruskin's 1884 lectures on 'The Storm Cloud of the Nineteenth Century' and Tennyson's 'Locksley Hall Sixty Years After' (1886), with its denunciation of 'the troughs of Zolaism' and its cry of 'Chaos, Cosmos! Cosmos, Chaos! who can tell how all will end?'. If these outbursts can be partly discounted as the cries of old men who had lost touch with their age, then the mood of certain younger writers was if anything more despairing, because more resignedly pessimistic. There was a widespread awareness that the social and intellectual problems inherited from the previous generation had not been solved, were perhaps insoluble, and had in any case to be confronted without the ethical idealism and moral energy available to their fathers. It was no longer so possible, as it had been for Tennyson in *In Memoriam* (1850), to harness the facts of evolution to an idea of moral development, when the bleaker implications of *The Descent of Man* (Darwin's book was published in 1871) began to sink home. A sense of drift and loss, of stoical resignation in the face of betrayed hopes, dominates the fiction of Hardy and Gissing, the poetry of A.E. Housman, and the writings of W.H. Mallock, author of such typical titles of the period as the novel *The Old Order Changes* (1886) and *Is Life Worth Living?* (1879). Two other late-Victorian 'isms' come to the fore at this time: Agnosticism, coined by T.H. Huxley in 1869, signifies the new intellectual respectability of the state of 'half-belief' which had so agonized earlier thinkers; and Pessimism, which starts to challenge Positivism with the spread of Schopenhauer's ideas to Britain. Positivism was attacked by W.H. Mallock in his satire *The New Paul and Virginia; or, Positivism on an Island* (1878), and was privately renounced by Gissing in 1882, whose conversion from Positivism to Pessimism is, in its way, as representative of 'advanced opinion' in the 80s as was George Eliot's conversion from Evangelical Christianity to the Religion of Humanity in the 40s. His essay 'The Hope of Pessimism', written in 1882 but unpublished in Gissing's lifetime, expresses a mood of pathos and stoic resolution widespread in the literature of the time; its message is essentially that of Hardy's line in 'In Tenebris II' – 'if way to the better there be, it exacts a full look at the worst'.[10]

The cultural fragmentation of the period is reflected in its fiction, which displays a wide variety of form and subject-matter. George Eliot's death in 1880 left behind no natural successor of comparable eminence, although

[9]See Clarence R. Decker, 'Zola's Literary Reputation in England', *PMLA* 49 (1934), pp. 1140–53, and W.C. Frierson, 'The English Controversy over Realism in Fiction', *PMLA* 43 (1928), pp. 533–50. See also Kenneth Graham, *English Criticism of the Novel, 1865–1900* (Oxford, Clarendon, 1965).

[10]The essay is published in *George Gissing: Essays and Fiction*, ed. Pierre Coustillas (Baltimore, Johns Hopkins Press, 1970).

Meredith's novels of the previous decade, especially *Beauchamp's Career* (1876) and *The Egoist* (1879), had won him an enthusiastic following among younger writers. The novelists we think of today as her chief heirs, Hardy and James, had produced fine and characteristic work well before her death, although the influence is more obvious in Hardy's three provincial or 'Wessex' novels – *Under the Greenwood Tree* (1872), *Far From the Madding Crowd* (1874), and *The Return of the Native* (1878) – than in James's *Roderick Hudson* (1875), *The American* (1876–7), and *The Europeans* (1878). New territories open up in the 1880s. As Donald Stone points out, the decade 'witnessed a rise simultaneously in the creation of fictional autobiographies, which described the loss of and the need for new spiritual values, and in romantic invitations to various forms of withdrawal or escapism'.[11] In the former category are William Hale White's two 'Mark Rutherford' novels, *The Autobiography* (1881) and *Mark Rutherford's Deliverance* (1885), which describe a Victorian pilgrim's progress from the certainties of Dissent, via a conversion to a Wordsworthian 'natural piety', to an agnosticism balanced by commitment to work among the poor of central London – a process not dissimilar to that undergone by the clergyman hero of Mrs Humphry Ward's more melodramatic and controversial *Robert Elsmere* (1888). The sales of *Elsmere*, estimated at from 30 to 40,000 within a year of publication in Britain alone, and some 200,000 in the United States, made it the runaway bestseller of the decade, and indicates the topicality of its subject, but it is the Mark Rutherford novels which offer the more sensitive portrait of the agnostic temper, capturing as they do with moving honesty the fluctuations of a mind which cannot rest either in the security of dogma or in the denial of unbelief, and whose attitude before the open grave is *'I do not know*; and in this there is an element of hope, now rising and now falling, but always sufficient to prevent that blank despair which we must feel if we consider it as settled that when we lie down under the grass there is an absolute end.'[12] Pater's *Marius the Epicurean* appeared in the same year as *Mark Rutherford's Deliverance*, and takes a rather more oblique route to the presentation of the unorthodox but yearning religious temperament, locating it in the figure of a second-century Roman aesthete who is brought to the threshold of Christian commitment by his discontent with the prevailing pagan philosophies of Epicureanism and Stoicism. When Mrs Humphry Ward reviewed Pater's novel, she classed it with Carlyle's *Sartor Resartus* and Froude's *Nemesis of Faith* as a type of confessional fiction peculiar to the age: it was in books like these rather than in formal autobiography, she suggested, 'that the future student of the nineteenth century will have to

---

[11]*Novelists in a Changing World: Meredith, James and the Transformation of English Fiction in the 1880s* (Cambridge, Mass., Harvard UP, 1972), p. 37.
[12]*Mark Rutherford's Deliverance* (T. Fisher Unwin, 1896), ch. 6, p. 86.

look for what is deepest, most intimate, and most real in its personal experience'.[13]

The intimacy of these fictional autobiographies is part of an increasing movement towards inwardness of presentation and subtlety of psychological analysis, initiated in the later novels of George Eliot and developed variously by Meredith and Henry James. When James comes to write the Preface to *The Portrait of a Lady* (1881) in 1908, he singled out chapter 42, which describes Isabel Archer's coming to terms with the failure of her marriage as she sits up through the night, and called it 'obviously the best thing in the book': 'It is a representation simply of her motionlessly *seeing*, and an attempt withal to make the mere still lucidity of her act as "interesting" as the surprise of a caravan or the identification of a pirate.' Not every reader of the time was happy to accept so stationary an ideal of fictional excellence; some would rather have had the caravans and the pirates, like Andrew Lang, whose cry for 'More claymores, less psychology' was answered by the clashing cutlasses of Stevenson's *Treasure Island* (1883) and *Kidnapped* (1886), and by the tales of adventure which the consciousness of Empire was starting to inspire. This is the age of Rider Haggard's African novels, *King Solomon's Mines* (1885) and *Allan Quatermain* (1887), of G.A. Henty's imperialistic interpretations of English history in his long series of novels for boys, as well as the less indulgent view of Empire to be found in Kipling's *Plain Tales from the Hills* (1888) and Stevenson's later South Seas tales, *The Beach of Falesá* (1892) and *The Ebb-Tide* (1893). All these works form the context in which Conrad's classic novella of Empire, *Heart of Darkness* (1899; 1902), was written and read.

The very diversity of the novels being written at this time, and the fragmentation of opinion about them, points to an important underlying development: the increasing specialization within fiction and its reading public, and a growing separation in both between the 'serious' and the 'popular'. To some extent that separation had always been there: popular novelists like 'Ouida' and Rhoda Broughton, and later Marie Corelli, were read by many who would have considered George Eliot too intimidating, and thousands more read the tales of G.W.M. Reynolds than read even so popular a serious novelist as Dickens. There was, however, a relative homogeneity about the mid-Victorian public – small, largely middle-class and centred around the lending-library, the monthly number and the magazine serial – which enabled the great novelists to be both popular and experimental, and to carry their audience with them into new territories by means of an appeal to shared experiences and tastes. The great increase in the reading public towards the end of the century, as a consequence of the 1870 Education Act, and the growth of cheap books and popular weeklies

[13]*Macmillan's Magazine* 52 (1885), p. 134.

to supply it, changed all that radically. It was in the 1880s that magazines like *Tit-Bits* and *Answers* started to appear, reaching a weekly audience of several hundred thousand each. Writing in 1896, H.G. Wells saw the 1870 act as marking an 'impassable gulf' between the popular novel of his day and that of the early Victorians; it was easy to see why 'our grandfathers and grandmothers went into ecstasies over *Jane Eyre*' and 'our fathers and mothers' over *The Woman in White*, but the popularity of *Tit-Bits* and novels like George du Maurier's *Trilby* (1894) and Marie Corelli's *The Sorrows of Satan* (1895) indicated that the reading public itself had changed through the 'advent of the Board-School scholar':

> 'Arry reads *Ally Sloper* and *Tit-Bits*, 'Arriet *Trilby* and *The Sorrows of Satan*. We only use these extreme examples to account for what would otherwise be unaccountable – the comparative popularity to-day of scores of books whose relation to life is of the slightest, and whose connexion with Art is purely accidental. It is scarcely too much to say that every writer of our time who can be called popular owes three-quarters of his or her fame to the girls who have been taught in Board schools.[14]

On the other hand, it is important to remember that there were gains in this development too. As Richard Altick says, 'the common reader in the last days of Victoria was more amply supplied with books than ever before', and it would be wrong to underestimate the number of Jude the Obscures who benefited from the Education Act and took advantage of the cheap reprints of good literature available at this time.[15] Perhaps, also, the late Victorians were inclined to be rather snooty about the new mass reading-public, and unduly pessimistic about its tastes.

The truth is that it was a largely unknown public, and with the boom in cheap printing an increasingly fissile one. After 1880 we need to think in terms of reading publics rather than a single reading public, each large enough to require and sustain different kinds of fiction at different levels of literacy. Of course, specialized categories of novel had existed before, but the striking thing about earlier novelists had been their ability to reabsorb these into the cultural mainstream, as Dickens had done with the Newgate Novel in *Oliver Twist* and the sensation novel in *Great Expectations* and *Our Mutual Friend*, or Thackeray with the silver-fork novel in *Vanity Fair*. Now the different categories start to go their different ways, into the various specialized forms we are familiar with today – the sentimental romance, the adventure story, the detective thriller, the psychological novel, the comedy of manners – when only an exceptional writer like Graham Greene is able to bridge the gulf between some of the different

[14]'An Informal Appreciation' in *H.G. Wells's Literary Criticism*, ed. Patrick Parrinder and Robert M. Philmus (Hassocks, Harvester, 1980), p. 74. See also Henry James, 'The Future of the Novel' (1899), in *The House of Fiction*, pp. 48–59.
[15]*The English Common Reader: A Social History of the Mass Reading Public 1800–1900* (Chicago, University of Chicago Press, 1957), p. 317.

publics, and the serious novelist is mostly resigned to writing for a minority readership. By the end of the nineteenth century the novelist's awareness of a fragmented public had started to weaken his confidence in being able to speak to, and about, the whole of his society. This was true of even a popular writer like Hardy, and many times more so of Henry James, whose attempt to reinterpret the high Victorian tradition in novels of the 1880s like *The Bostonians* and *The Princess Casamassima* was to end in a sense of failure and bafflement at his inability to reach a large public.[16] The subject of the unappreciated or wrongly appreciated artist is a recurrent theme in James's stories of the 1890s, and is one of many links between his work and the Aesthetic Movement. He discovered painfully and with regret what Whistler and Wilde celebrated with irresponsible relish: the growing separation of the serious artist from the middle-class public.

'All ages are ages of transition,' Tennyson told his grandson in 1886, 'but this is an awful moment of transition'.[17] His intuition of crisis was correct, although its roots lie deeper than any of the evils denounced in 'Locksley Hall Sixty Years After'. The challenge to the established order was not fundamentally a political one, as it had been in the 1840s: the threat of 'Demos' and Socialism, like the threat of 'Zolaism', was greatly exaggerated in the 1880s. The real crisis was a crisis of authority, and in particular of patriarchal authority; the fragmentation of late-Victorian culture is a symptom of this, not its cause. Here Dostoevsky's great novel *The Brothers Karamazov*, completed in 1880, is deeply suggestive in its preoccupation with the crime of parricide and its relation to anarchism. And although Samuel Butler's novel is not to be mentioned in the same breath as Dostoevsky's, it is significant that *The Way of All Flesh* was written at this time, between 1873 and 1885, and was received on its publication in 1903 for the parricidal work it undoubtedly is, a frontal assault on the Victorian father. Conflict between father and son, an archetypal literary subject, takes on a new sharpness and a wider cultural meaning in the fiction of the second half of the nineteenth century: one thinks of Meredith's *Ordeal of Richard Feverel* (1859), Turgenev's *Fathers and Sons* (1862), Stevenson's *Weir of Hermiston* (1896), Edmund Gosse's semi-fictional autobiography *Father and Son* (1907).

But the challenge to the Victorian father in these works is only one manifestation of a wider challenge to masculine authority and dominance, or 'patriarchy' as feminist criticism has taught us to call it. The growth of the Women's Movement in the second half of the nineteenth century is a fact of considerable importance of the student of later Victorian fiction, and not only for its bearing on the 'New Woman' novels of the 1890s. The story is by now a familiar one and its salient features can be briefly

[16]See *Henry James Letters*, ed. Leon Edel (3 vols., Macmillan, 1974–80) III, pp. 208–10; letter of 2 January 1888.
[17]Charles Tennyson, *Alfred Tennyson* (Macmillan, 1949), p. 491.

summarized: defeat on the suffrage issue balanced by such modest but real legal gains as the Matrimonial Causes Act of 1857 and the Married Woman's Property Acts of 1870 and 1882; a new seriousness of intellectual debate stimulated by John Stuart Mill's *The Subjection of Women* (1869); the publicity given to contraception by the Bradlaugh–Besant trial of 1877, and a greater frankness in the discussion of sexual questions; solid advances in girl's secondary and higher education, and a great expansion after 1870 in the jobs available to women outside the home.[18] These developments are variously reflected in the fiction of the period, as what Thackeray called 'the matrimonial barrier' is crossed, first by George Eliot in her detailed explorations of unhappy marriages in *Middlemarch* and *Daniel Deronda*, and then by James in *The Portrait of a Lady*; while the issue of sexual emancipation was publicized in bestsellers like Grant Allen's *The Woman Who Did* (1895), and its psychological consequences examined by James in *The Bostonians* and by Hardy in *Jude the Obscure*. A less obvious but perhaps more far-reaching result of this new awareness of women's needs and frustrations is the challenge it posed to the conventional images of masculine dignity in which fiction had traditionally dealt. Chief among these images is the notion of the gentleman, a focus for the writer's concern with male honour from Richardson to Thackeray and Trollope, and one way to understand the crisis in masculine authority in this transitional phase of English fiction is to trace the dwindling fortunes of the gentlemanly idea in three important novels of the 1870s – *The Way We Live Now* (1875), *Daniel Deronda* (1876), and *The Egoist* (1879).

Of these three novels, Trollope's is by far the most traditional. *The Way We Live Now* is a large-scale anatomy of society after the manner of *Little Dorrit* and *The Newcomes*, and in it the corrupt financier Melmotte plays a role similar to that of Merdle in Dickens's novel, which may well have influenced Trollope. Melmotte is both symptom and symbol of a widespread collapse of standards in contemporary society; not a gentleman himself, he presides over a novel in which gambling is the controlling metaphor for the betrayal of gentlemanly honour on the Stock Exchange, in the marriage market and among the landed aristocracy. Trollope's is a powerful denunciation, but a denunciation phrased in terms of the gentlemanly values currently being flouted, which are incarnated in the book's one true if pallid gentleman, the unmarried and childless squire, Roger Carbury. The way we live now is the way 'we' gentlemen, who ought to know better, have come to behave in a world where Melmotte is the uncrowned king. For much of its length, until Trollope's characteristic sympathy for the outsider takes over, the novel is a growl from the club armchair, a lament for standards which the narrator holds to and others are betraying.

[18]See Patricia Hollis, *Women in Public: The Women's Movement 1850–1900* (Allen & Unwin, 1979); Martha Vicinus (ed.), *A Widening Sphere: Changing Roles of Victorian Women* (Bloomington, Indiana UP, 1977); and Gail Cunningham, *The New Woman and the Victorian Novel* (Macmillan, 1978).

In *Daniel Deronda*, however, gentlemanliness is itself part of the crisis in contemporary life with which the novel deals. This remarkable last novel shows George Eliot abandoning the temporal middle distance of her previous novels for the near-present of the 1860s, and in doing so forfeiting the equilibrium of *Middlemarch*. Although there are significant continuities between the two novels, not least in the sympathetic handling of painful and unhappy marriages, *Deronda* is a more radically troubled work in which her previously cautious meliorism seems to falter, leading her to portray contemporary society as almost devoid of hope, while at the same time investing the visionary idealism of the Jewish outsiders – Deronda, the musician Klesmer, and the hieratic Mordecai – with an unwonted degree of authorial approval. This split between pessimism and sponsored idealism corresponds to a formal split in the novel between the realism of the English scenes and the visionary romance of the Jewish scenes, where George Eliot finally abandons the unadorned, terrestrial realism with which she had begun her career in 'Amos Barton'. *Deronda* is also a work which travels further than any previous Victorian novel down a road she had made peculiarly her own, the exploration of those 'dark seed-growths of consciousness' (26) in the individual psyche, that 'great deal of unmapped country within us' (24) which, in Gwendolen's struggles to confront the 'dread' in her unconscious, was so deeply to impress and influence Henry James. The corruption in contemporary England is focused in the figure of Grandcourt, the cold, selfish, sadistic aristocrat Gwendolen marries after the bank failure which ruins her family (and *Deronda*, which opens in a casino, shares with Trollope's novel the motif of gambling as a metaphor for the instability of contemporary capitalism). It is surely significant that Grandcourt's name should echo that of Sir Charles Grandison, the idealized baronet and pattern gentleman of Richardson's famous novel, which was, we know, one of George Eliot's favourites. For Grandcourt is the antithesis of Grandison. The moral feeling with which Richardson had tried to invest gentlemanliness in his novel has drained away in Grandcourt to leave only a sterile social form, and in this, George Eliot suggests, he is as symbolic a figurehead for her society as Grandison was for Richardson's. His laziness and cynicism, his readiness to exploit his rank while denying its responsibilities, are typical of a divorce between form and function in the contemporary 'polite' world. Notions of artistic discipline, like those of spiritual dedication, are alien to 'a society where everything, from low arithmetic to high art, is of the amateur kind politely supposed to fall short of perfection only because gentlemen and ladies are not obliged to do more than they like' (23). So the *nouveaux riches* Arrowpoints can dismiss Klesmer's pretensions to their daughter's hand because he is 'only' a distinguished musician, and Sir Hugo Mallinger can feel no qualms about turning the choir and cloisters of the 'Abbey', his country house, into stabling for his horses.

Grandcourt stands at the end of a dying tradition, Daniel Deronda at the outset of the more modern one, where the search for personal authenticity takes the hero beyond class. He is a fluid and somewhat uncertainly conceived character, and George Eliot's handling of his development undermines the conventional pattern of the Victorian *bildungsroman*. In the meeting with his dying actress mother in Genoa, Deronda rejects the aristocratic gentlemanliness she has acquired for him and embraces the discovery of his Jewish ancestry with an enthusiasm which jolts his mother, and was clearly meant to jolt the Victorian reader: ' "Why do you say you are glad? You are an English gentleman. I secured you that".' (51). But being an 'English gentleman' is no longer a sufficient destiny in life, and Deronda must pass beyond it into action and commitment.

The paralysis of the gentleman, evident in Grandcourt, becomes the central subject of *The Egoist*. Meredith's novel is a comprehensive comic subversion of *Sir Charles Grandison*, in which the 'pattern' baronet, Sir Willoughby Patterne, ensconced like Richardson's hero in a country-house and surrounded by an initially admiring circle of ladies, is in the course of the novel gradually picked clean of his authority not only as a gentleman but as a man. The cosy little harem of *Grandison* turns into a battle of the sexes. *The Egoist*, in fact, marks a turning-point in Victorian fiction, the novel with which Meredith, always an interesting writer, becomes an important one.

George Meredith

George Meredith (1828–1909) is, and always has been, a difficult figure to see clearly in the landscape of Victorian fiction. Born almost ten years after George Eliot, he comes rather uneasily between her generation and the later, early modern generation of Hardy and James, and his novels reflect this, proto-modern in their interest in technique and feminine psychology, Victorian in their length, exuberance and moral didacticism. Meredith's transitional placing might not greatly matter, might indeed have been a decided asset, were it not for the notorious difficulty of his prose style, which cost him a popular readership in his own time and has made him the least read of the major Victorian novelists today. Meredith's prose is not difficult in the way that the prose of Henry James's later novels is difficult, where a tortuous style seeks an ambiguous subject; its difficulties are all on the surface, so to speak, in the almost continual stylistic bustle which makes him such a tiring and at times exasperating writer to read. Meredith was a poet, and the tendency of his imagination was to embellish every detail, to make every observation an epigram and every twitch of his characters' minds a flash of poetic illumination. Thus Clara Middleton in *The Egoist* does not blush, but 'was in fine sunset colour, unable to arrest the mounting tide' (8). Where another character might simply close her eyes, we are told that 'Her lovely eyes troubled the lids to hide their softness' (48). This style has its successes as well as its excesses, but it is not a natural or happy medium for extended prose narrative, at least of the three-volume length Meredith was required to produce. The continually restless, nervous local life of his prose, by turns highfalutin and epigrammatic, flouncing and terse, works against the creation of steady narrative momentum, and when to this is added Meredith's tendency to an elliptical narrative method, presenting the essential obliquely and elaborating the peripheral, it is not surprising that even his admirers were moved to protest that his novels might be better if he would consent to be a little less brilliant: 'He is not content to be plain Jupiter', W.E. Henley wrote, 'his lightnings are less to him than the fireworks he delights in, and his pages so teem with fine sayings, and magniloquent epigrams, and gorgeous images, and fantastic locutions, that the mind would welcome dullness as a glad relief.'[19] Or as V.S. Pritchett, Meredith's most eloquent modern defender, wittily puts it: 'To read some stretches of Meredith's prose is like living on a continuous diet of lobster and champagne: lobster done in every known sauce and champagne only too knowingly addressed as the Veuve'.[20]

The richness of the diet is not confined to style. The reader of Meredith soon becomes aware of moving in a glamorous realm of Romance, rather than the realm of history which most Victorian novels acknowledge. His characters, or at least his young heroes, seem to enjoy a perpetual holiday from the social and economic probabilities that press so insistently on the characters in other fiction of the period. The typical Meredithian protagonist – Richard Feverel, Harry Richmond, Sir Willoughby Patterne – is a young patrician of almost fabulous wealth, heir to a landed estate where he presides like a princeling over a court of dependent relatives and resident tutors; if he stays at home, like Sir Willoughby, he is free to indulge every whim of his heart; if he travels abroad, as Harry Richmond does, it is to encounter adventures of Ruritanian extravagance. The justification for the improbable plots and high-flown sentiment of his novels is that Meredith was writing Romance, indeed rediscovering its possibilities for readers attuned to the sobriety of Thackeray, Trollope and George Eliot. By ditching the constraints of character analysis which went with the novel of domestic realism, so the defence goes, he was setting himself free to explore the psychology of the individual in a new way. *Beauchamp's Career* (1876) apart, one would not go to Meredith for an interpretation of the social and political life of Victorian England. He had a distinctive vision of his times, but this is expressed not through topicality or surface realism, but through the relationships his strange novels imagine, in particular through his interest in the relations of fathers and sons, and in the situation and psychology of women.

[19]Ioan Williams (ed.), *Meredith: The Critical Heritage* (Routledge & Kegan Paul, 1971), p. 207.
[20]*George Meredith and English Comedy* (Chatto & Windus, 1970), p. 41.

'A History of a Father and Son' is the subtitle of his first and most accessible novel, *The Ordeal of Richard Feverel* (1859). This is the story of Sir Austin Feverel, a wealthy baronet whose wife has deserted him, leaving behind an infant son, Richard (Meredith's own situation at the time of writing the novel: his first wife had left him and their five-year-old son Arthur for the painter Henry Wallis). Wounded by this betrayal, Sir Austin resolves to rear his son on a pseudo-scientific educational 'system' which, by isolating the boy from the world and sexuality, is meant to produce a pure young man ready at the age of 25 to marry a noble young lady of his father's choosing. Nature takes an ironic revenge on the pretensions of this 'scientific humanist' when Richard falls in love with and marries a local farmer's niece, the irony lying in the fact that the girl is both lovely and good, and their marriage the truly virtuous relationship which the father had planned. But Sir Austin is too blinded by pride of mind and caste to see this, and his opposition to the marriage leads, by a further irony, to Richard's involvement in those same worldly experiences which the 'system' was designed to circumvent. The novel recounts the painful process by which the hero learns the hard way a truth he has always known instinctively, and when at last he returns chastened to his wife and baby son the damage has been done, and in an improbable and melodramatic ending she dies of brain fever. Richard is left at the end in the same situation as his father at the start of the novel, but more desolate, without even the false hopefulness of 'scientific humanism' to sustain him.

The 'ordeal' of the title is twofold: the 'romantic' love, corruption, purification and final loss of the son, and the embittering humiliation of the ironist father at the hands of Lady Feverel, which takes place before the novel starts – as in real life it did for Meredith himself – and yet seems to dominate the action, much as the misogynistic sayings from his book of aphorisms, 'The Pilgrim's Scrip', frame the narrative. First novels are nearly always revealing, and in the two versions of the ordeal it is possible to see the seeds of Meredith's subsequent fiction. Broadly speaking, the novels up to *Beauchamp's Career* (1876) explore the possibilities and the dangers of Romance. The heroines are brilliant, brave and beautiful; the young heroes are dashing patricians for whom the ordeal by woman takes a flattering rather than humiliating form: they are placed, Gail Cunningham observes, 'rather comfortably at the centre of a whirling galaxy of beauties with conflicting claims to [their] attention, and allowed. . .to reach out at the end and pluck the best'.[21] These novels were important historically in re-establishing the respectability of romantic fiction, which a more subtle writer like Stevenson could build upon, but only *Harry Richmond* (1871) seems salvageable today, and even that work is arrested in a pre-Victorian

[21] *The New Woman and the Victorian Novel*, pp. 123–4.

form of the *bildungsroman*, stranded somewhere between *Tom Jones* and *David Copperfield*.

The Egoist, however, is a different matter. Here Meredith returned to what one suspects was the deeper subject for him, the bitter ordeal of the father. The 'Egoist is the Son of Himself. He is likewise the Father' (xxxix): the father and son of *Richard Feverel* meet in Sir Willoughby, who is both dashing young patrician and (twice) rejected lover. The ordeal at the hands of woman which preceded the early novel becomes the substance of the action in *The Egoist*, and the woman in question, Clara Middleton, although invested with the Romance characteristics of beauty, wealth and breeding, is a much more critical observer of masculine posturing than any of her predecessors. While this development can be and has been related to Meredith's feminist convictions, it also shows the surfacing of a certain fear of women which is never far away in his work, an awareness of their power to challenge and humiliate the male ego. Fear sharpened insight, helped to make him acutely sensitive to the woman's view of masculine dominance, but it is revealing that he does not appear to have been able to imagine a balanced relationship between the sexes in his later fiction. The rise of the independent women in his novels, the Clara Middletons and Diana Warwicks, involves the defeat of masculine force and independence; the mates they find are colourless, neutral figures like Vernon Whitford in *The Egoist* and Tom Redworth in *Diana of the Crossways*.

The Egoist is subtitled 'A Comedy in Narrative', and inevitably invites comparison with the idea of comedy set out in Meredith's famous *Essay on Comedy* (1897), which he delivered as a lecture in 1877. It is a high, intellectual comedy that Meredith advocates, the comedy of Molière and Congreve, in which women play a civilizing role through their powers of mind: 'Comedy lifts women to a station offering them free play for their wit, as they usually show it, when they have it, on the side of sound sense. The higher the Comedy, the more prominent the part they enjoy in it.'[22] *The Egoist* comes closest in English fiction to Restoration comedy, or at least to Meredith's idea of Restoration comedy – a battle of the sexes, awakening 'thoughtful laughter' which 'is impersonal and of unrivalled politeness, nearer a smile; often no more than a smile' (p. 88). If this seems a somewhat chilling idea of the comic, then it has to be said that the reader coming to *The Egoist* with expectations based on the more familiar English tradition of comedy is likely to be disappointed. He will soon encounter rococo passages like the following, in which Meredith elaborates on Mrs Mountstuart Jenkinson's observation on Sir Willoughby, '*You see he has a leg*':

He has the leg of Rochester, Buckingham, Dorset, Suckling; the leg that smiles, that winks, is obsequious to you, yet perforce of beauty self-satisfied;

---

[22] *An Essay on Comedy and the Uses of the Comic Spirit* (Constable, 2nd edn, 1898), p. 28.

that twinkles to a tender midway between imperiousness and seductiveness, audacity and discretion; between 'you shall worship me', and 'I am devoted to you'; is your lord, your slave, alternately and in one. It is a leg of ebb and flow and high-tide ripples. Such a leg, when it has done with pretending to retire, will walk straight into the hearts of women. Nothing so fatal to them. (ii)

As a piece of comic writing this is certainly very different from, say, Dickens's Mrs Waterbrook: ' "We see Blood in a nose, and we know it. We meet with it in a chin, and we say, 'There it is! That's Blood!' " ' (*David Copperfield*, 25). Beside this sharp flash of absurdity Meredith's prose may well seem laboured and artificial, until one realizes that artificiality is very much the point: what he is hunting in Sir Willoughby are not only the more obvious vices of snobbery and pride, but also an insinuating softness, sexual in basis, which seeks out feminine sympathy and ruthlessly exploits it. The leg 'that twinkles to a tender midway between imperiousness and seductiveness' is in fact satirically right and thematically relevant, for it captures the unstable combination of chivalric deference and inner will which is the essence of Sir Willoughby's character and the subject of the novel.

The Egoist is like an elaborate dance in which the various characters pair off in a series of elegant formal encounters. The influence of Meredith's reading in Molière and Congreve for the *Essay on Comedy* can perhaps be seen in the book's unity of place and action, so different from the usual picaresque bustle of his novels. The country-house setting, the limited cast of characters, and the theatrical nature of much of the dialogue all contribute to a rare concentration of dramatic effect. And if Sir Willoughby does not quite come to life as a character, he is vibrant as a type, 'a picture of an English gentleman' (xxxv), seen in the representative splendour of the wealthy baronet: 'Rich, handsome, courteous, generous, lord of the Hall, the feast and the dance. . .' (ii). Meredith is clear about the reality behind this 'pattern' gentleman: Sir Willoughby may be a latter-day Sir Charles Grandison, but – Meredith had read his Darwin – he is also 'the heir of successful competitors' (v), his aristocratic prominence made possible by the ruthless pruning of younger sons in previous generations; and it is as a successful competitor that he wins Clara Middleton.

The irony at the centre of the novel is that while Sir Willoughby speaks the language of deferential courtship, his will to dominate others is monstrous and tenacious. All his energies are devoted to preserving his seigneurial image in the eyes of the world, and for this it is necessary that he control the admiring but watchful circle of women who guard public opinion in the county. As the queen of this circle Clara is required to be what Meredith calls in a brilliant phrase, 'essentially feminine, in other words, a parasite and a chalice' (v). This self-regarding attitude to women is the root of Sir Willoughby's sterility, as a man and as a proprietor; it is responsible for the claustrophobic stasis of Patterne Hall, which is broken only by the boyish enthusiasm of his 12-year-old relative Crossjay who, significantly, would rather be a sailor than a 'gentleman' in Sir Willoughby's mould. The action of the novel is as static as its setting, little more than a story of courtship in reverse. As Clara comes to perceive the fierce possessiveness beneath her suitor's sentimental rhetoric, and struggles to extricate herself from an imprisoning engagement, Sir Willoughby, dreading a second humiliation (he has been jilted by Constantia Durham before the start of the novel) makes a desperate match with his once adoring but now disillusioned childhood sweetheart Laetitia Dale. Much has been made of Clara's 'wit' in this battle of the sexes, following Meredith's remarks on Millamant and the witty woman in the *Essay on Comedy*; the 'Comic Spirit' invoked in the 'Prelude' is also female – 'the ultimate civilizer, the polisher, a sweet cook'. In reality, Clara is not a particularly witty character, certainly not in the same league as Elizabeth Bennet or Becky Sharp; what she does possess is intelligence, independence of spirit, physical energy (she is often seen running in the novel, plays the tomboy with Crossjay, and loves nature and mountain scenery), all qualities which are necessarily at war with the carefully preserved immobility of Patterne Hall. They throw into relief what is genuinely if savagely comic in *The Egoist*, the disparity between Willoughby's 'fluting' rhetoric in public and his increasingly desperate awareness that Clara's rebellion threatens what he most dreads, the shameful exposure of 'his naked eidolon, the tender infant Self swaddled in his name before the world, for which he felt as the most highly civilized of men alone can feel, and which it was impossible for him to stretch out hands to protect' (xxix). And when that 'infant self' is exposed, the action becomes almost too painful for comedy.

It is at those moments, when the rather brittle comedy of manners gives way to a battle for psychic survival, that we are most aware of Meredith's equivocal modernity. Clara discovering the 'subterranean sunlessness' (vii) of Willoughby's nature – 'without any substantial quality that she could grasp, only the mystery of the inefficient tallow-light in those caverns of the complacent-talking man' – and struggling to articulate her revulsion from a rhetoric of sentiment which her culture has taught her to esteem, is in a recognizable line of psychological development which links her to George Eliot's Dorothea and Gwendolen, and forward to Henry James's Isabel Archer. And Willoughby's dread of humiliation, the dizzying gulfs of masculine insecurity which are opened up when his social persona starts to crack and the 'tender infant self' is exposed, anticipate D.H. Lawrence's much fuller treatment of this subject in Anton Skrebensky, Gerald Crich and Sir Clifford Chatterley. Indeed, by giving Clara to the self-effacing scholar, Vernon Whitford, Meredith seems to pinpoint an important change in the character of the hero in modern fiction: 'One [Sir Willoughby] was the English gentleman wherever he went; the other was a new kind of thing, nondescript, produced in England of late, and not likely to come to much good himself, or do much good to the country' (iv).

Henry James

The Egoist apart, Meredith's reputation seems shaky today. A question-mark continues to hang over his achievement. There are no such question-marks over the fiction of Henry James (1843–1916). He is the supreme example in the period of a novelist in whose work all the available possibilities seem to have been realized, of an imagination almost invariably in control of its material. He was also a great critic of the novel, who brought to the appreciation of his immediate predecessors a penetrating intelligence nourished on a wider reading in European, and especially French fiction than any of his contemporaries. His total *oeuvre*, in tales and novels, essays, prefaces and reviews, has a massive integrity and an unprecedented self-consciousness which have given his pronouncements on the novel a special authority. It is hardly an exaggeration to say that the critical rediscovery of Victorian fiction in the last 30 years has been possible only by re-examining the notion of form in the novel set out by James in his Prefaces, and by finding ways of refuting the charge of formlessness implicit in such influential asides as his description of *War and Peace* and *The Newcomes* as 'large loose baggy monsters' (Preface to *The Tragic Muse*).

It is important to begin with the obvious point that James was an American. In a famous early letter, written when he was 24, he spoke of the 'complex fate' of his nationality:

> We are Americans born – *il faut en prendre son parti*. I look upon it as a great blessing; and I think that to be an American is an excellent preparation for culture. We have exquisite qualities as a race, and it seems to me that we are ahead of the European races in the fact that more than either of them we can deal freely with forms of civilization not our own, can pick and choose and assimilate and in short (aesthetically &c) claim our property wherever we find it. . .We must of course have something of our own – something distinctive and homogeneous – and I take it that we shall find it in our moral consciousness, our unprecedented spiritual lightness and vigour.[23]

This is a brave manifesto, although in some ways – the cool detachment of 'pick and choose and assimilate', for instance – a slightly disquieting one. The phrase 'preparation for culture', besides suggesting that James had been reading Matthew Arnold, reveals an attitude which Philip Larkin has aptly characterized, apropos of Eliot and Pound, as 'the belief that you can order culture whole, that it is a separate item on the menu'.[24] But of course

[23]*Henry James Letters* I, p. 77; letter of 20 September 1867.
[24]Ian Hamilton, 'Four Conversations', *London Magazine* IV (November 1964), p. 71.

'culture' does not present itself in this way to the native writer, who cannot 'pick and choose' with quite this degree of detachment, and who is inevitably involved in his society's debate about itself, involved therefore in certain choices and conflicts, from which James was exempt. His exemption was a great opportunity, and what James did with it was noble, but it did not go unattended by limitations. In his fiction a crucial shift takes place, from the Victorian sense of society as a shared predicament between author and reader, to a sense of society as a background against which the sensitive and unconditioned individual defines his or her self; and the shift is implicit in the last sentence of the passage quoted above. Not all James's central characters are American, of course, but most of them are endowed with an 'unprecedented spiritual lightness and vigour'. They are aristocrats of the spirit, and the development of James's art was all in the direction of enlarging the space in the novel devoted to the drama of their consciousnesses.

James's masters were Balzac, George Eliot and, especially, Turgenev, but his Victorian bearings are best taken from two very different writers, Trollope and Walter Pater. He had crossed the Atlantic with Trollope in 1875 and found him 'the dullest Briton of them all', and that judgement, although later modified, surfaces in his reading of Trollope's novels.[25] Trollope figured for James as a primitive ancestor, the very type of the copious, naive Victorian realist, 'gross' and 'importunate' in his 'fertility' but deficient in intellectual power and artistic control. The 1883 essay is the classic formulation of the roast-beef-and-Yorkshire-pudding view of Trollope, seeing him as the unreflective producer of solid but shapeless novels – baggy monsters. It is a tactical statement, and should be read in conjunction with 'The Art of Fiction' the following year, where he set out the principles by which the baggy monster was to be slimmed down and toned up. 'One can speak best from one's own taste, and I may therefore venture to say that the air of reality (solidity of specification) seems to me to be the supreme virtue of a novel.' The means to this end is art, but the art which conceals art:

> Catching the very note and trick, the strange irregular rhythm of life, that is the attempt whose strenuous force keeps Fiction upon her feet. In proportion as in what she offers we see life *without* rearrangement do we feel that we are touching the truth; in proportion as we see it *with* rearrangement do we feel that we are being put off with a substitute, a compromise and convention. . . .Art is essentially selection, but it is a selection whose main care is to be typical, to be inclusive.[26]

James here makes a necessary and useful clarification, shifting the ground from the naive mimetic view of reality as something the novelist passively

[25]Leon Edel, *The Life of Henry James* (2 vols., Harmondsworth, Penguin, 1977) I, p. 428.
[26]*The House of Fiction*, pp. 33, 38.

mirrors, to the 'air of reality', an impression the novelist creates through the practice of selection and shaping. The distinction implies an ideal of realist fiction in which inclusiveness and concentration reinforce one another, a goal James was working towards in the 'Victorian' novels he was writing at this time.

The name of Pater suggests a different context in which James's fiction can be seen, but an equally important one. He read *The Renaissance* on its appearance in 1873, and wrote a review which has not survived.[27] There are various echoes of Pater in his early writings, and it is possible that the title of *The Wings of the Dove* owes something to the fact that the biblical phrase from which it comes, 'Yet shall ye be as the wings of a dove', formed the epigraph to *The Renaissance*. Needless to say, James is a much greater writer than Pater; for all his 'aestheticism' he had an altogether more robust sensibility and a larger appetite for life than the man he was later to refer to as 'faint, pale, embarrassed, exquisite Pater'.[28] What they have in common is a devotion to art, a rare delicacy and scrupulosity of taste, and a tendency to treat life with a certain fascinated detachment, as a spectacle capable of yielding a rich harvest of sensation and impression – 'this fruit of a quickened, multiplied consciousness', as the closing words of *The Renaissance* put it. Just as Pater turned the objectivity of the Arnoldian critical ideal inwards – ' "To see the object as in itself it really is," has been justly said to be the aim of all true criticism whatever; and in aesthetic criticism the first step towards seeing one's object as it really is, is to know one's own impression as it really is. . .' (Preface) – so James was to try to turn the novel from social panorama to the drama of consciousness. And 'consciousness' in the enriched Paterian sense is a central value in all James's work. Writing a letter of consolation to Grace Norton in 1883, he could not say '*why* we live' but offered as a reason for going on living the reflection that

> life is the most valuable thing we know anything about and it is therefore presumptively a great mistake to surrender it while there is any yet left in the cup. In other words consciousness is an illimitable power, and though at times it may seem to be all consciousness of misery, yet in the way it propagates itself from wave to wave, so that we never cease to feel, though at moments we appear to, try to, pray to, there is something that holds one in one's place, makes it a standpoint in the universe which it is probably good not to forsake.[29]

So it is for James's characters: enlarged consciousness, even if it seems to be

---

[27]See *Letters* I, p. 412.

[28]In a letter of 13 December 1894 to Edmund Gosse: *Letters* III, p. 492. The affinities between Pater and James are discussed in James J. Kirschke, *Henry James and Impressionism* (Troy, NY, Whitston Publishing Co., 1981) and Alwyn Berland, *Culture and Conduct in the Novels of Henry James* (Cambridge, CUP, 1981). See also Stewart P. Sherman, 'The Aesthetic Idealism of Henry James', in F.W. Dupee (ed.), *The Question of Henry James: A Collection of Critical Essays* (Allan Wingate, 1947), pp. 86–106.

[29]*Letters* II, p. 424; letter of 28 July 1883.

'consciousness of misery', is a value and an end in itself, and the one sure consolation for defeat at the hands of life.

'I saw that I should be an eternal outsider', James wrote in his journal, as he prepared to cross the Channel in 1876 to settle in England.[30] For the 'eternal outsider', life becomes a matter of contemplation or 'appreciation' in the detached, evaluative sense of connoisseurship common to Pater and James. *Appreciations* (1889) is the title of a collection of Pater's essays, and 'appreciation' is a key word in James's vocabulary too. In the Preface to *The Princess Casamassima* he wrote that 'the affair of the painter is not the immediate, it is the reflected field of life, the realm not of application, but of *appreciation*. . .'. The novelist 'appreciates' his subject like a painter his canvas,[31] noting its qualities of composition and lighting, and his characters, or the more sensitive among them, 'appreciate' life and one another. Thus the invalid Ralph Touchett in *The Portrait of a Lady* 'indulged in a boundless liberty of appreciation' (I, 5) as a young man, because 'his outward conformity to the manners that surrounded him was. . .the mark of a mind that greatly enjoyed its independence' (I, 5); and Isabel Archer in the same novel reflects on Madame Merle's sophistication:

> 'That is the great thing. . .that is the supreme good fortune: to be in a better position for appreciating people than they are for appreciating you.' And she added that this, when one considered it, was simply the essence of the aristocratic situation. (I, 19)

Isabel is of course deceived about Madame Merle, but the link she makes here between the capacity for subtle 'appreciation' and the aristocratic character runs throughout James's fiction. If, to return to that early letter on the 'adantages of being an American', James's central characters, and especially his Americans, are natural aristocrats, they are so by virtue of the capacity for appreciation which their detachment and intelligence give them, and the Paterian 'fruit of a quickened, multiplied consciousness' which this yields.

James's world in his English novels is that of Trollope's 'Upper Ten Thousand'. The letters he wrote in his early years in London reveal how assiduously he set out to acquaint himself with the life of the upper classes, but also how exceptionally clear-eyed he was about their limitations. Of one scandal, in 1886, he wrote to an American friend that it 'will besmirch exceedingly the already very damaged prestige of the English upper-class', and went on with the words he had put in the mouth of the revolutionary Princess Casamassima: 'The condition of that body seems to me to be in many ways very much the same rotten and *collapsible* one as that of the French aristocracy before the revolution – minus cleverness and

[30]Edel, *Life of Henry James* I, p. 486.

[31]For a detailed discussion of this aspect of Henry James, see Viola Hopkins Winner, *Henry James and the Visual Arts* (Charlottesville, University Press of Virginia, 1970).

conversation.'[32] But the *idea* of aristocracy was dear to James, and like Disraeli before him he was to create in his books an ideal or myth of aristocracy built around his own outsider status. From Clement Searle in 'A Passionate Pilgrim' (1871) to Lambert Strether in *The Ambassadors* (1903), a recurring figure in his work is the outsider, usually American, who brings to the appreciation of European social forms a finer and richer awareness of their possibilities than the natives have. Clement Searle is a broken-down, penniless American who feels he has been born in exile: ' "I came into the world an aristocrat" ', he tells the narrator at Hampton Court, ' "I was born with a soul for the picturesque" ', and the picturesque he responds to is the England of literary associations. At his ancestral home, which bears the Tennysonian name of Lockley Park, the irony – and the comedy, for James's use of a narrator implies distance from his pilgrim's rhapsodies – turn on the fact that it is the poor American relation who has the deeper aristocratic sense, the finer feeling for the storied past, than the Searle in possession of the estate. ' "Suppose I should turn out a better Searle than you? Better than you, nursed here in romance and picturesqueness." '[33] When the owner throws him out, he goes to Oxford to die. Similarly Bessie Alden, the American girl in 'An International Episode' (1878), is more intelligent, better-read and simply more responsive to the past than Lord Lambeth, and shows her fineness of moral scruple and social tact in declining to take up his offer of marriage.

The most ambitious of James's novels on this theme, and his first extensive exploration of the English scene, is *The Portrait of a Lady* (1881). This book and its immediate successors should put to rout the mistaken but still common view that James's interests are narrowly 'aesthetic'. As one perceptive contemporary critic observed in 1891: 'In *The Portrait of a Lady*, in *The Bostonians*, *The Princess Casamassima*, *The Tragic Muse*. . .we feel less that the curtain has risen on a comedy of manners or of plot, than on a vast section of society, and of society considered with especial reference to some of its more modern developments.'[34] The modernity of *The Portrait* lay partly in its subject, which with the 'American invasion' of heiresses at the time was highly topical,[35] and partly in the striking similarities of theme and character it shared with the most advanced works of the period, *Daniel Deronda* and *The Egoist*: each is a novel with a lively and independent heroine who makes a disastrous marriage to, or engagement with, an egoist. The preoccupation with egoism, and the family likeness between Grandcourt and Osmond, and

[32]*Letters* III, p. 146; letter of 6 December 1886.

[33]*The Complete Tales of Henry James*, ed. Leon Edel (12 vols., Hart-Davis, 1962–5) II, pp. 245, 263.

[34]From an unsigned article in *Murray's*, November 1891: see Roger Gard (ed.), *Henry James: The Critical Heritage* (Routledge & Kegan Paul, 1968), p. 227.

[35]See Hesketh Pearson, *The Pilgrim Daughters* (Heinemann, 1961).

Gwendolen and Isabel, suggest that James was making a deliberate bid for the mantle of George Eliot, although this often made comparison needs to be qualified in one important respect. George Eliot, like Meredith, seems obsessed with egoism; it is the serpent in the garden of her Victorian humanism, and she hunts it relentlessly through the pages of her last novel. *The Portrait of a Lady* can be read in this way, and James provides some of the materials for such a reading, but the deeper impulse of the book is not really moralistic in the Victorian manner. The narrator's attitude is at once more detached in the analysis of psychology and motive, and more lenient in the matter of judgement. Consider the long opening paragraph of the sixth chapter, which offers a very complete inventory of Isabel's strengths and weaknesses – her intelligence, high spirit, liability to 'the sin of self-esteem', ignorance of life, 'nobleness of imagination' and proneness to self-deception – but keeps them in suspension, as it were, refusing the precision and finality of judgement George Eliot would reach for, and ending instead with an appeal to the reader's charity: 'she would be an easy victim of scientific criticism, if she were not intended to awaken on the reader's part an impulse more tender and more purely expectant.'

And 'expectant' is the right word to describe the effect of those wonderful opening chapters. For although Isabel has many ancestors, she was essentially a new kind of heroine, an unconditioned spirit at large in the normally highly conditioned landscape of Victorian fiction. It is here that the familiar comparison with Dorothea Brooke and Gwendolen Harleth breaks down. The important sources are American – James's beloved cousin Minny Temple, about whose love of life and early death he was to write so movingly in *Notes of a Son and Brother* (1914), and, as Professor Edel and many others have pointed out, James himself, the passionate pilgrim. Something of the classical richness of the first 19 chapters comes from the fact that Isabel's discovery of a social and cultural tradition is filtered through her creator's exploitation of a literary tradition. The afternoon sunlight on the country-house lawn in the opening chapter; Gardencourt itself, the Tudor house which has entertained 'the great Elizabeth' and now holds the American Princess, for whom its 'rich perfection. . .at once revealed a world and gratified a need' (I, 6); the meeting with Lord Warburton and the visit to Lockleigh (the Tennysonian name reappearing from 'The Passionate Pilgrim') with its 'ache of antiquity' (I, 9) – we have been here before, in the novels of Jane Austen, George Eliot and Trollope, and at moments James seems to go out of his way to remind us of this:

> It suddenly came upon her that her situation was one which a few weeks ago she would have deemed deeply romantic; the park of an old English country-house, with the foreground embellished by a local nobleman in the act of making love to a young lady who, on careful inspection, should be found to present remarkable analogies with herself. But if she were now the heroine of the situation, she succeeded scarcely the less in looking at it from the outside. (I, 12)

James invokes the novelistic convention only to rub home the essential difference, which is Isabel's very American detachment, her capacity to look at things 'from the outside'. Unlike Isabel Boncassen, the compliant American girl in Trollope's *The Duke's Children* (1880), she turns down her aristocratic suitor.

In *Notes of a Son and Brother,* James wrote of his cousin Minny Temple that 'she was to remain for us the very figure and image of a felt interest in life. . .of a taste for life as life, as personal living.'[36] The tall, grey-eyed Isabel has this quality, and the architecture of the novel is designed to bring out a rich potentiality in her situation. Installed in Gardencourt by her aunt Mrs Touchett, she turns down the obvious possibilities in marriage represented by Caspar Goodwood's new-world energy and (as she sees it) Lord Warburton's old-world grandeur: 'A certain instinct, not imperious, but persuasive, told her to resist – it murmured to her that virtually she had a system and an orbit of her own' (I, 12). Quite what Isabel's 'orbit' might be James never makes plain. The first third of the novel is taken up with suggesting, largely in terms of contrast with other more limited figures such as Henrietta Stackpole, her go-getting American journalist friend, that her true element is some unconditioned realm of the 'personal'. Her cousin Ralph, who loves her and whose fatal illness absolves him 'from all professional and official emotions and left him with the luxury of being simply personal' (II, 14), ministers to her destiny as a free spirit by arranging the legacy that makes her an heiress, and by advising her to ' "Spread your wings; rise above the ground" ' (II, 2). This is a new kind of destiny for a Victorian heroine. Not for Isabel Archer the modest ambition of a Lucy Snowe to set up her own school, or Dorothea Brooke in her plan for model cottages; the realm of the 'exclusively personal' in which she is encouraged to move has none of the restraints or the sustaining disciplines and obligations of a real community, and it is significant that when she returns to earth, weighed down by her fortune, it should be into the arms of the sterile Gilbert Osmond. The essence of the aristocratic situation for Isabel turns out to be marriage to a middle-aged dilettante, and life among the etiolated American colony in Florence. From this point of view, *The Portrait of a Lady* can be seen as an American tragedy, not in its Romance form of New World innocence betrayed by Old World experience, but – since the principal characters are all American – of the perils of detached 'appreciation', of that dangerous freedom 'to pick and choose and assimilate' James had welcomed in his youthful letter. For even Ralph has 'something of this same quality, the appearance of thinking that life was a matter of connoisseurship' (II, 5). James clearly intends a critique of connoisseurship, though how largely this should figure in our reading of the novel is difficult to judge.

[36] *Notes of a Son and Brother* (Macmillan, 1914), p. 73.

It is difficult to judge, as is a good deal else in the later sections of the novel, partly because of the narrative method James increasingly adopts. The leisurely omniscient narration which contributes to the Victorian richness of the early scenes gives way in the second half of the novel to narration by implication and through point of view. The transition comes in chapters 16 and 17 of the second volume, 35 and 36 in most modern editions. In the first Isabel is in love with Osmond and about to marry him; in the next three years have passed and we learn, through Madame Merle's conversation, that they have married, lost a child and, it is hinted, are now unhappy with one another. In the gap between two chapters matter essential to our understanding of the novel's central relationship has simply slipped away; we are not told the reasons for the breakdown of the marriage, the nature of Osmond's villainy, or the extent of Isabel's responsibility for the failure. James's justification of his refusal to 'do' the marriage is implicit in the Preface he wrote for the New York edition, where he discussed his intention to 'place the centre of the subject in the young woman's own consciousness' and declared Isabel's 'extraordinary meditative vigil' in chapter 42 as 'obviously the best thing in the book'. It is a judgement that might well be disputed, but what is surely revealing is James's unawareness of the extent to which the increased concentration on the heroine's drama of consciousness in effect privileges her view of the marriage. One recalls George Eliot's narrator breaking off at the start of chapter 29 of *Middlemarch*: '– but why always Dorothea? Was her point of view the only possible one with regard to this marriage?' The intervention is clumsy, but serves a wider sense of justice, as does the omniscient convention generally. James's selective use of point of view gives a greater yield of dramatized consciousness, but at the expense of those other points of view which might answer some of the more troubling questions about Isabel's character, particularly the hints of inhibition and cold connoisseurship, which the narrative raises. Above all, concentrating on her perspective smooths the way for a tragic ending, when Ralph on his deathbed voices a more generously tragic interpretation of Isabel's fate – ' "You wanted to look at life for yourself – but you were not allowed; you were punished for your wish" ' (III, 15) – than the reader at this point may be willing to concede.

The use of a central narrative consciousness is carried much further in James's next novel of English life, *The Princess Casamassima* (1886). This is the most Victorian of his books, in the sense that it recalls *Alton Locke* and *Great Expectations*, and also the most insistently topical; it is James's ambitious response to what his characters call the 'great social question', the awakening sense in the 1880s of urban poverty and the challenge of revolutionary socialism and anarchism. Like Gissing's *Demos* (1886), it expresses a feeling of crisis, of turbulence working 'irreconcilably, subversively, beneath the vast smug surface' (Preface) of society; but it is also something of a Victorian *bildungsroman*, with a protagonist, like Alton Locke, who grows up in an impoverished background into radical politics, and like Pip, whose feelings of social disinheritance are compounded by the conviction that he is innately a 'gentleman'. Hyacinth Robinson is the illegitimate son of an English nobleman and a French seamstress, daughter of a Paris revolutionary and the convicted murderess of her aristocratic lover. The novel opens powerfully with the young Hyacinth's visit to his dying mother in Millbank Prison, a scene of symbolic melodrama in the Dickens–Wilkie Collins sensation tradition which serves to establish unforgettably the contradictory nature of the child's heredity. Hyacinth grows up to become a bookbinder, and through this trade he comes in contact with an élite group of radical artisans, attends their meetings, and in a rash moment pledges himself to a future act of revolutionary violence should the cause require it. But his sense of social justice is at war with his feeling for aristocracy, he is drawn to the fashionable parade in Hyde Park as well as to the political meeting in the East End, and when he is taken up by the Princess Casamassima, a bored aristocrat seeking excitement in revolutionary politics, the 'gentleman' in him starts to dominate. His visit to the Princess's rented English country-house, Medley, is the turning-point in the novel. As he walks in the garden before breakfast, he experiences a religious sense of 'breathless ecstasy'. Like Gilbert Searle and Isabel Archer before him, the natural aristocrat has come home:

> Round the admirable house he revolved repeatedly; catching every point and tone, feasting on its expression. . . .There was something in the way the gray walls rose from the green lawn that brought tears to his eyes; the spectacle of long duration unassociated with some sordid infirmity or poverty was new to him; he had lived with people among whom old age meant, for the most part, a grudged and degraded survival. In the majestic preservation of Medley there was a kind of serenity of success, an accumulation of dignity and honour. (22)

The irony is that his enchantment with Medley is the start of the Princess's disenchantment with him; hoping for a proletarian revolutionary, she finds a gentleman, and turns to the real thing in Hyacinth's friend Paul Muniment. More honest and more consistent, Hyacinth finds that a visit to Paris and Venice only confirms the process Medley has begun, and that he cannot square his love of culture with his commitment to overthrow the social order: 'What was supreme in his mind today was not the idea of how the society that surrounded him should be destroyed; it was, much more, the sense of the wonderful, precious things it had produced, of the brilliant, impressive fabric it had raised' (29). Faced with the task of assassinating a duke in fulfilment of his rash oath, Hyacinth refuses to repeat his mother's crime and shoots himself.

Deeply 'social' as the matter of *The Princess Casamassima* is, however, the impression we take away from the novel is of the drama of Hyacinth's consciousness, and his 'power to be finely aware and richly responsible' (Preface). Nor is it fair to see this as a failure on James's part, for the Preface makes it clear that such was his intention: 'The interest of the attitude and the act would be the actor's imagination and vision of them, together with the nature and degree of their felt return upon him'. What may legitimately be questioned is the adequacy of this treatment to the subject proposed, for the effect of illuminating a central consciousness is to focus out other factors, other characters and relationships, necessary to the fullest development of the theme. The weakness of *The Princess Casamassima* lies not so much in the obvious failures of verisimiltude, in the fact, for example, that Hyacinth in scarcely more the product of his environment than Oliver Twist, or that he should read the *Revue des Deux Mondes* and speak the educated slang of the well-born, as in the absence of any felt image of the social injustice which makes him a revolutionary in the first place. James asks us to see Hyacinth 'divided, to the point of torture. . .split open by sympathies that pulled him in different ways' (11), but when it comes to the injustice all he can manage is a dim, sympathetic groan. In contrast to the evocation of aristocratic culture, the language in which the 'social question' is broached is, like the phrase itself, vague and general: 'the deep perpetual groan of London misery seemed to swell and swell and form the whole undertone of life' (21), and so on.

The Princess Casamassima marks the point at which James took his departure from the inherited tradition of Victorian fiction. An honest and courageous attempt to do a Dickens and imagine the sacrifices that made his world possible, James's resolution of the conflict between two worlds is already implicit in his concentration on Hyacinth's consciousness, and in the exclusive nature of that consciousness; and it leads naturally to the much simpler and more relaxed opposition of art and politics in his next novel, *The Tragic Muse* (1890). Thereafter, and following his unhappy involvement with the theatre in the 1890s, James was to take the high road of consciousness. 'I confess', he wrote in the Preface to *The Princess*, 'I never see the *leading* interest of any human hazard but in a consciousness (on the part of the moved and moving creature) subject to fine intensification and wide enlargement.' And in the Preface to *The Spoils of Poynton* (1897), he writes of 'Life being all inclusion and confusion, and art being all discrimination and selection', and thus of the need for 'the sublime economy of art, which rescues, which saves and hoards and "banks", investing and reinvesting these fruits of toil in wondrous useful "works" and thus making up for us, desperate spendthrifts that we all naturally are, the most princely of incomes.' James's playful elaboration of his financial metaphor is disarming, but the choice of metaphor is surely revealing. Fecund genius though he was, his attitude to the quantity and range of experience the novel could carry came increasingly to resemble that of some great financier setting his mind to reinvesting a widow's pension: a narrowing amount of life had to be made to yield a maximum amount of interest. The artistic economy is impressive, but it is not possible without losses of a kind that previous novelists, however 'spendthrift', had not incurred – the loss of the crowded canvas, the rich variety of character and incident which gives the great Victorian novels their normative balance and power of cultural generalization.

This is not to say, as is too often and easily said, that James's concerns are narrowly aesthetic; on the contrary, the life of his 'finely aware and richly responsible' figures is intense and dramatic, and their antennae remain subtly tuned to the discontents of their civilization. But it is a subjective life they lead, and as the space devoted to their inner dramas is enlarged, an increasingly ambiguous one, until in the later novels the relativity of the individual consciousness becomes almost James's central subject. What, for example, are we to make of Fleda Vetch's failure to seize the man she loves at the crucial moment in *The Spoils of Poynton*: the superfine scruple of an inhibited woman, ' "a stiff little beggar" ' as Mrs Gereth calls her (18), or a noble attempt to behave honourably that ends in tragic waste? The objectivity with which James handles Fleda's consciousness is so delicately poised that it is difficult to be finally sure, and in that poise there are pleasures, and critical opportunities, not available in earlier Victorian fiction. It is foolish to wish James's later novels other than they are, but necessary also to be clear about the change they portend: their setting may be the Victorian world, but their techniques and preoccupations belong to the history of the modern novel.

Robert Louis Stevenson

In the later stages of his career James had to endure a shrinking demand for his novels and critical incomprehension in quarters from which he had a right to expect sympathetic understanding. The letters he wrote in 1915 to Edmund Gosse about the commercial failure of the New York edition ('I remain at my age. . .and after my long career, utterly, insurmountably, unsaleable'), and to H.G. Wells after the latter's attack on him in *Boon* (1915), make particularly poignant reading.[37] Happily, his friendship with Robert Louis Stevenson (1850–94) was another matter. Different as the two men were as writers, they met on a common ground of concern for the craft of fiction. James did not have to spell out to Stevenson the elementary principles of art as he later had to do with Wells ('It is art that *makes* life, makes interest, makes importance, for our consideration and application of these things. . .'). Rather, it was Stevenson who took the lead in affirming the primacy of art. In his reply to James's 'The Art of Fiction', called 'A Humble Remonstrance' (1884), he discussed the relations of art and life in

[37] *Henry James Letters* IV (Cambridge, Mass., Belknap Press, 1984), pp. 766–70; these letters are conveniently reprinted in the *Critical Heritage* volume, pp. 527–32.

terms that now seem uncannily modern. 'So far as it imitates at all, [art] imitates not life but speech: not the facts of human destiny, but the emphasis and the suppressions with which the human actor tells of them.' Life presents a 'welter of impressions', art harmonizes them.

> From all its chapters, from all its pages, from all its sentences, the well-written novel echoes and re-echoes its one creative and controlling thought; to this must every incident and character contribute; the style must have been pitched in unison with this; and if there is anywhere a word that looks another way, the book would be stronger, clearer, and. . .fuller without it. Life is monstrous, infinite, illogical, abrupt and poignant; a work of art, in comparison, is neat, finite, self-contained, rational, flowing and emasculate.[38]

This was going much further than James himself had done in 'The Art of Fiction': there he had argued for selection as a means to the effect of inclusiveness ('Art is essentially selection, but it is a selection whose main care is to be typical, to be inclusive'). Stevenson's analogy is more abstract: 'A proposition of geometry does not compete with life; and a proposition of geometry is a fair and luminous parallel for a work of art.'

Stevenson was obsessed with technique, and at first glance this obsession consorts oddly with the traditional ends which technique is made to serve in his fiction. A novel, he argued in 'A Humble Remonstrance', was 'not a transcript from life, to be judged by its exactitude; but a simplification of some side or point of life, to stand or fall by its significant simplicity'. He admired, and in his own work tried to emulate, the 'significant simplicity' of epic, ballad and romance. This makes him a somewhat elusive figure, modern in his self-consciousness and preoccupation with art, but temperamentally and philosophically at odds with the naturalistic novel of his day. It is revealing that 'A Humble Remonstrance' should end with a resounding antithesis between 'the novel of society' and 'the romance of man': let the writer beware of limiting himself to the contemporary and everyday 'lest, in seeking to draw the normal, a man should draw the null, and write the novel of society instead of the romance of man.'

In electing for 'the romance of man' Stevenson turned inevitably to the past – to the past seen not as Scott had seen it, as the nursery of the present, but to a now safely picturesque past, and to the past of genre. He was not a great originator like Scott; rather, he was a hermit-crab, forever trying on the available fictional forms and transforming them from within. John Jay Chapman thought Stevenson 'the most extraordinary mimic that has ever appeared in literature'.[39] The mimicry began early, with

[38]This essay, with its companion-piece 'A Gossip on Romance', can be found in the volume *Memories and Portraits* in collected editions of Stevenson's work, of which there are several. My quotations are taken from the Vailima Edition XXII, pp. 212–13.
[39]*Robert Louis Stevenson: The Critical Heritage*, ed. Paul Maixner (Routledge & Kegan Paul, 1981), p. 490.

Stevenson playing what he called 'the sedulous ape' to the style of writers he admired, and continued in some form for the rest of his writing life. Each of his masterpieces draws upon the subject-matter or setting, and sometimes the themes of previous literature (usually Scottish, although Alexandre Dumas *père* and Emily Brontë are important influences) and rings sophisticated changes on them. Behind *Treasure Island* (1883) is R.M. Ballantyne's *Coral Island* (1857) and the pirate tale, behind *Dr Jekyll and Mr Hyde* (1886) and *The Master of Ballantrae* (1889) is Hogg's master-piece of moral dualism, *The Memoirs and Confessions of a Justified Sinner* (1824), behind *Kidnapped* (1886) is *Redgauntlet* (1824) and Scott's other Jacobite novels. *Jekyll* apart, each of these works is set in the historical past and involves an element of stylistic pastiche. Mimicry seems to have been an essential preliminary to the release of his imagination; even his last, uncompleted novel, *Weir of Hermiston* (1896), considered by many critics his masterpiece, is a kind of prose equivalent of a border ballad. Stevenson worked with great self-consciousness within the traditions of romance, in order to achieve the effect of 'significant simplicity' which he felt the realistic novel had lost. Or as Henry James put it, 'he is an artist accomplished even to sophistication, whose constant theme is the unsophisticated.'[40]

To the sophisticated pursuit of the unsophisticated Stevenson brought rare gifts. There is, firstly, the uncluttered efficiency of his narrative line, moving from episode to episode in a brisk progression, so well suited to the novel of adventure. Related to this is his power of conveying physical movement and sensation, of which the chapters in *Kidnapped* describing 'The Flight in the Heather' are a classic example. Then there is the grace and economy of his prose. Stevenson liked to rail at 'the besotting *particularity* of fiction',[41] yet it was his eye for the exactly right detail, allied to the fluency of his narrative, which brings his world of romance to life (the comparison with his master Meredith in this respect seems to me all in Stevenson's favour). Consider the setting for the duel in *The Master of Ballantrae*:

> I took up the candlesticks and went before them, steps that I would give my hands to recall; but a coward is a slave at the best; and even as I went, my teeth smote each other in my mouth. It was as he had said: there was no breath stirring; a windless stricture of frost had bound the air; and as we went forth in the shine of the candles, the blackness was like a roof over our heads. Never a word was said; there was never a sound but the creaking of our steps along the frozen path. The cold of the night fell about me like a bucket of water; I shook as I went with more than terror; but my companions, bare-headed like myself, and fresh from the warm hall, appeared not even conscious of the change.

[40] *Partial Portraits* (Macmillan, 1888), p. 145.
[41] *Henry James and Robert Louis Stevenson: A Record of Friendship and Criticism*, ed. Janet Adam Smith (Hart-Davis, 1948), p. 233; letter of July 1893.

"Here is the place," said the Master. "Set down the candles."

I did as he bid me, and presently the flames went up, as steady as in a chamber, in the midst of the frosted trees, and I beheld these two brothers take their places. (v)

It is the candles and the stillness of the frost that make this scene live in the memory: a lesser writer would have settled for moonlight and storm. And note the sensuous efficiency of the image used to create the impression of cold – 'The cold of the night fell about me like a bucket of water. . .'

Stevenson's vivid immediacy of narrative is laced with a characteristically Scottish sense of the perils and attractions of evil. He recalled in an autobiographical passage how his nurse 'Cummy' had overheated his imagination with the dangers of sin, so that the idea of sin and rebellion against God came to seem irresistibly fascinating: 'the worst consequence is the romance conferred on doubtful actions; until the child grows to think nothing more glorious than to be struck dead in the act of some surprising wickedness.'[42] The awareness of evil and 'the romance conferred on doubtful actions' contribute to the successful moral *frissons* in Stevenson's work. No one who has read *Treasure Island* ever forgets Blind Pew and the black spot, or the genial but brutal roguery of Long John Silver. Alan Breck in *Kidnapped* is not exactly a rogue, but the fight aboard ship reveals his uncivilized otherness, as he cutlasses his dead and dying enemies and tumbles them out of the round-house, whistling the while, his eyes 'as bright as a five-year-old child's with a new toy' (x). Violence is endemic to the novel of adventure and Stevenson was capable of treating it without the usual conventions, as when Wiltshire despatches Case in *The Beach of Falesá*: 'With that I gave him the cold steel for all I was worth. His body kicked under me like a spring sofa; he gave a dreadful kind of a long moan, and lay still.'[43] Moral dualism is central to *Dr Jekyll and Mr Hyde*, that moral fable of the divided self which now seems increasingly a prophetic work, and to *The Master of Ballantrae*, where in the story of the two brothers he transformed the Scott-derived antithesis of the bourgeois and the Jacobite into a study in the degeneration of a decent man under the spell of the Master, decribed by Stevenson as 'all I know of the devil'.[44]

With *Weir of Hermiston* Stevenson was moving in new directions, to some extent away from the moral ambivalences of *The Master* and *Dr Jekyll* towards a more stark and purely tragic clash of character. The story of Archie Weir's conflict with his powerful father, the 'hanging judge' Lord Hermiston, deals directly with a subject that is never far away in Stevenson's work (one thinks of the various surrogate fathers encountered by the fatherless young heroes of *Treasure Island* and *Kidnapped*) and may

[42]'Memoirs of Himself', *Miscellanea* (Vailima edn, 1923) XXVI, p. 221.

[43]*'Dr Jekyll and Mr Hyde' and Other Stories* (Harmondsworth, Penguin, 1979), p. 166.

[44]*Letters of Robert Louis Stevenson*, ed. Sidney Colvin (2 vols., Methuen, 1901) II, p. 88; letter of 24 December 1887.

owe its power here to the memory of his troubled but loving relations with his own father. Lord Hermiston is a magnificent creation, with a kind of coarse grandeur that is outside the normal range of characterization in Victorian fiction. There is a new power, too, in his handling of the love-affair between Archie and Kirstie, reminiscent of comparable passages in another novel of father–son conflict that he much admired, *The Ordeal of Richard Feverel,* and a taut symbolic force about the moorland setting where the young lovers meet. The historical associations of their trysting-place, the Weaver's Stone, scene of a Covenanter's murder, serve, like the back-dating to the start of the century, to sink the action in time, giving it an archaic, legendary quality. Character, place and destiny come together in a style that aspires to a tragic impersonality:

> It was late in the afternoon when Archie drew near by the hill path to the Praying Weaver's Stone. The Hags were in shadow. But still, through the gate of the Slap, the sun shot a last arrow, which sped far and straight across the surface of the moss, here and there touching and shining on a tussock, and lighted at length on the gravestone and the small figure awaiting him there. The emptiness and solitude of the great moors seemed to be concentrated there, and Kirstie pointed out by that finger of sunshine for the only inhab-itant. His first sight of her was thus excruciatingly sad, like a glimpse of a world from which all light, comfort, and society were on the point of van-ishing. (ix)

It is difficult to see how Stevenson could have married the static, monu-mental quality of scenes like these to the later action of murder, trial and prison-rescue he had planned, and perhaps it is as well that he did not do so. As it stands, *Weir of Hermiston* is unique in Victorian fiction, as suggestive and unfinished as the fragment of a ballad, 'like the bones of a giant buried there and half dug up. . .naked and imperfect' ('Introduc-tory').

The variety of forms and styles in Stevenson points to something rest-less and unsettled in his imagination which cannot be accounted for entirely in terms of the continual travel in search of health of his later years. It there a central theme, a controlling vision? In so far as we are prepared to consider Stevenson in the light of the aims he set himself, then the best definition remains that of his friend Henry James: 'He would say we ought to make believe that the extraordinary is the best part of life even if it were not, and to do so because the finest feelings – suspense, daring, decision, passion, curiosity, gallantry, eloquence, friendship – are involved in it, and it is of infinite importance that the tradition of these precious things should not perish.'[45] The ordinary universe of Victorian fiction did not leave too much room for these feelings, and Stevenson will always be an important figure because of his attempt, in Chesterton's

---

[45]*Partial Portraits,* p. 166.

words, 'to urge the neglected things'.[46] But even if we miss a controlling centre in his work, or find James's estimate too generous, there is significance in his restless ransacking of popular forms and his stylistic eclecticism. He points the way, not to the Modernists – who might have learned from him, but were put off by the romantic legend of RLS – but to a later generation of novelists living in the aftermath of the Victorian and Modern novel. Writers as different as Graham Greene and Jorge Luis Borges have found his narrative skill and formal self-consciousness, as well as his 'romance conferred on doubtful actions', liberating. If there is life after Joyce, Stevenson has an honoured place among those who have helped novelists to find it.

---

[46] *The Victorian Age in Literature* (Williams & Norgate, 1913), p. 243.

7

The Ache of Modernism: Hardy, Moore, Gissing, Butler and Mary Ward

The revival of romance in the 1880s around the figure of Stevenson is yet another chapter in the continuing debate between 'realism' and 'idealism' in the history of Victorian fiction, sharpened by an awareness of two contemporary developments: the feeling that realism had entered a new and virulent phase with the publication of Zola's novels and Ibsen's plays in translation, and a deepening mood of pessimism in late-Victorian culture. Stevenson's novels promised escape not only from the depressing influence of Zola but from depression itself, from that mood of agnostic anxiety which Hardy in *Tess of the d'Urbervilles* called 'the ache of modernism' (19). 'Modern' in this sense means much what it does in the writings of Matthew Arnold: a prevailing mood of self-consciousness, bewilderment and melancholy brought on by the ebbing of the Sea of Faith, a sense of being stranded between epochs—

> Wandering between two worlds, one dead,
> The other powerless to be born. . .[1]

To wander between two worlds is the peculiar fate of the agnostic intellectual of the period, cut off from the consolations of traditional Christianity by the discoveries of biblical scholarship and Victorian science, but unable to reach a new synthesis which would release energy and optimism. The air of defeat in so many late-Victorian novels is epitomized in the figure of Father Time in *Jude the Obscure*, the child prematurely aware of life's sorrow and evanescence, harbinger of 'the coming universal wish not to live' (VI, 2). In formal terms, too, these novels seem caught between two worlds, feeling the unavailability of comic resolution as an 'ache', a stasis, and unable to break through into new fictional forms. Victorianism is

---

Texts: References to Gissing's novels are to the first editions; those to Hardy's are to The New Wessex Edition, ed. P.N. Furbank (Macmillan, 1974–). The World's Classics edition of *Esther Waters* has been used, and the Penguin English Library editions of *The Way of All Flesh* and *Helbeck of Bannisdale*.

[1]'Stanzas from the Grande Chartreuse' (1855). Hardy's response to Arnold's ideas, and in particular his theological writings, is explored in David de Laura's valuable article, ' "The Ache of Modernism" in Hardy's Later Novels', *ELH* 34 (1967), pp. 380–99.

rebelled against but rarely transcended, and even the most rebellious of novels, *The Way of All Flesh* or *Jude the Obscure*, exhaust their rebellion in a no-man's-land between the Victorian and the Modern novel.

This mood of stasis and exhaustion is in keeping with the mood of the literary movement known today as Naturalism but then, confusingly, as Realism. It is tempting, and not entirely misleading, to define Naturalism as being like Realism but only more so. The terms were (and are) used interchangeably to describe a literary method which attempts to portray reality objectively, in its ordinary rather than exceptional manifestations, and with an emphasis on the power of environment to condition the individual. Naturalism, however, differs not only in the degree of emphasis it puts on the conditioning power of environment, but also in its underlying ideology, which is that of a scientism derived from biology and applied with aggressive literalism to the human world. Mankind is seen as a species like any other species in nature, subject to evolutionary 'laws' and the determining forces of environment and heredity; and the novelist adopts a stance of scientific objectivity, observing human behaviour with the clinical detachment of an anatomist. So Zola can write of his aims in the famous Preface to the second (1868) edition of *Thérèse Raquin*:

> In *Thérèse Raquin* my aim has been to study temperaments and not characters. That is the whole point of the book. I have chosen people completely dominated by their nerves and blood, without free will, drawn into each action of their lives by the inexorable laws of their physical nature. Thérèse and Laurent are human animals, nothing more. . . .my object has been first and foremost a scientific one. . . .I simply applied to two living bodies the analytical method that surgeons apply to corpses.[2]

This is a deeply depressing view of both human nature and art: to see individuals as devoid of free will and at the mercy of their genes and instincts is to cut oneself off from almost everything that makes them interesting. It is also self-defeating as a programme for fiction, since a stance of value-free detachment is an impossible goal for a creative artist, even if it were desirable. In practice, as Zola's readers discovered, his novels transcended his theories about them, and in Britain, where he was denounced for his subject-matter, he was read, when he was read, in spite of theory. 'The doctrine of M. Zola', Henry James observed with his usual percipience, 'so jejune if literally taken, is fruitful, inasmuch as in practice he romantically departs from it.'[3]

Realism also draws on scientific analogies, as we saw in the case of George Eliot and her attempt to write a 'natural history' of English life in *Adam Bede*. But her scientism was historical and developmental, allowing positivist notions of progress to higher goals and requiring a moral

[2] *Thérèse Raquin*, trans. L. Tancock (Penguin, Harmondsworth, 1962), pp. 22–3.
[3] *The House of Fiction*, ed. L. Edel (Hart-Davis, 1957), p. 131.

engagement with her material. The difference between her brand of moral realism and the later naturalism can be seen by comparing the ending of *Middlemarch* with the ending of Gissing's *The Nether World* (1889), a fine naturalistic novel by a writer who admired George Eliot and seems here to be deliberately echoing the conclusion of her greatest novel:

> In each life little for congratulation. He with the ambitions of his youth frustrated; neither an artist, nor a leader of men in the battle for justice. She, no saviour of society by the force of a superb example; no daughter of the people, holding wealth in trust for the people's needs. Yet to both was their work given. Unmarked, unencouraged save by their love of uprightness and mercy, they stood by the side of those more hapless, brought some comfort to hearts less courageous than their own. Where they abode it was not all dark. Sorrow certainly awaited them, perchance defeat in even the humble aims they had set themselves; but at least their lives would remain a protest against those brute forces of society which fill with wreck the abysses of the nether world.

In contrast to George Eliot's muted faith in the 'unhistoric acts' which will contribute to 'the growing good of the world', Gissing records the stoic dignity of those who cannot hope to change the world, but whose lives 'remain a protest against those brute forces of society'. What makes the difference is, in part, Gissing's awareness of late–Victorian London, which in *The Nether World* is the City of Dreadful Night (Thomson's poem of that name was published in 1874), where those 'brute forces' of the Darwinian struggle for existence could be observed at their most intransigent. The modern city, vast, sprawling, chaotic, seemingly unmanageable, confirmed the impression of mankind as a species swayed by blind forces.

Yet English Naturalism was a relatively short-lived affair. The native tradition of realism was too strong for the movement to have the revolutionary impact it had in France, and was later to have with Joyce in Ireland and Dreiser in the United States. Its main Victorian monuments are *The Nether World* and the early novels of George Moore (1852–1933). Moore had encountered Zolaism directly as a young art student in Paris, and he came to London determined to put the new 'scientific' art into practice. With *A Mummer's Wife* (1885) he produced the first Zolaesque novel in English. It is the story of Kate Ede, a linen draper's wife living in the Potteries, who is seduced by a travelling actor, leaves middle-class respectability for a bohemian life on the stage, and soon degenerates into drunkenness, dying a sordid death which is described in painstaking naturalistic detail. Banned by Mudie's, like its predecessor *A Modern Lover* (1883), *A Mummer's Wife* was the occasion of Moore's pamphlet *Literature at Nurse, or Circulating Morals* (1885), in which he demonstrated that the offending passage in his novel was no stronger than comparable passages in novels Mudie already stocked, and accused him of being a 'narrow-minded tradesman' unfit to wield the power he enjoyed. The pamphlet created a stir (as well as giving some shrewd publicity to the six-shilling first edition of the novel) but it was the success of *Esther Waters* nine years later which forced Mudie and Smith to lift their ban on Moore's work. Gladstone declared his approval, the climate was changing, and Moore himself had changed, dropping the scientific pretensions of naturalism for a more warmly 'English' treatment of his servant-girl heroine.

Esther Waters (1894) makes for a revealing comparison with *Tess of the d'Urbervilles* (1891). Moore read Hardy's novel while he was working on his own and disliked it, and *Esther Waters* can be read as an implicit critique of the more sensational treatment of a similar subject in *Tess*. Tess begins as a dairymaid, Esther as a kitchenmaid; both are girls of simple piety, uneducated, and naive in sexual matters; both are seduced early in their careers, Tess by her employer, Esther by a footman in the house where she is a servant; both become pregnant and give birth to illegitimate children; both make fresh starts thereafter, only through chance encounters to meet their seducers again and be drawn back into living with them. But there is a world of difference in the treatment. For a start, Esther's baby does not conveniently die like Tess's, but lives to become the central care of his mother's life, her struggle to bring him up decently forming the main action of the novel. Her seducer is not a melodramatic villain like Alec d'Urberville but a fellow-servant who loves her in his way, and when he reappears in her life does his best to provide for her and her child until his early death. There is no murder of the seducer, bloodstains on the ceiling, flight from the police and arrest at Stonehenge; no President of the Immortals and 'Fulfilment' (the title of Phase Seven of *Tess*) leading to a tragic death. Esther returns to her first employer at the end, to stay with her in the now deserted big house; her fulfilment is the quiet pride she takes in the son she has reared:

> A tall soldier came through the gate. He wore a long red cloak, and a small cap jauntily set on the side of his close-clipped head. Esther uttered a little exclamation, and ran to meet him. He took his mother in his arms, kissed her, and they walked towards Mrs. Barfield together. All was forgotten in the happiness of the moment – the long fight for his life, and the possibility that any moment might declare him to be mere food for powder and shot. She was only conscious that she had accomplished her woman's work – she had brought him up to man's estate; and that was her sufficient reward. (47)

One is not obliged to choose between the two novels, but there will always be readers for whom *Esther Waters* is the truer book, who are unmoved or even repelled by Hardy's immense act of special pleading on Tess's behalf. Esther too is a heroine, not merely the passive victim of circumstances. 'Hers is a heroic adventure if one considers it – a mother's fight for the life of her child against all the forces that civilization arrays against the lowly and the illegitimate' (20). Esther has unusual powers of endurance and the goodness of her simple piety, but given these endowments, there is nothing improbable in her survival, and the circumstances she has to struggle against are rendered with unsensational exactitude. Moore describes the servant's hall, the working-class home, the maternity hospital, the baby-farm, the injustices of the wet-nursing system, as these appear to the eyes of an illiterate servant-girl anxious for her child and constantly worried about money. There is little symbolism, but a motif of gambling threads the novel together, bringing about the downfall of masters and servants and the failure of the public-house that is Esther's one chance of an independent life, and serving as a kind of implicit metaphor for the instability of life in a chance-directed universe.

When Esther returns to Mrs Barfield at the end, Moore repeats the opening paragraph of the novel: 'She stood on the platform watching the receding train. . .'. The matter-of-factness of that opening, describing Esther's 'short, strong arms and. . .plump neck' and her 'oblong box painted reddish brown and tied with a rough rope' (it reappears at the end), is in marked contrast to the scene in *Tess* where Angel and Tess take the milk to the London train:

> Then there was the hissing of a train, which drew up almost silently upon the wet rails, and the milk was rapidly swung can by can into the truck. The light of the engine flashed for a second upon Tess Durbeyfield's figure, motionless under the great holly tree. No object could have looked more foreign to the gleaming cranks and wheels than this unsophisticated girl, with the round bare arms, the rainy face and hair, the suspended attitude of a friendly leopard at pause, the print gown of no date or fashion, and the cotton bonnet drooping on her brow. (30)

It is impossible to miss the symbolism of this passage. Tess is not, like Esther, simply a girl on a railway platform watching a train. Her 'round bare arms' and leopard's poise is brought into menaced conjunction with those 'gleaming cranks and wheels', and 'the great holly tree' is there to underline the impression that what we are being offered here is the emblem of an archetypal opposition. Tess is 'foreign' to the railway engine because she stands for something at odds with the modern Victorian world it symbolizes: an older, vulnerable world of instinctual living and natural femininity. The central interests of the novel move through this scene and direct our response to it, and we cannot read it, as we cannot read the novel as a whole, in naturalistic terms. *Tess* is a tragic poem in prose. If it is a greater novel than *Esther Waters*, this is because in the last analysis – melodrama, improbabilities and all – it risks more and penetrates more deeply into the life of its time. In this it is characteristic of Hardy's achievement as a whole.

Hardy

It is part of our increasing sense today of the importance of Thomas Hardy (1840–1928) that so many of the characteristic concerns of late-Victorian culture should find a place in his work. He is a novelist of provincial life in the tradition of George Eliot, and also of country life, sharing with writers like Richard Jefferies, the author of *Bevis* (1882) and *Amaryllis at the Fair* (1887), a concern for the changing ways of rural England at the end of the century. He was a late-Victorian intellectual, and more impressively one than is often allowed, who continued to keep abreast with 'advanced' thought from Darwin and Mill in the 1860s to Bergson and Einstein in the early twentieth century. His novels are at the centre of both the woman question and tragedy in this period, and the two subjects are inseparably linked in *Tess* and *Jude the Obscure*. Although he rejected the aesthetic premises of Naturalism, traces of its influence can be found in his later novels, and its philosophical basis – the theories of evolutionary biology – are present in his fiction almost from the start. Indeed, if we wish to know why tragedy makes such a decisive appearance in Hardy's novels after the muted tragic sense of George Eliot, part of the answer lies in his troubled response to the evolutionary world view.

The Life of Thomas Hardy by his second wife, which we now know was written largely by Hardy himself, records that 'As a young man he had been among the earliest acclaimers of *The Origin of Species*'.[4] He remained loyal to this intellectual discovery for the rest of his life. When a clergyman wrote to him of his problems in reconciling 'the horrors of human and animal life, particularly parasitic. . .with the absolute goodness and non-limitation of God', Hardy replied that he was unable to reconcile them, but that 'Perhaps Dr. Grosart might be helped to a provisional view of the universe by the recently published Life of Darwin, and the works of Herbert Spencer and other agnostics'.[5] Hardy did not of course need Darwin to teach him that life for the majority of creatures on earth was a harsh struggle for survival. Two of his abiding childhood memories were of a bird his father killed with a stone on a bitterly cold day which they then discovered to be 'all skin and bone, practically starved', and of a local boy who had died of starvation, the post-mortem revealing nothing but raw turnips in his stomach.[6] But *The Origin of Species* provided a systematic explanation of this 'struggle for existence', as Darwin called his third chapter. The natural world might seem 'bright with gladness' but in reality it was a battleground. 'Lighten any check, mitigate the destruction ever so little, and the number of the species will almost instantaneously increase to any amount. The face of Nature may be compared to a yielding

---

[4]F.E. Hardy, *The Life of Thomas Hardy* (Macmillan, 1962), p. 153. Hereafter cited as *Life*.
[5]*Life*, p. 205.
[6]*Life*, pp. 444, 312.

surface, with ten thousand sharp wedges packed close together and driven inwards by incessant blows, sometimes one wedge being struck, and then another with greater force.'[7] Darwin gave the name Natural Selection to the process by which, in the wasteful fecundity of nature, the chance variation of a species favourable to further adaptation and development was preserved. It was in this way, by chance mutation over immense stretches of time, that life on earth had developed, and that individual species had grown up, changed and become extinct.

Hardy was peculiarly well placed to take the full disturbing impact of the Darwinian theory. An heir, like his contemporaries, to both the Christian view of Providence and the special creation of man, and the Romantic or Wordsworthian view of the natural world as morally and spiritually beneficent, he was also by choice and temperament a novelist of rural life rather than of the city where Zola and Gissing made their naturalistic readings of life. He classified his Wessex novels as 'Novels of Character and Environment',[8] and the environment through which his characters move is a natural landscape seen intermittently through the Darwinian lens. This new evolutionary perspective encouraged a shift in the novel from society to the human condition. By heightening awareness of mankind as a species, it helped foster a sense of life as a general condition obeying universal laws. In Hardy's novels we are aware of more than individual men and women living their lives in society; we are aware of mankind, the human predicament. This is potentially a tragic perception, and in Hardy's case cannot be separated from consideration of the mode of vision peculiar to his novels.

Our typical impression of a Hardy novel is of a narrator/observer who stands at a distance from his characters and observes their movements against a large background of earth and sky and through a long temporal perspective. W.H. Auden spoke of his 'hawk's vision, his way of looking at life from a very great height'.[9] One thinks of Eustacia Vye at the start of *The Return of the Native*:

> There the form stood, motionless as the hill beneath. Above the plain rose the hill, above the hill rose the barrow, and above the barrow rose the figure. Above the figure was nothing that could be mapped elsewhere than on a celestial globe. (I, 2)

That effortless shift from the terrestrial to the cosmic is Hardy's artistic 'signature', and it comes in part from the distance at which he stands from his created world. His narrative stance sometimes suggests the detachment of a scientist taking his readings of natural phenomena, and in defence of

[7] *The Origin of Species*, ed. J.W. Burrow (Penguin, Harmondsworth, 1968), p. 119.
[8] See his General Preface to the Wessex Edition of 1912.
[9] 'A Literary Transference', *The Southern Review* VI (1940); reprinted in A.J. Guerard (ed.), *Hardy: A Collection of Critical Essays* (Prentice-Hall, Englewood Cliffs, NJ, 1963), p. 139.

his art against those who wanted to pin him down to a philosophy he would stress its provisional character, as of a scientist carefully recording effects but holding back from conclusions. (The scientific analogy is implicit and metaphorical in Hardy's case, rather than explicit and programmatic as in Zola's.) A novel is 'an impression, not an argument' (1892 Preface to *Tess*), 'a series of seemings' (Preface to *Jude*). The 'road to a true philosophy of life', he wrote in the Preface to *Poems of the Past and Present* (1901), 'seems to lie in humbly recording diverse readings of its phenomena.' The scene on which this observer looks down is one of evolutionary struggle. The trees Grace Melbury notices in the woods are 'close together, wrestling for existence, their branches disfigured with wounds resulting from their mutual rubbings and blows' (*Woodlanders*, 42). The dairymaids in *Tess* pine hopelessly for Angel Clare, and Hardy comments that 'They writhed feverishly under the oppressiveness of an emotion thrust on them by cruel Nature's law' (23). And society also shows its surviving and defeated species, like the reddleman in *The Return of the Native* – 'a curious, interesting, and nearly perished link between obsolete forms of life and those which generally prevail' (I, 2). It is the evolutionary perspective which enables us to see these figures as both individuals and participants in a larger cosmic drama. Men and women are, so to speak, silhouetted in Hardy as not before in Victorian fiction.

The heightened vulnerability of Hardy's characters is reflected in the prominence he gives to plot in his novels. He recovered the resources of melodrama from the sensation novel of the 1860s, and sensational elements are never far away even in his greatest novels. *Tess* is not usually thought of in these terms, yet it deals in murder and adultery, the motif of blood runs throughout the narrative, and the plot, it has been shown, has a good deal in common with Mary Braddon's well-known sensation novel *Aurora Floyd* (1863).[10] Violent incidents and elaborate plots were means by which Hardy escaped from the plainness of the realistic novel, but they also reflect his metaphysic, his sense of men and women at the mercy of forces larger than themselves. E.S. Dallas's comment on the sensation novel in the 1860s reads like a prophecy of Hardy's novels:

> In the novel of character man appears moulding circumstances to his will, directing the action for himself, supreme over incident and plot. In the opposite class of novel [sensation] man is represented as made and ruled by circumstance; he is the victim of change and the puppet of intrigue.[11]

The sensation novel restored the primacy of plot and the subservience of character to event, and Hardy, turning his back on the high Victorian novel of character, found in it a way of expressing his sense of human destiny in the evolutionary universe. He wrote in 1888: 'A "sensation-

[10]See Winifred Hughes, *The Maniac in the Cellar*, pp. 187–9.
[11]*The Gay Science*, II, p. 293.

novel" is possible in which sensationalism is not casualty, but evolution.'[12]

Hardy's response to Darwin and other evolutionary writers contributed to the cosmic sweep of his fiction, and to his sense of tragedy as a general condition, but it was marked by ambivalence and resistances too. He spoke of his 'infinite trying to reconcile a scientific view of life with the emotional and spiritual',[13] and his novels record that struggle. Just as he did not lose his religious sense by losing his faith, so he retained some of the Wordsworthian sense of a beneficence in nature in the teeth of Darwinian theory, as *Tess* shows. His novels are an affirmation of the 'emotional and spiritual' in the face of scientific determinism; his chance-driven plots test his tragic heroes and heroines to breaking-point, but they refuse to accept the anonymity and insignificance of their biological destiny, asserting a precious individuality to which the Life Force is seemingly indifferent. So, at the end of *The Mayor of Casterbridge*, the defeated Henchard can shoulder his rush-basket and declare, ' "But my punishment is *not* greater than I can bear!" ' (43), and even in the act of writing his will requesting that 'no man remember me', sign it with his name in capital letters – 'MICHAEL HENCHARD' (45).[14]

Hardy's hawk's vision is compassionate, but it is not morally engaged in the way previous Victorian novelists were. 'He is concerned with life as a spectacle,' P.N. Furbank writes, 'a spectacle engaging our deepest feelings and appealing to our imagination but not capable of providing lessons . . . .It can only confuse us to think of him in the humanistic and moralistic tradition of George Eliot and Dickens.'[15] Life seen as a spectacle is life seen in its comic as well as its tragic aspects, and with an eye for the picturesque and the grotesque. Dickens and George Eliot could never have described the drowned Eustacia as Hardy does, noting the beauty of her complexion, the 'pleasant' expression of 'her finely carved mouth', and the fact that the 'stateliness of look which had been almost too marked for a dweller in a country domicile had at last found an artistically happy background' (*Return*, V, 9). The presence of aesthetic values at this moment is a reminder that Hardy belongs to the age of Pater as well as to the age of Darwin. He has something of the painter's eye for bright sensuous particulars and for the compositional qualities of a scene, and he cannot resist the incongruously picturesque. The fact that the death of the Durbeyfield horse is to be the trigger of Tess's downfall does not deter him from recording the strange sight of the horse being carted away: 'All that was left of Prince was now hoisted into the wagon he had formerly hauled, and with

[12]*Life*, p. 204.
[13]*Life*, p. 148.
[14]A point well made by Roger Robinson in his excellent essay on 'Hardy and Darwin' in *Thomas Hardy: The Writer and his Background*, ed. N. Page (Bell & Hyman, 1980), pp. 128–50.
[15]Introduction to *Tess* (Macmillan paperback edn, 1974), p. 12.

his hoofs in the air, and his shoes shining in the setting sunlight, he retraced the eight or nine miles to Marlott' (4). Comic, poetic and grotesque, the detail is as quintessentially Hardyan in its delight in incongruity as the great scene in *The Return of the Native* where Wildeve and Diggory Venn dice on the heath by the light of glowworms:

> The incongruity between the men's deeds and their environment was great. Amid the soft juicy vegetation of the hollow in which they sat, the motionless and the uninhabited solitude, intruded the chink of guineas, the rattle of dice, the exclamations of the reckless players. (III, 8)

Such visual incongruities reinforce the deeper incongruities of destiny in his work, the irony at the heart of things. Hardy is a much more thorough-going ironist than any other Victorian novelist apart from Thackeray, from whom he obviously learnt much in this respect. His novels are propelled by the ironies of desire, as his characters invariably seek (or in Tess's case, get) the wrong mate, or discover too late who they really love; and by the irony within desire, as Hardy sees it, his belief that 'Love lives on propinquity, but dies of contact'.[16] And the perception of incongruity is behind his quarrel with the equable surface of mid-Victorian realism, his repeatedly stated conviction that 'Art is a disproportioning – (*i.e.* distorting, throwing out of proportion) – of realities, to show more clearly the features that matter in those realities'.[17]

Hardy's greatness is bound up with his creation and elaboration of that 'partly real, partly dream country' he called Wessex, the most distinctive region in English fiction.[18] His attitude to Wessex combines the detachment of the disenchanted intellectual with the inwardness of a local man who has moved among the people he describes, and his development takes the form of a steadily deepening imaginative possession of this territory. What begins in *Under the Greenwood Tree* and *Far From the Madding Crowd* as a version of Victorian pastoral ends in *Tess* and *Jude* carrying the full burden of contemporary angst, the ache of modernism. The ache is scarcely felt in *Far from the Madding Crowd* (1874), which celebrates enduring and restorative rural stabilities in a manner reminiscent of *Adam Bede* and *Silas Marner*. Yet to compare Hardy with George Eliot, as the first reviewers inevitably did, is to become aware of two important differences: the greater authenticity in his evocation of rural life and labour, and the power of sexual passion in his novel. The first gives us the great set-piece descriptions of the sheep-shearing (22), and Gabriel Oak's rescue of the sheep (21) and of the ricks from the storm (37); the second shows in Hardy's unmoralizing understanding of sexual obsession, so different

[16]*Life*, p. 220.
[17]*Life*, p. 229. See also pp. 150, 185 and many other places where Hardy's dissatisfaction with the tenets of realism is expressed.
[18]See his Preface to *Far from the Madding Crowd*.

from George Eliot's finger-wagging treatment of Hetty and Arthur. It is worth noting that the gain in directness here is achieved not by any greater explicitness of treatment, but comes from Hardy's command of the symbolism inherent in the elements of melodrama and folk-tale he characteristically draws on. The famous scene of Troy's swordplay before the awed and finally overwhelmed Bathsheba (28) is an excellent example of the power of suggestion available to a pre-Freudian author working well within the confines set by Mudie's and the three-decker.

Far from the Madding Crowd portrays a world in balance. Boldwood's obsession with Bathsheba has a tragic outcome, but is contained within the customary mixed form in which the faithful lover, Gabriel Oak, wins the fair lady. Subsequent novels move closer to tragedy by bringing the conflict between traditional and modern to the centre of the stage, and by making it increasingly the catalyst of tragic feeling and event. Clym Yeobright in *The Return of the Native* (1878) is Hardy's first attempt to portray a specifically modern form of consciousness in interaction with traditional ways, but his 'culture scheme' (IV, 2) for the locals is very unsatisfactorily handled in the novel, and the tragic import of the theme is developed not through the myopic Clym but through the disappointment which the restless Eustacia finds in her marriage to him. Far from initiating change in Egdon Heath, this man who has lived in Paris digs back into his roots by becoming a furze-cutter – 'a mere parasite of the heath, fretting its surface in his daily labour as a moth frets a garment' (IV, 5) – while the unwillingly rooted Eustacia feels all the bitterness of betrayed hopes when she finds the promised escape-route of marriage a dead-end. The further, tragic irony is that she is more deeply bound to the life of the heath than she knows, an impression established as early as the second chapter when her emblematic silhouette on Rainbarrow appears 'an organic part of the entire motionless structure', completing its shape 'like a spike from a helmet'. Both rooted and restless, it is Eustacia rather than Clym who comes closest to realizing the 'tragical possibilities' (I, 1) legible on the face of the heath. The modern theme, like Clym's scholar-gipsy ambition, remains undeveloped.

With his next Wessex novel, *The Mayor of Casterbridge* (1886), Hardy found a more satisfying embodiment of the conflict between the traditional and the modern. The rise and fall of Michael Henchard, the itinerant hay-trusser become grain merchant and Mayor, is subtitled 'The Story of a Man of Character', and character in its traditional sense counts for more in this novel than it usually does in Hardy. 'Character is Fate', he comments (17), quoting Novalis, and Henchard's character is displayed in all its reckless will and energy in the first chapters, when he sells his wife and daughter in a bout of drunkenness and then takes an oath forswearing drink for 21 years. This folk-tale opening creates a legendary atmosphere which enriches and deepens the account of his downfall. Henchard is an early-

Victorian self-made man who is supplanted by the young Scot, Donald Farfrae, and the new methods and technology he brings to the Casterbridge grain business; but he is also Saul to Farfrae's David,[19] the old leader supplanted by the new, and a casualty of social evolution in a landscape littered with such casualties. The perspective is archaeological, as Hardy cuts beneath the surface of Wessex to reveal the layered past. 'Casterbridge announced old Rome in every street, alley, and precinct. It looked Roman, bespoke the art of Rome, concealed dead men of Rome' (11). Henchard meets his wife again in the Roman Amphitheatre (11), and when she dies her 'dust mingled with the dust of women who lay ornamented with glass hair-pins and amber necklaces, and men who held in their mouths coins of Hadrian, Posthumus, and the Constantines' (20). Beneath the Roman past is a more distant pagan past shading into the mists of pre-history. Henchard's last wandering takes him away from Roman Casterbridge to the primeval landscape north of Egdon Heath, to 'that ancient country whose surface never had been stirred to a finger's depth, save by the scratchings of rabbits, since brushed by the feet of the earliest tribes' (45). In this way the Wessex landscape defines, dignifies and universalizes the nineteenth-century tragedy, setting Henchard's defeat in a long series of similar supplantings.

The Mayor of Casterbridge is a key text in considerations of Hardy as a novelist of social change, and can usefully be studied in connection with his essay on 'The Dorsetshire Labourer' (1883) and his letter of 1902 to Rider Haggard on this subject.[20] The relative neutrality of these statements, and the careful impartiality of the novel itself, where Farfrae is portrayed as a decent if limited man, unwilling to oust his former friend and employer, should put us on our guard against a too elegiac reading of this theme in the novel. Henchard, after all, the 'self-alienated man' (45), brings many of his woes on himself. And yet one cannot read the novel sympathetically without feeling that Henchard is a larger man than Farfrae, and that in his passing something of unique value has gone. The loss cannot be expressed easily in moral or sociological terms. Farfrae will make a better corn-merchant than Henchard, a better husband and a better Mayor, but he lacks his rival's wholeness and fullness of being. Farfrae is the professional exile, his feelings are available to him to turn on and off at will, like his sentimental songs of Scotland, and the scene in which he is heard singing 'The Lass of Gowrie' from inside the mechanical seed-drill (24) establishes the link between his modernity of feeling and his role as social innovator with Hardy's characteristic symbolic expressiveness. Henchard's susceptibility to music, on the other hand, his helplessness before melody, is a sign of the integrity of feeling and action in his character;

[19]See Julian Moynahan, '*The Mayor of Casterbridge* and the Old Testament's First Book of Samuel', *PMLA* 71 (1956), pp. 118–30.

[20]See *Life*, pp. 312–14; also Select Bibliography for relevant articles and books on this topic.

and it aligns him with features in the traditional rural culture which Hardy sees as doomed – with physical and intuitive ways of doing business, with the old-fashioned rural customs (Henchard's public 'entertainment' offers the old village sports, free; Farfrae offers dancing in a tent, and charges), and with magic and superstition, pagan survivals in the Wessex world which are especially prominent here. What goes down with the defeat of this 'Man of Character' is not so much a way of life as a way of feeling and being, a certain deep-seated vitality of instinctive life – felt in his physical strength and in our sense of him at the end as a 'netted lion' (42) – which has its roots in a pre-industrial world.

The action of *The Mayor of Casterbridge* takes place in the 1840s, that of *Tess of the d'Urbervilles* (1891) in the near-present, in the Wessex world that has come about as a consequence of the social changes seen to be set in motion in the earlier novel. It is Hardy's most deeply felt work, drawing into the sensuously imagined figure of the heroine all his creative interests. Tess is seen from many angles. She is a heroine of ballad and folk tale, the 'maid who went to the merry green wood and came back a changed state' (14). She is the heroine of a Victorian sensation novel which might be called 'The Woman Pays' (the title Hardy gave to Phase the Fifth), a story of betrayal and revenge ending on the scaffold. Then there is Tess the victim of modern society, both as the representative of a rural way of life increasingly vulnerable and uprooted in the industrial age, and as the victim of double standards in contemporary Victorian attitudes to sex and religion – Alec D'Urberville representing the one, Angel Clare the other. There is Tess the victim of heredity, playing out the last tragic act of the d'Urberville destiny; and Tess the evolutionary victim, hunted from her territory and brought to bay on the sacrificial stone at Stonehenge. These different aspects of her destiny are not given equal prominence, and they are not always in play at the same time, but their presence is a sign of the richness of Hardy's conception. His ability to concentrate so many meanings in a single character comes from the intense sensuous immediacy with which he imagined her and the landscape in which she moves, a landscape which simultaneously figures her nature and defines her tragic predicament.

Like *Jane Eyre* and so many other works of the period, *Tess* is a novel of pilgrimage, and the allegorical meaning of its various stages and places is unusually plain: we are much closer to *Pilgrim's Progress* than we expect to be in a novel of this date, and like the folk-tale elements, this contributes an archaic feel to the narrative. We read Tess's unfolding destiny in the places she lives in or passes through: her childhood home in the Vale of Blackmoor, 'an engirdled and secluded region' (2); her journey to The Slopes, the fake farm of the Stoke-d'Urbervilles, 'which rose like a geranium bloom against the subdued colours around' (5), and her seduction in the primeval setting of The Chase; the rising sap and flowing juices of Talbothays Farm at midsummer where she stages her 'Rally' and feels 'the invincible instinct towards self-delight' (15) stirring in her again; the starve-acre grimness of the swede-field at Flintcomb-Ash, a face without features over which Tess and Marian are seen crawling 'like flies' (43). An art so pictorial and allegorical does not lend itself easily to the portrayal of fluctuating movements of character, nor to the kind of speculation which goes with the novel of character about how tragedy might have been avoided had Tess acted differently at certain points. Hardy occasionally gestures towards such a reading of Tess's fate – her 'feminine loss of courage' (44), for instance, in judging the likely response of Angel's father by his priggish brothers – but most of the time she is presented as an exemplary figure: exemplary in her honesty, her purity in refusing to keep hidden the impurity she has suffered, her powers of endurance and capacity for love and constancy. Being as she is, Tess is necessarily in conflict with the modern Victorian world, and the novel's greatest scenes display that necessary opposition with emblematic force. When Tess on the threshing-machine swings her glove-gauntlet, 'heavy and thick as a warrior's' (47), in Alec's face, the different strands in Hardy's conception of her fuse in an action of great symbolic resonance – Tess the violated maid of ballad, Tess the victim of modern economic forces, Tess the last of the d'Urbervilles, but also Tess rebelling against her imprisonment, striking out and drawing blood. Similarly, when the police come over the dawn horizon to arrest her at Stonehenge (58), we are aware of a tragedy that is both historically specific and timeless, the victim of the modern world who is at one with the victims of pagan Britain. The knowledge of tragic recurrence written into the Wessex landscape makes Tess's fate richly symbolic. A character who, like Henchard, is intensely susceptible to music and in touch with the old world of folklore and superstition, who suffers in the body and whose career is shadowed by the motif of blood, Tess is finally seen as a sacrificial victim in the world of the railway train and the threshing machine, and what is sacrificed is the fullness and purity of her passional being, which that world is hostile to and is driven to violate.

In *Tess* the modern is inescapable. The *nouveau riche* Alec and the mechanical threshing-machine are only the more dramatic manifestations of a new order whose self-division can be traced in the refined sensibility of Angel Clare as well. In *Jude the Obscure* (1894–5) the self-division of the modern consciousness becomes the central subject of the novel, and Wessex shrinks from the richly figured allegorical landscape of *Tess* to the Great Wessex Agricultural Show, which Jude and Sue visit by excursion train (V, 5). It is now a place of large towns linked by railways, and these give their names to the different parts of the novel – Aldbrickham (Reading), Christminster (Oxford), Melchester (Salisbury). Contrast and division marked Hardy's original conception. 'Of course the book is all contrasts', he wrote to Edmund Gosse. '. . .Sue and her heathen gods set against Jude's reading the Greek testament; Christminster academical, Christminster in the slums; Jude the saint, Jude the sinner; Sue the Pagan, Sue the saint; marriage, no marriage; &c., &c..'[21] Although the Arabella–Jude–Sue triangle repeats the Alec–Tess–Angel triangle of *Tess*, the contrast between the earthly partner (Arabella) and the spiritual (Sue) is more extreme, and Jude is radically divided between flesh and spirit as Tess is not. The contrasts in the book are a sign of strain in Hardy's relation to his fictional world, a strain also reflected in the tone of bitter, sometimes jeering pessimism in his handling of marriage and institutional Christianity. 'What has Providence done to Mr. Hardy that he should rise up in the arable land of Wessex and shake his fist at his Creator?', Gosse asked, and many readers have shared his perplexity.[22] The novel has no answer to that question, nor to the problems faced by the central characters, who are indeed 'wandering between two worlds', a fossilized past and an unreachable future. Jude can see the emptiness of his dream of becoming a Christminster don, and has a 'true illumination' that the stonemason's yard 'was a centre of effort as worthy as that dignified by the name of scholarly study within the noblest of the colleges' (II, 2), but a dead medievalism holds his imagination even after he has lost the faith that originally animated it, and he returns to Christminster to die. Sue travels in the opposite direction intellectually, from Swinburnian Hellenism to dogmatic Christianity, but at the cost of violating her true being by returning to a husband she finds repulsive. 'The letter killeth', as the book's epigraph has it. In Hardy's last novel there is nowhere for the troubled modern spirit to go. It is significant that in this world of railway travelling the effect of the many journeys undertaken by the central characters should be to return them, exhausted and defeated, to their starting-points: Sue to Phillotson, Jude to Arabella and death in the hearing of the college festivities he has never been able to join.

Jude stands at the centre of our understanding of English fiction in the 1890s. Other novelists were treating the subject of the emancipated woman – Gissing in *The Emancipated* (1890) and *The Odd Women* (1893), 'Mark Rutherford' in *Clara Hopgood* (1896) – but none explored so thoroughly as Hardy did in Sue the human cost of living out the premises of sexual and religious emancipation. The conflict between belief and scepticism had been handled before, but not interwoven with the tensions of intimate human relationships as Hardy shows it in Jude and Sue. The figure of the young man of humble origins seeking to educate himself is a familiar one in Victorian fiction, but Hardy gave it a contemporary twist by focusing on the deadlock between intellectual ambition and educational

[21] *Life*, pp. 272–3.
[22] In a review of *Jude the Obscure* in *Cosmopolis*, January 1896: see *Thomas Hardy: The Critical Heritage*, ed. R.G. Cox (Routhedge & Kegan Paul 1970), p. 269.

opportunity, so crucial for those like Jude who were the disappointed heirs of the 1870 Education Act. In all these respects *Jude* is the most topical of Hardy's novels, and it was also his last. Its anguished contraries take his fictional universe, and the world of the Victorian novel as a whole, to a point of no return, and I want to end this study by looking briefly at three novels of the time which develop aspects of the contemporary crisis which *Jude* embodies and explores. Each is a work with significant autobiographical elements, each deals centrally with the religious issue, and each portrays a character at odds with his or her environment, experiencing, and failing to resolve, the conflict between modern forms of consciousness and traditional ways and beliefs.

Conclusion: Three Late Victorian Novels

The first of these is *Born in Exile* (1892) by George Gissing (1857–1903). It is customary to regard *New Grub Street* (1891) as his best novel, and certainly it is almost the only one in which his drab but honest vision of human failure is raised to the level of objective art. But in many ways *Born in Exile* is the deeper book, since it gives definitive expression to what Gissing himself recognized as his chief subject, the plight of 'a class of young men distinctive of our time – well educated, fairly bred, but *without money*'.[23] Like his creator, Godwin Peak is a young man from the lower middle classes, brilliant, arrogant and freethinking, who when the novel opens is a student at Whitelaw College (based on Owens College, Manchester). Gissing was expelled from Owens because at the age of 18 he fell in love with a prostitute and, quite uncharacteristically, stole from his fellow-students to support her. Godwin Peak leaves Whitelaw through shame rather than guilt, because his vulgar cockney uncle plans to set up a cheap eating-house opposite the college gates. He is obsessed with class, declaring his hatred of 'low, uneducated people' (I, 2), and he is just as contemptuous of organized religion, despising the 'pious jugglery' (II, 1) of those who attempt to reconcile evolutionary theory with Christian revelation. But just as Jude finds his flesh at war with his intellect, so Peak's corruscating rationalism and hatred of intellectual convention coexists with admiration for, and even idealization of the cultured middle-class home from which he feels excluded by poverty and class. His ambition is to marry a lady, and when he meets one, the sister of a college friend, and sees her in the civilizing context of her home (II, 4), he conceives a daring plan: he will render himself fit to marry her through the one route to gentility open to him, by becoming a clergyman of the Established Church. The novel tells the story of that deceit and its unmasking by the girl's brother. *Born in Exile* has something in common with earlier novels

[23]See John Halperin, *Gissing: A Life in Books* (Oxford, OUP, 1982), p. 213.

on a similar theme, such as *Alton Locke* and *Great Expectations*, but Godwin Peak stands apart from his predecessors by virtue of the ruthless intellectual logic he brings to his predicament. He is not tender-minded like Alton, Pip or Hyacinth Robinson; he does not, like Jude, tiptoe round the earthworms for fear of treading on them; he accepts the implications of the evolutionary universe and acts accordingly, pursuing his conventional goal with a Nietzschean indifference to the usual Victorian agnostic longings and regrets. Gissing's portrayal of this arrogant, doomed character is something quite unusual, even unique, in Victorian fiction. For a comparable understanding of the nihilist implications of the rationalist position one has to turn to the great Russian novels Gissing read and admired before writing *Born in Exile* – to Bazarov in Turgenev's *Fathers and Sons* and Raskolnikov in *Crime and Punishment*.

Exile from the middle-class home is also the fate, but the wished-for fate, of Ernest Pontifex in *The Way of All Flesh* (1903) by Samuel Butler (1835–1902). Whereas Godwin Peak looks longingly in on the charmed circle of the clerical Warricombe family, seeing it as 'the best result of civilization in an age devoted to material progress' (II, 4), to Ernest and Butler it is a machine for the manufacture of hypocrisy and unhappiness. The novel stands the Victorian *bildungsroman* on its head. Instead of the usual progress of a lonely child through rebellion and the education of the heart to love, marriage and the experience of moral and spiritual maturing, Ernest proceeds by unlearning the pieties of home and public school, and discovering through imprisonment and a failed marriage to a working-class girl that life's true goal is to be a worldly bachelor like his friend Towneley. He learns the very unVictorian 'wisdom' of the narrator, his guardian Overton, that 'Pleasure, after all, is a safer guide than either right or duty' (19). His final destination in the novel, life in chambers on the inheritance his guardian has preserved for him, is curiously similar to the country-cottage version of bachelor life in Gissing's *The Private Papers of Henry Ryecroft* (1903), and suggests that Hardy's 'coming universal wish not to live' was also a wish not to marry – there is a strong vein of misogyny in the *fin-de-siècle* agnostic temperament. *The Way of All Flesh* was a profoundly liberating book for its first readers, and we can still feel that power in the vigour of its irony and the mercilessness of its caricature. Mr Pontifex thrashing the infant Ernest for being unable to pronounce 'come' and then ringing the bell for family prayers, 'red-handed as he was' (22), is a memorable satirical icon, but it has only a fraction of the dramatic power of the similar scene in *David Copperfield* (4). Butler's characters are simple and one-dimensional in a rather old-fashioned way, suggesting that his own affinities were with eighteenth-century moralists like Fielding and Gibbon (it is significant that Ernest's development should be backward, into the kindly worldliness of his great-grandfather). The argument matters more than the characters, and turns out to be not a very good argument after all. To replace Theobald Pontifex with Townely, the spiritual bully with the man-about-town, is to exchange one impoverished way of life for another. As a credible moral alternative to Victorianism, Ernest's later life of epicurean bachelorhood, with his two natural children safely farmed out, is a symbol of exhaustion, not new life.

The Bloomsbury which welcomed *The Way of All Flesh* so enthusiastically treated the work of Mrs Humphry Ward (1851–1920) with disdain, seeing her as the humourless embodiment of a dying Victorianism. It is true that her novels lack the wit and sparkle of Butler, and her best-known work, *Robert Elsmere*, has dated in the way that only the topical bestseller can date. Yet there is at least one of her books, *Helbeck of Bannisdale* (1898), which deserves to be rescued from the wreck of her reputation. A good case can be made for considering it the finest novel of religious conflict in the period. It has a grand and enduring subject – the clash between free thought and Catholic authority and tradition – successfully realized in character and action, and carried through to an inevitable tragic conclusion. No Victorian novel fulfils better the Hegelian notion of tragedy as the 'collision of equally justified powers and individuals'.[24] *Helbeck* is the story of Laura Fountain, the daughter of a freethinking Cambridge scientist, who after her father's death goes with her stepmother to stay with her stepmother's brother in Westmorland. Alan Helbeck is a devout Catholic squire from an old recusant family, living a lonely and austere life on his impoverished estate, Bannisdale. Opposites attract and they fall in love, but after a painful struggle Laura finds that she cannot bring herself to accept Helbeck's religion, and commits suicide. It was a subject, Mary Ward wrote, which 'seemed to challenge the modern in oneself',[25] and it had autobiographical roots: she was drawing on memories of her own father, Thomas Arnold (Matthew's brother), and his lifelong fascination with Newman and Catholicism which had caused bitter unhappiness to her Huguenot mother. But the autobiographical element, like the intellectual conflict, is transmuted into art. It is not just that she presents Helbeck's Catholicism with sympathetic insight and intellectual fairness, she also 'challenges the modern' in Laura by showing how a background of free thought has left her without resources in the crisis of her life. Like Sue Bridehead, Laura is torn between intellectual negation and emotional need, and her tragedy is that the father she has lost and the father she finds in Helbeck pull in opposite directions. She is destroyed by forces larger than herself, by the hostile traditions of free thought and Catholicism inscribed in their natures – 'those facts of character and individuality. . .which are always, and in all cases, the true facts of the world' (V, 3). The tragic effect is enhanced by the powerful symbolic presence of the Westmorland landscape in the novel, as Laura is drawn by its intimations

---

[24]Quoted in R.P.: Draper (ed.), *Tragedy: Developments in Criticism* (Macmillan, 1980), p. 113.
[25]From her Introduction to the Westmorland Edition (1911–12).

of transcendent grandeur and freedom to her death by drowning at the end, a 'blind witness to august things'.

Hardy looks forward to D.H. Lawrence, Samuel Butler to E.M. Forster; Mary Ward in her finest novel looks back – to the moral earnestness and intellectual ambition of George Eliot in *Middlemarch*, and to Charlotte Brontë in *Villette*. Hers is a lesser achievement, needless to say, but it is an achievement in a similar mode, and may therefore serve as a fitting conclusion to the present study. As the English novel passes into the twentieth century, to a new and more challenging sense of Modernism than Matthew Arnold or his niece knew, *Helbeck of Bannisdale* is a reminder of the strength, seriousness and humanity of the high Victorian tradition.

Select Bibliography

Abbreviations

NCF   *Nineteenth Century Fiction*
PMLA *Publications of the Modern Languages Association of America*
RES   *Review of English Studies*
VS   *Victorian Studies*

Bibliographies

The standard reference work for the period is vol. III (1800–1900) of *The New Cambridge Bibliography of English Literature,* edited by George Watson. More detailed guidance to scholarship and criticism can be found in *Victorian Fiction: A Guide to Research,* edited by Lionel Stevenson (Cambridge, Mass., Harvard UP, 1964), and its sequel, *Victorian Fiction: A Second Guide to Research,* edited by G.H. Ford (New York, Modern Languages Association of America, 1978). A guide to more recent work in the field can be found in the comprehensive annual bibliographies in the journal *Victorian Studies.* Shorter works of reference are A.E. Dyson (ed.), *The English Novel: A Select Bibliographical Guide* (OUP, 1974) and *The Novel to 1900* volume in the 'Great Writers Student Library', edited by James Vinson and introduced by A.O.J. Cockshut (Macmillan, 1980).

There are a number of annotated bibliographies of writing on individual novelists, which include the following: A. Passel, *Charlotte and Emily Bronte* (New York, Garland, 1979); C.M. Fulmer, *George Eliot: A Reference Guide* (Boston, G.K. Hall, 1977); R.L. Selig, *Elizabeth Gaskell: A Reference Guide* (Boston, G.K. Hall, 1977), and J. Welch, *Elizabeth Gaskell: 1929–1975* (New York, Garland, 1977); J.L. Wolff, *George Gissing* (De Kalb, Northern Illinois UP, 1974); W.E. Davis and H.E. Gerber, *Thomas Hardy* (2 vols., De Kalb, Northern Illinois UP, 1973, 1983); J.C. Olmsted, *George Meredith: 1925–1975* (New York, Garland, 1978); D. Flamm, *Thackeray's Critics: 1836–1901* (Chapel Hill, University of North Carolina Press, 1967), and J.C. Olmsted, *Thackeray and his Twentieth-Century Critics: 1900–1975* (New York, Garland, 1977); J.C. Olmsted and J.E. Welch, *The Reputation of Trollope: 1925–1975* (New York, Garland, 1978). The secondary literature on Dickens is now so vast that no single bibliography is likely to be comprehensive, a fact recognized by the setting up of the *Garland Dickens Bibliographies* series, under the general editorship of Duane De Vries: individual volumes on *David Copperfield, Hard Times, Our Mutual Friend* and *The Christmas Books* have so far appeared.

General Histories

The best single-volume history remains Walter Allen's *The English Novel* (1954; Harmondsworth, Penguin, 1958). Michael Wheeler, *English Fiction of the Victorian Period 1830-1890* (Longman, 1985) is a good survey of the field, with useful bibliographical and biographical sections. Ernest Baker's 10-volume *History of the English Novel* (Witherby, 1924-39) is comprehensive but now rather dated, although still worth consulting on the minor figures. Kathleen Tillotson, *Novels of the Eighteen-Forties* (Oxford, Clarendon, 1954) is less limited than its title suggests, and is in fact an indispensable scholarly introduction to early Victorian fiction. More specialized studies are mentioned in the bibliographies to the separate chapters of this study.

Publishing, Reading-Public, Illustration

Amy Cruse, *The Victorians and their Books* (Allen & Unwin, 1935) is lively and readable, but now needs supplementing by modern scholarship. Pioneering studies in the field of Victorian publishing are Richard Altick, *The English Common Reader: A Social History of the Mass Reading Public 1800-1900* (Chicago, University of Chicago Press, 1957) and J.A. Sutherland, *Victorian Novelists and Publishers* (Athlone Press, 1976). Guinevere L. Griest, *Mudie's Circulating Library and the Victorian Novel* (Bloomington, Indiana UP, 1970) is a fascinating account of a great Victorian institution. Illustration was an important part of Victorian novel production, especially in serialization, and is explored in J.R. Harvey, *Victorian Novelists and their Illustrators* (Sidgwick & Jackson, 1970).

1 The Novel and Aristocracy

Pre-Victorian fiction is discussed in Elliot Engel and Margaret F. King, *The Victorian Novel Before Victoria* (Macmillan, 1984), which has chapters on Bulwer-Lytton and Disraeli. Specialized studies of early Victorian themes and genres mentioned in this chapter are: Keith Hollingsworth, *The Newgate Novel: 1830-47* (Detroit, Wayne State UP, 1963), Susanne N. Howe, *Wilhelm Meister and his English Kinsmen* (New York, Columbia UP, 1930), and Matthew W. Rosa, *The Silver-Fork School: Novels of Fashion Preceding Vanity Fair* (New York, Columbia UP, 1936). Also relevant to the understanding of the fashionable novel, and of the conflict between aristocracy and middle classes at this time, are Alison Adburgham, *Silver Fork Society: Fashionable Life and Literature 1814 to 1840* (Constable, 1983), and Ellen Moers's classic study, *The Dandy: Brummell to Beerbohm* (Secker & Warburg, 1960). Norman Gash, *Aristocracy and People: Britain 1815-1865* (Edward Arnold, 1979) is a modern general history in which the question of aristocratic leadership figures prominently.

There has been no modern biography of Bulwer-Lytton after Michael Sadleir's *Bulwer: A Panorama. I. Edward and Rosina, 1803-36* (Constable, 1931). Attempts to consider his novels on their own terms are made in A.C. Christiansen, *Edward Bulwer-Lytton: The Fiction of New Regions* (Athens, Georgia, University of Georgia Press, 1976) and Edwin Eigner, *The Metaphysical Novel in England and America: Dickens, Bulwer, Melville, and Hawthorne* (Berkeley & Los Angeles,

University of California Press, 1978). The relevant sections of the books by Hollingsworth, Howe, Rosa and Moers, cited above, are also of value.

Disraeli has been better served by biographers, Robert Blake's *Disraeli* (Eyre & Spottiswoode, 1966) being the authoritative modern life. There are three book-length studies of the fiction: Richard A. Levine, *Benjamin Disraeli* (New York, Twayne, 1968), Daniel Schwarz, *Disraeli's Fiction* (Macmillan, 1979), and Thom Braun, *Disraeli the Novelist* (Allen & Unwin, 1981). Of particular value to the student of *Coningsby* is an article by Robert O'Kell, 'Disraeli's *Coningsby*: Political Manifesto or Psychological Romance', *VS* 23 (1979), pp. 57–78. Other useful essays can be found in V.S. Pritchett, *The Living Novel* (Chatto & Windus, 1946) and John Holloway, *The Victorian Sage* (Macmillan, 1953). Young England is well explored by Alice Chandler in *A Dream of Order: The Medieval Ideal in Nineteenth-Century English Literature* (Routledge & Kegan Paul, 1971), and its wider context is the subject of Mark Girouard's *The Return to Camelot: Chivalry and the English Gentleman* (Yale UP, 1981).

Gordon Ray's two-volume life of Thackeray, *Thackeray: The Uses of Adversity 1811–1846* and *Thackeray: The Age of Wisdom 1847–63* (OUP, 1955, 1958), is far and away the best modern biography of any Victorian novelist, and is indispensable for anyone studying Thackeray. His edition of *The Letters and Private Papers* (4 vols., OUP, 1945–6) is also a fascinating source of information. Thackeray's connection with *Fraser's Magazine* is explored in Miriam Thrall, *Rebellious Fraser's* (New York, Columbia UP, 1934). Victorian criticism of Thackeray, much of it of a high standard, is collected in the *Critical Heritage* volume, edited by Geoffrey Tillotson and Donald Hawes (Routledge & Kegan Paul, 1968): the longer essays by Bagehot, W.C. Roscoe and Leslie Stephen are of particular value. More recent collections of essays are the *Twentieth-Century Views* volume, edited by Alexander Welsh (Englewood Cliffs, NJ, Prentice-Hall, 1968), and the special Thackeray issue of the journal *Costerus*, New Series II (1974).

Trollope's *Thackeray* in the 'English Men of Letters' series (Macmillan, 1879) is of special interest as a study by a novelist who was Thackeray's natural successor. George Saintsbury's *A Consideration of Thackeray* (OUP, 1931) reprints his introductions from the *Oxford Thackeray*. The traditional vew of Thackeray is presented in Geoffrey Tillotson's wise study, *Thackeray the Novelist* (Cambridge, CUP, 1954); the case for a more subversive artist is argued by Barbara Hardy in *The Exposure of Luxury: Radical Themes in Thackeray* (Peter Owen, 1972), and by John Carey in *Thackeray: Prodigal Genius* (Faber, 1977). Jack P. Rawlins, *Thackeray's Novels: A Fiction that is True* (Berkeley & Los Angeles, University of California Press, 1974) is a sophisticated study of Thackeray's narrative methods and the problematic nature of his realism. His working methods are explored by John Sutherland in *Thackeray at Work* (Athlone Press, 1974), and by Edgar Harden in *The Emergence of Thackeray's Serial Fiction* (Athens, Georgia, University of Georgia Press, 1979). Robert Colby's *Thackeray's Canvass of Humanity* (Columbus, Ohio UP, 1979) is the most comprehensive survey of the fiction to date, setting it in the literary context of the time.

The relevant chapters in the following books shed differing lights on Thackeray's work: Percy Lubbock, *The Craft of Fiction* (Cape, 1921), Kathleen Tillotson, *Novels of the Eighteen-Forties* (Oxford, Clarendon, 1954), A.E. Dyson,

The Crazy Fabric: Essays in Irony (Macmillan, 1966), Robin Gilmour, *The Idea of the Gentleman in the Victorian Novel* (Allen & Unwin, 1981). The last author has also written a monograph on *Vanity Fair* for the 'Studies in English Literature' series (Edward Arnold, 1982). There is an outstanding article on Thackeray's handling of time by Jean Sudrann, ' "The Philosopher's Property": Thackeray and the Use of Time', *VS* 10 (1967), pp. 355–88. Finally, Philip Collins has brought together, in *Thackeray: Interviews and Recollections* (Macmillan, 1983), many contemporary impressions of a man who, while not larger than his novels, was a large man in all senses of the word, and remains a fascinating figure in his own right.

2 The Sense of the Present

The standard work on the early Victorian social-problem novel remains Louis Cazamian, *The Social Novel in England 1830–1850*, first published in French in 1903 and since translated by Martin Fido (Routledge & Kegan Paul, 1973). It has dated in many respects but is unrivalled in its comprehensiveness. P.J. Keating, *The Working Classes in Victorian Fiction* (Routledge & Kegan Paul, 1971) deals mainly with the later Victorians but has some thoughtful pages on the industrial novels of the 1840s and 50s, as does Raymond Williams in *Culture and Society 1780–1950* (Harmondsworth, Penguin, 1961). The question of the novelists' use of documentary material is explored by Sheila Smith in *The Other Nation: The Poor in English Novels of the 1840s and 1850s* (Oxford, Clarendon, 1980). Guidance to the larger context in which the novelists worked can be found in J.F.C. Harrison, *The Early Victorians* (Weidenfeld & Nicolson, 1971), Harold Perkin, *The Origins of Modern English Society 1780–1880* (Routledge & Kegan Paul, 1969), and Asa Briggs, 'The Language of Class in Early Nineteenth-Century England', *Essays in Labour History*, edited by A. Briggs and J. Saville (Macmillan, 1960).

The best brief introduction to Carlyle is A.L. Le Quesne, *Carlyle* (Oxford, OUP, 1982). There is a fascinating account of one working-man's interpretation of *Chartism*, and Dickens's reaction, in Sheila Smith, 'John Overs to Charles Dickens: A Working-Man's Letter and its Implications', *VS* 18 (1974), pp. 195–217. The question of the novelists' response to trade unionism is explored in Geoffrey Carnall, 'Dickens, Mrs Gaskell, and the Preston Strike', *VS* 8 (1964), pp. 31–48, and Patrick Brantlinger, 'The Case Against Trade Unions in Early Victorian Fiction', *VS* 13 (1969), pp. 37–52.

There has been relatively little criticism of Kingsley outside the studies of the industrial novel already mentioned, although R.B. Martin's *The Dust of Combat* (Faber, 1959) is a good critical biography. His novels are approached from a Christian Social perspective in A.J. Hartley, *The Novels of Charles Kingsley* (Folkestone, Hour-Glass Press, 1977). There are useful essays on Kingsley by Thomas Hughes in his 'Prefatory Memoir' to later editions of *Alton Locke*, Leslie Stephen in volume 3 of *Hours in a Library* (Smith, Elder, 1879), and on *Alton Locke* in Carl Dawson, *Victorian Noon* (Baltimore, Johns Hopkins UP, 1979).

Winifred Gérin's *Elizabeth Gaskell* (Oxford, Clarendon, 1976) is the standard life, the first to draw upon *The Letters of Mrs. Gaskell*, edited by J.A.V. Chapple and A. Pollard (Manchester, Manchester UP, 1966). Angus Easson, *Elizabeth*

Gaskell (Routledge & Kegan Paul, 1979) is a good scholarly and biographical introduction. Of critical books, W.A. Craik, *Elizabeth Gaskell and the English Provincial Novel* (Methuen, 1975) can be recommended, as can Coral Lansbury, *Elizabeth Gaskell: The Novel of Social Crisis* (Elek, 1975), which gives some consideration to Gaskell's Unitarianism. Some of the best recent criticism has been in essay form: see the chapters on Gaskell by John Lucas in *Tradition and Tolerance in Nineteenth-Century Fiction*, edited by J. Goode, D. Howard and J. Lucas (Routledge & Kegan Paul, 1966), and in his *The Literature of Change: Studies in the Nineteenth-Century Provincial Novel* (Hassocks, Harvester, 1977); also Peter Keating's introduction to the Penguin English Library edition of *Cranford and Cousin Phillis* (1976).

A great deal of attention has been paid to the working classes in Victorian fiction, not much to their employers. A study which attempts to redress the balance is John McVeagh, *Tradefull Merchants: The Portrayal of the Capitalist in Literature* (Routledge & Kegan Paul, 1981). Two other studies which bear on this side of the question are S.G. Checkland, *The Rise of Industrial Society in England 1815-1885* (Longman, 1964) and M.J. Wiener, *English Culture and the Decline of the Industrial Spirit, 1850-1980* (Cambridge, CUP, 1981).

3 The Sense of the Self

The Victorian sense of the past is discussed succinctly by J.W. Burrow in *The Victorians*, ed. Laurence Lerner (Methuen, 1978), pp. 120–38, and in greater detail by J.H. Buckley in *The Triumph of Time: A Study of the Victorian Concepts of Time, History, Progress, and Decadence* (Cambridge, Mass., Harvard UP, 1967). Andrew Sanders in *The Victorian Historical Novel, 1840-1880* (Macmillan, 1978), and J.C. Simmons in *The Novelist as Historian: Essays on the Victorian Historical Novel* (The Hague, Mouton, 1973), explore various aspects of the novelists' treatment of history. The standard work on the later *bildungsroman* is J.H. Buckley, *Season of Youth: The Bildungsroman from Dickens to Golding* (Cambridge, Mass., Harvard UP, 1974), which, however, curiously omits Charlotte Brontë. There has been much recent work on the Romantic and religious influences on Victorian fiction. D.D. Stone, *The Romantic Impulse in Victorian Fiction* (Cambridge, Mass., Harvard UP, 1980) has separate chapters on Trollope, Disraeli, Charlotte Brontë, Elizabeth Gaskell, George Eliot, Dickens and Meredith. Barry Qualls, *The Secular Pilgrims of Victorian Fiction* (Cambridge, CUP, 1982). concentrates on the Christian, and specifically Carlylean, allegorical mode in Charlotte Brontë, Dickens and George Eliot. Also of interest is the discussion of religous allusion by Michael Wheeler in *The Art of Allusion in Victorian Fiction* (Macmillan, 1979), which has a chapter on *Jane Eyre*.

There is a vast literature on the Brontës. Elizabeth Gaskell's *Life of Charlotte Brontë* (1857, variously reprinted) remains indispensable, as do the 4 volumes of *The Brontës: Their Lives, Friendships and Correspondence*, ed. T.J. Wise and J.A. Symington (Oxford, Shakespeare Head, 1932). Winifred Gérin's *Charlotte Brontë: The Evolution of Genius* (Oxford, Clarendon, 1967) and *Emily Brontë: A Biography* (Oxford, Clarendon, 1971) are the fullest modern biographies. The background to the lives and novels is explored by T. Winnifrith in *The Brontës and their Background* (Macmillan, 1973; revised edn, 1977). There is an *Everyman's Companion to the Brontës* by Barbara and Gareth Lloyd Evans (Dent, 1982), which contains a useful 'Calendar of Events 1812–1861' and summary of the Juvenilia. The latter are the subject of studies by F.E. Ratchford, *The Brontës' Web of Childhood* (New York, Columbia UP, 1941), and Christine Alexander, *The Early Writings of Charlotte Brontë* (Oxford, Blackwell, 1983).

Victorian criticism of the Brontes is usefully collected in Miriam Allott's *Critical Heritage* volume (Routledge & Kegan Paul, 1974). The most stimulating modern introductions are by Q.D. Leavis, to the Penguin English Library edition of *Jane Eyre* (1966) and to the Harper edition of *Villette* (1972); these, and her more controversial 'Fresh Approach to *Wuthering Heights*', are available in volume I of her *Collected Essays*, ed. G. Singh (Cambridge, CUP, 1983). Other valuable short studies are the chapters on Emily Brontë in Lord David Cecil, *Early Victorian Novelists* (Constable, 1934); Dorothy Van Ghent, *The English Novel: Form and Function* (New York, Rinehart, 1953; Harper, 1961); J.H. Miller, *The Disappearance of God* (Cambridge, Mass., Harvard UP, 1963); and Mark Roberts, *The Tradition of Romantic Morality* (Macmillan, 1973). On *Jane Eyre*, the chapters in Kathleen Tillotson's *Novels of the Eighteen-Forties* and David Lodge, *The Language of Fiction* (Routledge & Kegan Paul, 1966) can be recommended, as can R.B. Heilman, 'Charlotte Brontë's 'New' Gothic', in *From Jane Austen to Joseph Conrad*, ed. R.C. Rathburn and M. Steinmann (Minneapolis, University of Minnesota Press, 1958), which also discusses *Villette*. The following essays on *Villette* are worth consulting: R.A. Colby, '*Villette* and the Life of the Mind', *PMLA* 75 (1960), pp. 410–19, and 'Lucy Snowe and the Good Governess', in his *Fiction With a Purpose* (Bloomington, Indiana UP, 1967); M. Jacobus, 'The Buried Letter: Feminism and Romanticism in *Villette*', in *Women Writing and Writing About Women*, ed. M. Jacobus (Croom Helm, 1979). Some of these essays are reprinted in Miriam Allott's two *Casebooks* on *Wuthering Heights* (Macmillan, 1970) and '*Jane Eyre' and 'Villette*' (Macmillan, 1973), and in Ian Gregor's *Twentieth Century Views* volume (Englewood Cliffs, NJ, Prentice-Hall, 1970), which in addition to reprinting Heilman and Lodge, has excellent new essays on 'The Place of Love in *Jane Eyre* and *Wuthering Heights*' by Mark Kinkead-Weekes and on 'Charlotte Brontë, the Imagination, and *Villette*', by Andrew Hook. Gregor also reprints C.P. Sanger's important essay on 'The Structure of Wuthering Heights'.

R.B. Martin, *The Accents of Persuasion: Charlotte Brontë's Novels* (Faber, 1966) and W.A. Craik, *The Brontë Novels* (Methuen, 1968) are good book-length studies. The near 200 pages on Emily and Charlotte Brontë in S.M. Gilbert and S. Gubar, *The Madwoman in the Attic: The Woman Writer and the Nineteenth-Century Literary Imagination* (New Haven, Yale UP, 1979) is almost a book within a book, and represents the most ambitious feminist reading of their work. Also important from this angle is the discussion of Charlotte Brontë by Elaine Showalter in *A Literature of Their Own: British Women Novelists from Brontë to Lessing* (Princeton, NJ, Princeton UP, 1977). A more modest, but illuminating, approach through style is made by Margot Peters in *Charlotte Brontë, Style in the Novel* (Madison, Wisconsin UP, 1973).

4 Dickens

The one indispensable source for information about Dickens's life remains *The Life of Charles Dickens* (1872–4) by his friend John Forster, best consulted in the annotated edition of J.W.T. Ley (Cecil Palmer, 1928) or A.J. Hoppé's Everyman reprint (2 vols., Dent, 1966). Edgar Johnson, *Charles Dickens: His Tragedy and Triumph* (2 vols., Gollancz, 1953), available in a revised and abbreviated Penguin edition (1 vol., Harmondsworth, 1978) is the most comprehensive modern biography, although since it was written much new information about Dicken's life and career has come to light. An example of the biographical revision this might lead to can be seen in the new light thrown on Dickens's marriage by Michael Slater in his excellent *Dickens and Women* (Dent, 1983). The best short critical biographies are by K.J. Fielding, *Charles Dickens: A Critical Introduction* (2nd edn, Longman, 1965) and Angus Wilson, *The World of Charles Dickens* (Secker & Warburg, 1970; Penguin, 1972).

Walter Dexter's edition of *The Letters of Charles Dickens* (3 vols., Nonesuch, 1938) is gradually being superseded by the Pilgrim Edition of *The Letters of Charles Dickens*, ed. Madeline House, Graham Storey, and Kathleen Tillotson (Oxford, Clarendon, 1965–), of which five volumes have to date been published. Dickens's activities as public speaker and reader can be studied in *The Speeches of Charles Dickens*, ed. K.J. Fielding (Oxford, Clarendon, 1960) and *Charles Dickens: The Public Readings* ed. Philip Collins (Oxford, Clarendon, 1975). His journalism is available in *The Uncommercial Traveller, Reprinted Pieces*, and *Miscellaneous Papers* (ed. B.W. Matz) in collected editions of his work, and in *The Uncollected Writings of Charles Dickens: 'Household Words' 1850-1859*, ed. Harry Stone (2 vols., Allen Lane, 1969). Also of interest is *Charles Dickens's Book of Memoranda*, ed. Fred Kaplan (New York, New York Public Library, 1981).

Serious modern Dickens scholarship begins with Humphry House's *The Dickens World* (Oxford, OUP, 1941) and with the study of Dickens's working methods by John Butt and Kathleen Tillotson in *Dickens at Work* (Methuen, 1957). Since then a large number of 'Dickens and' studies have explored various aspects of his work and its relation to the contemporary Victorian world. Special mention may be made here of Philip Collins's two studies, *Dickens and Crime* (Macmillan, 1962) and *Dickens and Education* (Macmillan, (1963), of Robert L. Patten's *Charles Dickens and His Publishers* (Oxford, Clarendon, 1978), and of the following recent studies: Norris Pope, *Dickens and Charity* (Macmillan, 1978), Dennis Walder, *Dickens and Religion* (Allen & Unwin, 1981), Michael Slater, *Dickens and Women* (Dent, 1983), Paul Schlicke, *Dickens and Popular Entertainment* (Allen & Unwin, 1985).

Criticism of Dickens is a fascinating subject in its own right, and was first thoroughly explored by George Ford in *Dickens and His Readers: Aspects of Novel-Criticism Since 1836* (Princeton, NJ, Princeton UP, 1955). Victorian criticism is usefully collected by Philip Collins in his *Critical Heritage* volume (Routledge & Kegan Paul, 1971). The *Penguin Critical Anthology*, ed. Stephen Wall (Harmondsworth, 1970) is not so full as Collins in its selection of contemporary material, but is valuable for Dickens criticism of the early modern period, and reprints some more recent essays as well. Of studies published between Dickens's death and 1940, the books by George Gissing (Blackie, 1898) and G.K.

Chesterton (Methuen, 1906), remain indispensable, as does the latter's *Criticisms and Appreciations of the Works of Charles Dickens* (Dent, 1911). Modern criticism of Dickens effectively dates from Edmund Wilson's essay, 'Dickens: the Two Scrooges', in *The Wound and the Bow* (W.H. Allen, 1941), although George Orwell's more traditional account in *Inside the Whale* (Secker & Warburg, 1940) has also been influential. Of the many good critical books published since then it is possible here to mention only a handful. The best study of the early novels is Steven Marcus, *Dickens: From Pickwick to Dombey* (Chatto & Windus, 1965). There is no equivalent study for the later novels, although the challenging *Dickens the Novelist* by F.R. and Q.D. Leavis (Chatto & Windus, 1970) is exclusively devoted to them. J. Hillis Miller, *Charles Dickens: The World of his Novels* (Cambridge, Mass., Harvard UP, 1958) has a banal central thesis but many local insights, and Sylvère Monod, *Dickens the Novelist* (Norman, Oklahoma, Oklahoma UP, 1968) is always worth consulting, especially for the sensitivity this French scholar brings to the study of Dickens's language, which is the subject of a book by G.L. Brook (Andre Deutsch, 1970), and an article by Randolph Quirk reprinted in the *Penguin Critical Anthology*. The mythic dimension in Dickens's art is explored from different angles in Harry Stone, *Dickens and the Invisible World: Fairy Tales, Fantasy, and Novel-Making* (Macmillan, 1979) and in Geoffrey Thurley, *The Dickens Myth: Its Genesis and Structure* (Routledge & Kegan Paul, 1976). The Dickensian *bildungsroman* is discussed in Jerome Buckley, *Season of Youth: The Bildungsroman from Dickens to Golding* (Cambridge, Mass., Harvard UP, 1974) and is the subject of a book by Barry Westburg, *The Confessional Fictions of Charles Dickens* (Dekalb, Northern Illinois UP, 1977). Grahame Smith, *Dickens, Money, and Society* (Berkeley & Los Angeles, University of California Press, 1968) and Alexander Welsh, *The City of Dickens* (Oxford, Clarendon, 1971) deal in interesting ways with topics of obvious importance in Dickens's novels. Finally, H.M. Daleski explores the use of analogy as an ordering principle in *Dickens and the Art of Analogy* (Faber, 1970).

Much of the best criticism of Dickens, as of most authors, is in essay form, and *The Dickens Critics*, ed. G.H. Ford and L. Lane (Ithaca, NY, Cornell UP, 1961) reprints a valuable selection: the essays by Santayana, Dorothy Van Ghent ('The Dickens World: A View from Todgers's'), Lionel Trilling (on *Little Dorrit*), V.S. Pritchett ('The Comic World of Dickens'), are especially recommended. To these classic studies a future anthologist would certainly add W.H. Auden's brilliant essay on *Pickwick Papers*, 'Dingley Dell and the Fleet', in *The Dyer's Hand* (Faber, 1963).

Finally, mention should be made of two publications, one old and one new. *The Dickensian* (1906–) is unique among specialist journals in having been sustained for much of its life by enthusiastic amateurs, and for the high quality of its biographical, scholarly, and occasionally critical contributions: it is a mine of information about Dickens's life, friendships and the background of his novels. The 19 volumes of the proposed *Dickens Companions*, ed. Susan Shatto and Michael Cotsell (Allen & Unwin, 1986–), will provide the first comprehensive annotation of Dickens's novels, identifying their literary and topical references.

5 The Novel in the Age of Equipoise

There is no study of English fiction in the 1850s and 1860s comparable to Kathleen Tillotson's *Novels of the Eighteen-Forties,* although the critical assumptions of the period are examined by Richard Stang in *The Theory of the Novel in England, 1850–70* (Routledge & Kegan Paul, 1959), and the fiction industry by R.C. Terry in *Victorian Popular Fiction, 1860–80* (Macmillan, 1983), which also has separate chapters on Mrs Oliphant, Rhoda Broughton and James Payn. The social history of the period is discussed by Geoffrey Best in *Mid-Victorian Britain 1851–75* (Weidenfeld & Nicolson, 1971), a lively and accessible study by a historian unusually hospitable to the evidence of the novelists. The concept of a mid-Victorian 'equipoise' is explored in W.L. Burn's classic *The Age of Equipoise* (Allen & Unwin, 1964). The religious context of mid-Victorian fiction, particularly important in the case of George Eliot and Trollope, is the subject of books by Elisabeth Jay, *The Religion of the Heart: Anglican Evangelicalism and the Nineteenth-Century Novel* (Oxford, Clarendon, 1979), Valentine Cunningham, *Everywhere Spoken Against: Dissent in the Victorian Novel* (Oxford, Clarendon, 1975), and Robert Lee Wolff, *Gains and Losses: Novels of Faith and Doubt in Victorian England* (New York, Garland, 1977).

The best study of the sensation novel genre is Winifred Hughes, *The Maniac in the Cellar: Sensation Novels of the 1860s* (Princeton, NJ, Princeton UP, 1980). In addition to T.S. Eliot's important essay on 'Wilkie Collins and Dickens' in his *Selected Essays* (3rd edn, Faber, 1951), there are valuable discussions of the genre by Kathleen Tillotson in her introduction to the Riverside edition of *The Woman in White* (Boston, Houghton Mifflin, 1969), by Anthea Trodd in her introduction to the World's Classics edition of *The Moonstone* (Oxford OUP, 1982), and by Patrick Brantlinger in his article, 'What Is "Sensational" about the "Sensation Novel"?', *NCF* 37 (1982), pp. 1–28. The relations between Collins and Dickens have recently been explored afresh by Sue Lonoff in 'Charles Dickens and Wilkie Collins', *NCF* 35 (1980), pp. 150–70. She is also the author of the most thorough critical study of Collins to date, *Wilkie Collins and His Victorian Readers* (New York, AMS Press, 1982). W.H. Marshall's *Wilkie Collins* (New York, Twayne, 1970) is a biographical and critical introduction which surveys all his writings. Contemporary reviews of Collins's novels, some of considerable interest to the student of Victorian critical assumptions, are collected in the *Critical Heritage* volume, edited by Norman Page (Routledge & Kegan Paul, 1974).

There is no adequate modern biography of Trollope, although one is in preparation by N. John Hall, who has compiled the authoritative edition of *The Letters of Anthony Trollope* (2 vols., Stanford, Stanford UP, 1983). Michael Sadleir's *Trollope: A Commentary* (Constable, 1927) remains a valuable source of biographical material, and C.P. Snow's *Trollope* (Macmillan, 1975) is a lively introduction by a novelist who had an affinity with his subject. Trollope's *Autobiography* (1883, variously reprinted) is indispensable, as fascinating for its reticences as for its revelations. Non-fictional works by Trollope of relevance to the student of his novels include his *Clergymen of the Church of England* (1866, reprinted with an introduction by Ruth apRoberts, Leicester UP, 1974), and *The New Zealander,* ed. N. John Hall (Oxford, Clarendon, 1972). Contemporary criticism of Trollope is collected in the *Critical Heritage* volume, ed. Donald Smalley

(Routledge & Kegan Paul, 1969), and analysed by David Skilton in *Anthony Trollope and his Contemporaries* (Longman, 1972).

The traditional view of Trollope's fiction as robust and conventional is most eloquently expressed in Henry James's influential 'Partial Portrait' (reprinted in *Critical Heritage* and elsewhere). The modern view of him as a more subtle and pessimistic artist dates from A.O.J. Cockshut's *Anthony Trollope* (Collins, 1955), a view developed by Robert Polhemus in *The Changing World of Anthony Trollope* (Berkeley & Los Angeles, University of California Press, 1968) and modified by Ruth apRoberts in her *Trollope: Artist and Moralist* (Chatto & Windus, 1971). Arthur Pollard's *Anthony Trollope* (Routledge & Kegan Paul, 1978) is a useful introductory survey. Recent critical interpretations of the *oeuvre* can be found in James Kincaid, *The Novels of Anthony Trollope* (Oxford, Clarendon, 1977), P.D. Edwards, *Anthony Trollope: his Art and Scope* (Hassocks, Harvester Press, 1978), Bill Overton, *The Unofficial Trollope* (Hassocks, Harvester Press, 1982), and Andrew Wright, *Anthony Trollope: Dream and Art* (Macmillan, 1983). More specialized studies of value are John Halperin, *Trollope and Politics* (Macmillan, 1977) and Robert Tracy, *Trollope's Later Novels* (Berkeley & Los Angeles, University of California Press, 1978). There is a Casebook on *The Barsetshire Novels*, ed. T. Bareham (Macmillan, 1983), and a selection of criticism, including James's essay, in *The Trollope Critics*, ed. N. John Hall (Macmillan, 1980).

George Eliot has been well served by modern scholarship. The foundation for serious study was laid by Gordon Haight's nine-volume edition of *The George Eliot Letters* (New Haven, Yale UP, 1954–78), and by his *George Eliot: A Biography* (Oxford, Clarendon, 1968), the most factually informative life. Professor Haight is also general editor of the Clarendon Edition of her novels, currently in progress, which will be the authoritative modern edition. George Eliot's essays are available in *The Impressions of Theophrastus Such*, in *Essays of George Eliot*, ed. Thomas Pinney (Routledge & Kegan Paul, 1963), and in *George Eliot: A Writer's Notebook 1854–79 and Uncollected Writings*, ed. Joseph Wiesenfarth (Charlottesville, University of Virginia Press, 1981). Contemporary criticism is collected in the *Critical Heritage* volume, ed. David Carroll (Routledge & Kegan Paul, 1971). *A Century of George Eliot Criticism*, ed. Gordon Haight (Methuen, 1966) brings together some of the best criticism from the first reviews to the early 1960s.

Two good modern introductions are Walter Allen, *George Eliot* (Weidenfeld & Nicolson, 1965) and Rosemary Ashton, *George Eliot* (Oxford, OUP, 1983). Sympathetic modern criticism dates from Joan Bennett, *George Eliot: Her Mind and Art* (Cambridge, CUP, 1948) and F.R. Leavis, *The Great Tradition* (Chatto & Windus, 1948). Basil Willey mapped her intellectual development concisely in *Nineteenth-Century Studies* (Chatto & Windus, 1949). Barbara Hardy, *The Novels of George Eliot* (Athlone Press, 1959), and W.J. Harvey, *The Art of George Eliot* (Chatto & Windus, 1961), are pioneering studies of George Eliot's artistry. More specialized recent studies include U.C. Knoepflmacher, *George Eliot's Early Novels: The Limits of Realism* (Berkeley & Los Angeles, University of California Press, 1968), Henry Auster, *Local Habitations: Regionalism in the Early Novels of George Eliot* (Cambridge, Mass, Harvard UP, 1970), and Alan Mintz, *George Eliot and the Novel of Vocation* (Cambridge, Mass., Harvard UP, 1978). For feminist perspectives see the relevant sections in Elaine Showalter, *A Literature of Their Own* (Princeton, NJ, Princeton UP, 1977) and S.M. Gilbert and S. Gubar, *The Madwoman in the Attic* (New Haven, Yale UP, 1979). There are many stimulating pieces in *Critical Essays on George Eliot*, ed. Barbara Hardy (Routledge & Kegan Paul, 1970) and *George Eliot: A Collection of Critical Essays*, ed. George R. Creeger (Englewood Cliffs, NJ, Prentice-Hall, 1970).

Middlemarch has attracted extensive commentary. There are excellent monographs by David Daiches (Edward Arnold, 1963) and Kerry McSweeney (Allen & Unwin, 1984), and collections of essays edited by Barbara Hardy, *'Middlemarch': Critical Approaches to the Novel* (Athlone Press, 1967), and Ian Adam, *This Particular Web: Essays on 'Middlemarch'* (Toronto, Toronto UP, 1975). Among the many articles written on the novel, the following are valuable for the contextual perspectives they provide: Asa Briggs, *'Middlemarch* and the Doctors', *Cambridge Journal* I (1948), pp. 749–62; Jerome Beaty, 'History by Indirection: the Era of Reform in *Middlemarch*', *VS* I (1957), pp. 173–9 (reprinted Haight, *A Century of George Eliot Criticism*); Michael Y. Mason, *'Middlemarch* and History', *NCF* 25 (1971), pp. 417–31; Michael Y. Mason, *'Middlemarch* and Science: Problems of Life and Mind', *RES* 22 (1971), pp. 151–69; and John Sutherland, 'Marketing *Middlemarch*', in *Victorian Novelists and Publishers* (Athlone Press, 1976). Discussion of the novel in the perspectives of Victorian humanism and evolutionary theory can be found, respectively, in U.C. Knoepflmacher, *Religious Humanism and the Victorian Novel: George Eliot, Walter Pater and Samuel Butler* (Princeton, NJ, Princeton UP, 1965) and Gillian Beer, *Darwin's Plots: Evolutionary Narrative in Darwin, George Eliot and Nineteenth-Century Fiction* (Routledge & Kegan Paul, 1983).

6 Continuity and Change in the Later Victorian Novel

The fiction of the 1880s is comprehensively explored in Donald D. Stone, *Novelists in a Changing World: Meredith, James and the Transformation of English Fiction in the 1880s* (Cambridge, Mass., Harvard UP, 1972). The changing climate of critical opinion is discussed in Kenneth Graham, *English Criticism of the Novel 1865–1900* (Oxford, Clarendon, 1965), and of intellectual opinion in David Daiches, *Some Late Victorian Attitudes* (Andre Deutsch, 1969). As its title suggests, U.C. Knoepflmacher's *Religious Humanism and the Victorian Novel* (Princeton, NJ, Princeton UP, 1965) is a study of the agnostic temper in the later novels of George Eliot, in Pater, and in Samuel Butler. For consideration of the 'woman question' in this period see the books by Showalter and by Gilbert and Gubar mentioned in previous chapter bibliographies; Martha Vicinus's two collections of essays from *Victorian Studies*, published by Indiana UP, *Suffer and Be Still: Women in the Victorian Age* (1972) and *A Widening Sphere: Changing Roles of Victorian Women* (1977); and Gail Cunningham, *The New Woman and the Victorian Novel* (Macmillan, 1978). Of the many books on the subject, Alan Sandison's *The Wheel of Empire: A Study of the Imperial Idea in Some Late Nineteenth and Early Twentieth-Century Fiction* (Macmillan, 1967) can be recommended. A useful social and political history of the later Victorian period is Donald Read, *England 1868–1914* (Longman, 1979).

The groundwork for the study of George Meredith has been well laid by G.L. Cline's edition of his *Letters* (3 vols, Oxford, Clarendon, 1970), the lives by

Lionel Stevenson, *The Ordeal of George Meredith* (New York, Russell & Russell, 1953) and David Williams, *George Meredith: His Life and Lost Love* (Hamish Hamilton, 1977), and the *Critical Heritage* volume edited by Ioan Williams (Routledge & Kegan Paul, 1971). Meredith has also been fortunate in attracting a critic of the stature of V.S. Pritchett, whose *George Meredith and English Comedy* (Chatto & Windus, 1970) is the best critical starting-point. Other studies of value include Ian Fletcher (ed.), *Meredith Now* (Routledge & Kegan Paul, 1971), a collection of critical essays, Gillian Beer, *Meredith: A Change of Masks* (Athlone Press, 1971), and Judith Wilt, *The Readable People of George Meredith* (Princeton, NJ, Princeton UP, 1975).

The standard modern *Life* of Henry James is by Leon Edel (5 vols., Hart-Davis, 1953–73), available in a two-volume Penguin edition (Harmondsworth, 1977). Professor Edel has edited many volumes of James's writings, including the collected *Henry James Letters* (vols. I-III, Macmillan, 1974–80; vol. IV, Cambridge, Mass., Belknap Press, 1984), and a selection of his critical writings, *The House of Fiction* (Hart-Davis, 1957). Other volumes of James's literary criticism are Albert Mordell (ed.), *Literary Reviews and Essays by Henry James* (New York, Twayne, 1957), and Morris Shapira (ed.), *Selected Literary Criticism* (Heinemann, 1963; Cambridge, CUP, 1981). The Prefaces James wrote for the New York edition of his novels are available in *The Art of the Novel*, collected and introduced by R.P. Blackmur (New York, Scribner's, 1935), and his *Notebooks* have been edited by F.O. Matthiessen and K.B. Murdock (New York, OUP, 1947). The history of James's reputation in his lifetime is a fascinating subject in its own right, and can be studied in Roger Gard (ed.), *Henry James: The Critical Heritage* (Routledge & Kegan Paul, 1968). The best critical introduction is S. Gorley Putt, *The Fiction of Henry James: A Reader's Guide* (Thames & Hudson, 1966; Penguin, 1968). There is a vast secondary literature on Henry James, but those interested in his European and Victorian bearings will find the relevant sections of the following books helpful: F.R. Leavis, *The Great Tradition* (Chatto & Windus, 1948), David Gervais, *Flaubert and Henry James* (Macmillan, 1978), Alwyn Berland, *Culture and Conduct in the Novels of Henry James* (Cambridge, CUP, 1981), and Marcia Jacobson, *Henry James and the Mass Market* (Alabama, University of Alabama Press, 1983). Kenneth Graham, *Henry James: The Drama of Fulfilment* (Oxford, Clarendon, 1975) is an excellent critical study. The essays on James by Graham Greene in his *Collected Essays* (Bodley Head, 1969), and by Lionel Trilling (on *The Princess Casamassima*) in *The Liberal Imagination* (Secker & Warburg, 1951), are especially valuable. Two collections of more recent critical essays are Tony Tanner (ed.), *Henry James: Modern Judgments* (Macmillan, 1968) and John Goode (ed.), *The Air of Reality: New Essays on Henry James* (Methuen, 1972).

The letters of James and Stevenson to each other and their critical exchanges are collected in Janet Adam Smith (ed.), *Henry James and Robert Louis Stevenson: A Record of Friendship and Criticism* (Hart-Davis, 1948). The only collected edition of Stevenson's letters remains Sidney Colvin's *The Letters of Robert Louis Stevenson to his Family and Friends* (4 vols., Methuen, 1911). Of the many biographies, J.C. Furnas, *Voyage to Windward* (Faber, 1952) is the best, and Jenni Calder, *RLS: A Life Study* (Hamish Hamilton, 1980) the most recent. Modern rehabilitation of Stevenson began with David Daiches, *Robert Louis Stevenson*

(Glasgow, Maclellan, 1946), and Graham Greene's essay 'From Feathers to Iron' (1948) in *Collected Essays* (Bodley Head, 1969). More specialized studies are Robert Kiely, *Robert Louis Stevenson and the Fiction of Adventure* (Cambridge, Mass., Harvard UP, 1964) and Edwin Eigner, *Robert Louis Stevenson and Romantic Tradition* (Princeton, NJ, Princeton UP, 1966). There have been two recent collections of essays, Jenni Calder (ed.), *Stevenson and Victorian Scotland* (Edinburgh, Edinburgh UP, 1981), and Andrew Noble (ed.), *Robert Louis Stevenson* (Vision, 1983).

7 The Ache of Modernism

The books by Graham, Daiches and Knoepflmacher mentioned in the previous chapter bibliography are relevant to the concerns of this chapter also. On Naturalism, there is a good introduction by Lilian R. Furst and Peter N. Skrine in the 'Critical Idiom' series (Methuen, 1971), and an invaluable collection of contemporary and later writings in *Documents of Modern Literary Realism*, edited by George J. Becker (Princeton, NJ, Princeton UP, 1963). The Zola controversy is explored in Clarence R. Decker, 'Zola's Literary Reputation in England', *PMLA* 49 (1934), pp. 1140–53 and W.C. Frierson, 'The English Controversy over Realism in Fiction', *PMLA* 43 (1928), pp. 533–50, and a wider context of debate is provided by John Lucas in 'From Naturalism to Symbolism', in *Decadence and the 1890s*, ed. I. Fletcher (Edward Arnold, 1979). Specialist studies of relevance to issues raised in this chapter include P.J. Keating, *The Working Classes in Victorian Fiction* (Routledge & Kegan Paul, 1971), which has separate chapters on Gissing and 'French naturalism and English working-class fiction', Leo Henkin, *Darwinism in the English Novel* (New York, Corporate Press, 1940), Gillian Beer, *Darwin's Plots* (Routledge & Kegan Paul, 1983), and Jeanette King, *Tragedy in the Victorian Novel* (Cambridge, CUP, 1978).

The standard *Life* of George Moore is by Joseph M. Hone (Gollancz, 1936). Among book-length studies are Malcolm Brown, *George Moore: A Reconsideration* (Seattle, University of Washington Press, 1955) and Richard A. Cave, *A Study of the Novels of George Moore* (Gerrard's Cross, Colin Smythe, 1978). Graham Hough has two essays on Moore in his *Image and Experience* (Duckworth, 1960), and there are essays on *Esther Waters* by Katherine Mansfield in *Novels and Novelists* (Constable, 1930), Virginia Woolf in *The Death of the Moth and other Essays* (Hogarth, 1942), and by Brian Nicholas in I. Gregor and B. Nicholas, *The Moral and the Story* (Faber, 1962).

Recent biographical research has significantly altered our perception of Hardy the man. Robert Gittings in *Young Thomas Hardy* and *The Older Hardy* (Heinemann, 1975, 1978; Penguin, 1978, 1980) presents a more devious, class-conscious and sexually troubled figure than previous biographies allowed, based as these had been largely on *The Life of Thomas Hardy* by his second wife Florence (Macmillan, 1928, 1930; as single volume 1962), which we now know to be a covert autobiography. The original text and his widow's alterations can be studied in Michael Millgate's edition of Thomas Hardy, *The Life and Work of Thomas Hardy* (Macmillan, 1985). Professor Millgate is the author of the fullest and most balanced modern life, *Thomas Hardy: A Biography* (Oxford, OUP, 1982), and the editor, with R.L. Purdy, of a projected 7-volume edition of *The*

Collected Letters (Oxford, Clarendon, 1978–). Work on Hardy's texts has resulted in Clarendon editions of *The Woodlanders*, edited by Dale Kramer (Oxford, 1981), and *Tess of the d'Urbervilles*, edited by Juliet Grindle and Simon Gatrell (Oxford, 1983), the latter being a novel with a peculiarly complex and interesting textual history which is the subject of a fascinating study by J.T. Laird, *The Shaping of 'Tess of the d'Urbervilles'* (Oxford, Clarendon, 1975). *Thomas Hardy's Personal Writings* have been edited by H. Orel (Lawrence, Kansas, Kansas UP, 1966), *The Personal Notebooks* by Richard H. Taylor (Macmillan, 1979), and *The Literary Notebooks* by Lennart Björk (2 vols., Macmillan, 1985).

The best introductory study is Irving Howe, *Thomas Hardy* (Macmillan, 1967; 1985). Michael Millgate, *Thomas Hardy: His Career as a Novelist* (Bodley Head, 1971) is a most helpful survey, and the minor novels are the subject of a study by Richard H. Taylor, *The Neglected Hardy* (Macmillan, 1982). Of the many books on Hardy, the following may be recommended to those looking for a variety of viewpoints: John Bayley, *An Essay on Hardy* (Cambridge, CUP, 1978), Jean Brooks, *Thomas Hardy: The Poetic Structure* (Elek, 1971), Ian Gregor, *The Great Web: The Form of Hardy's Major Fiction* (Faber, 1974), J. Hillis Miller, *Thomas Hardy: Distance and Desire* (Cambridge, Mass., Harvard UP, 1970). There has been considerable recent debate about the treatment of social change in Hardy's novels, which has tended to focus around *The Mayor of Casterbridge* and his essay on 'The Dorsetshire Labourer' (in *Personal Writings*). See, in this connection, Douglas Brown's two books, *Thomas Hardy* (Longman, 1954; revised edn, 1961) and *Hardy: The Mayor of Casterbridge* (Edward Arnold, 1962), John Holloway's essay on 'Hardy's Major Fiction' in *From Jane Austen to Joseph Conrad*, edited by R.C. Rathburn and M. Steinmann (Minneapolis, University of Minnesota Press, 1958), and Raymond Williams's chapter on Hardy in *The Country and the City* (Chatto & Windus, 1973; Paladin, 1975). This approach is challenged by J.C. Maxwell in 'The "Sociological" Approach to *The Mayor of Casterbridge*' in *Imagined Worlds*, ed. I. Gregor and M. Mack (Methuen, 1968), and the issues are debated by Laurence Lerner in *Thomas Hardy's 'The Mayor of Casterbridge': Tragedy or Social History?* (Sussex UP, 1975).

Contemporary criticism of Hardy is available in the *Critical Heritage* volume, edited by R.G. Cox (Routledge & Kegan Paul, 1970). The *Twentieth Century Views* volume, edited by A. Guerard (Englewood Cliffs, NJ, Prentice-Hall, 1063), reprints the Holloway essay mentioned above, and important essays by Donald Davidson on 'The Traditional Basis of Thomas Hardy's Fiction', Mortan Dauwen Zabel on 'Hardy in Defense of His Art: The Aesthetic of Incongruity', and W.H. Auden on 'A Literary Transference'. A more recent selection of essays, including the Maxwell piece above and Tony Tanner's 'Colour and Movement in Hardy's *Tess*', is reprinted in *Thomas Hardy: The Tragic Novels*, edited by R.P. Draper (Macmillan, 1975). *Thomas Hardy: The Writer and his Background*, edited by Norman Page (Bell & Hyman, 1980), is a collection of original essays on various topics, ranging from class and education to the influence of Darwin and Hardy's reading, and containing a useful Reader's Guide and Select Bibliography. Finally, mention should be made of two essays on Hardy by novelists whose work shows the potency of his influence and example: D.H. Lawrence's 'Study of Thomas Hardy' in *Phoenix: The Posthumous Papers of D.H. Lawrence*, edited by E.D. McDonald (Heinemann, 1936), and John Fowles,

'Hardy and the Hag', in *Thomas Hardy After Fifty Years*, edited by L. St John Butler (Macmillan, 1977).

Much of the revived interest in Gissing has been biographical and sociological. Excellent biographies by Jacob Korg, *George Gissing: A Critical Biography* (Seattle, University of Washington Press, 1963), and John Halperin, *Gissing: A Life in Books* (Oxford, OUP, 1982), supplement the work of Pierre Coustillas in making reprints of the novels available, and editing the *Critical Heritage* volume (Routledge & Kegan Paul, 1972). Professor Coustillas has also edited *Collected Articles on George Gissing* (Frank Cass, 1968), which reprints essays by George Orwell and V.S. Pritchett, and Jacob Korg's essay on 'The Spiritual Theme of *Born in Exile*'. Adrian Poole, *Gissing in Context* (Macmillan, 1975) is a good starting-point for more specialized study.

Like Gissing, Samuel Butler has been the subject of much biographical study. Philip Henderson, *Samuel Butler: The Incarnate Bachelor* (Cohen & West, 1953) is the fullest modern life. Lee E. Holt, *Samuel Butler* (New York, Twayne, 1964) provides a useful survey of Butler's career and ideas, and U.C. Knoepflmacher the most searching exploration of the relations between his ideas and his art in *Religious Humanism and the Victorian Novel* (Princeton, NJ, Princeton UP, 1965). There are fine essays on *The Way of All Flesh* by V.S. Pritchett in *The Living Novel* (Chatto & Windus, 1946) and by Richard Hoggart in the introduction to the Penguin English Library edition (1966). The novel is considered in relation to the Victorian *bildungsroman* in J.H. Buckley, *Season of Youth* (Cambridge, Mass., Harvard UP, 1974).

There is no adequate modern biography of Mrs Humphry Ward, and the *Life* by her daughter J.P. Trevelyan (Constable, 1923) remains, with her own *A Writer's Recollections* (Collins, 1918), the chief source of information. The best introduction to her work and world is William S. Peterson, *Victorian Heretic: Mrs Humphry Ward's 'Robert Elsmere'* (Leicester, Leicester UP, 1976). Little has been written on *Helbeck of Bannisdale*, although Q.D. Leavis, who has done much to establish its claims to be considered a Victorian classic, discusses it in her essay on 'The Englishness of the English Novel' in her *Collected Essays*, I, edited by G. Singh (Cambridge, CUP, 1983), and the novel is set in its Victorian religious context by Robert Lee Wolff in *Gains and Losses: Novels of Faith and Doubt in Victorian England* (New York, Garland, 1977).

Index

Ackroyd, Tabitha, 58
aesthetic movement, 150
agnosticism, 151, 152
Ainsworth, W.H., 14, 59
All the Year Round, 7, 100, 113
Allen, Grant: *The Woman Who Did*, 156
Allen, Walter, 144
Altick, Richard, 154
Annan, Noel, 128, 130
Answers, 154
Arabian Nights, The, 38, 80
Arnold, Matthew, 1, 3, 61, 164, 198; poetry
    quoted, 71–2, 180; *Culture and Anar-
    chy*, 109
Arnold, Thomas, 197
Athenaeum, 59
Auden, W.H., 186; 'Musée des Beaux Arts',
    137
Austen, Jane, 74, 143, 169; *Northanger
    Abbey*, 112; *Persuasion*, 30; *Pride and
    Prejudice*, 143; *Sense and Sensibility*,
    121

Bagehot, Walter, 91, 108, 110; *The English
    Constitution*, 108, 109
Ballantyne, R.M.: *Coral Island*, 176
Balzac, Honoré de, 165
Bayley, John, 135
Beethoven, Ludvig van, 104
Bentley's Miscellany, 7
Bergson, Henri, 185
Best, Geoffrey, 3; quoted, 108
Bewick, Thomas: *History of British Birds*,
    64
bildungsroman, 5; defined, 17; in Charlotte
    Brontë, 65, 68–9; in Samuel Butler,
    196; in Dickens, 93–5, 99, 101; in
    George Eliot, 136–7, 158; mid-
    Victorian, 109; in Thackeray, 31–2
Bismarck, Otto, Prince von, 149

Blackwood's Magazine, 7
Blake, William, 79, 81; *Marriage of Heaven
    and Hell*, 73, 77
Blessington, Lady: *The Governess*, 62
Bonaparte, Napoleon, and Thackeray's
    Becky Sharp, 27
Booth, Charles: *Life and Labour*, 150
Booth, William: *In Darkest England*, 150
Borges, Jorge Luis, 179
Bradbury and Evans, 23
Braddon, Mary Elizabeth: *Aurora Floyd*,
    112, 187; *Lady Audley's Secret*, 112
Bradlaugh-Besant trial, 156
Briggs, Asa, 37
Bright, John, 124
Brontë, Anne: *Agnes Grey*, 62–3; *The
    Tenant of Wildfell Hall*, 61
Brontë, Branwell, 66
Brontë, Charlotte, 1, 32, 35, **60–72**, 112,
    116
    Jane Eyre, 4, 5, 10, 30, 35, 57, 60, 61,
    63–8, 69, 71, 77, 109, 112, 116, 154
    The Professor, 68
    Shirley, 57, 61, 69
    Villette, 12, 60, 61, 68–72, 77, 109, 198
Brontë, Emily, 1, 70, **72–7**, 176
    Wuthering Heights, 4, 10, 57, 59, 61,
    72–7, 137
Brontë family, 3, 58, 78
Broughton, Rhoda, 153
Brummell, Beau, 16, 26
Buchanan, Robert, 79
Bulwer-Lytton, Sir Edward, 15, **16–18**,
    30, 103; *Alice*, 17–18; *Ernest
    Maltravers*, 17–18, 27; *Pelham*, 16–17
Bunyan, John: *Pilgrim's Progress*, 46, 64,
    71, 86, 192
Burn, W.L., 4, 108
Butler, Samuel, 196–7, 198; *The Way of All
    Flesh*, 155, 181, 196–7

215

Woolf, Virginia, 72
Wordsworth, William, 14, 68, 129, 136, 186, 188; and Victorian novel, 59–60, 67, 88–9; 'Immortality Ode', 92; *Lyrical Ballads*, 60, 67, 134

Young England movement, 18–19; in *Coningsby*, 20–1; in *Sybil*, 44; in *Yeast*, 45
Zola, Émile, 146, 148, 150, 180, 181, 186, 187; *Thérèse Racquin*, 181